'Thoughtful and very timely. It captures much of what is contradictory in the relationship between the politics of the far-right and neoliberal world order and addresses some of the key questions, not only in terms of how we explain the rise of the far-right, but how the left/progressive forces should respond to it.'

Dr Richard Saull, Queen Mary University of London

'Owen Worth provides a much-needed historical and economic perspective to the study of present-day extremism. By lucidly tracing the differences and, importantly, the similarities to the development of and themes pushed by the far-right across the Western world, this book provides a useful guide to the emerging transnational nationalism. Without succumbing to the more dramatic and hysterical predictions for the future, *Morbid Symptoms* identifies the political danger of recent developments and, most intriguingly, hints at possible solutions.'

Michael Wendling, author of *Alt-Right: From 4chan to the White House*

MORBID SYMPTOMS

About The Author

OWEN WORTH is a senior lecturer in international relations at the University of Limerick. His previous books include *Resistance in the Age of Austerity: Nationalism, the Failure of the Left and the Return of God* (2013) and *Rethinking Hegemony* (2015).

MORBID SYMPTOMS

The Global Rise of the Far-Right

OWEN WORTH

ZED

Morbid Symptoms: The Global Rise of the Far-Right was first published in 2019 by Zed Books Ltd, The Foundry, 17 Oval Way, London SE11 5RR, UK.

www.zedbooks.net

Typeset in Bulmer by Swales and Willis Ltd, Exeter, Devon
Cover design by Burgess and Beech
Cover photo © Hossein Fatemi, Panos Pictures

Printed and bound by CPI Group (UK) Ltd, Croydon, CR0 4YY, UK

A catalogue record for this book is available from the British Library

ISBN 978-1-78699-335-9 hb
ISBN 978-1-78699-334-2 pb
ISBN 978-1-78699-336-6 pdf
ISBN 978-1-78699-337-3 epub
ISBN 978-1-78699-338-0 mobi

To Daisy June Gordon.
The world is yours to reclaim.

Contents

Acknowledgements

This book has been a long time in the making and, as events around us continue to move at pace, its content has continued to alter and develop. The study has also benefitted from a number of interventions and individuals to whom I am grateful. Firstly, this work was supported by the Ministry of Education of the Republic of Korea and the National Research Foundation of Korea (NRF-2015S1A5A2A03049866). I would like to thank Kwang-Yeong Shin and his team at Chung-Ang University in Seoul for collaboration in the project. I would also like to thank Lawrence Rosenthal and Christine Trost at the Berkeley Center for Right-Wing Studies for hosting me during the Spring Semester, 2018, which proved invaluable to my work on the US in particular. I would also like to thank the library staff both at Berkeley and at the Hoover Institution at Stanford for providing me with access to additional primary material. In addition, I would like to thank Andreas Bieler, Tony Burns and the Centre for the Study of Social and Global Justice at Nottingham University during the academic year 2017–2018. I would also like to acknowledge those who aided through discussions in different mediums or interviews with me during this research.

I would like to thank a number of other scholars who I have discussed, dissected and often drunk with that were invaluable to the book. In particular, Barry Gills, Rick Saull, Alex Anievas, Mark Rupert, Barry Gills, Chris Farrands, Gerry Strange,

Jason Abbott, Barry Ryan, Nick Kiersey, Phoebe Moore, Swati Parashar, Sabine Hirschauer, Stuart Shields, Daniela Tepe-Belfrage, Alex Nunn, Claes Belfrage, Dan Bulley, Alex Pritchard, Yuliya Yurchenko, Ruth Cain and David Bailey have all contributed to some of the main arguments in some form or other through engagement with some of this work. Closer to home, I would like to thank Neil Robinson, Maura Adshead, Scott Fitzsimmons and Rory Costello at the University of Limerick. At Zed Books, I particular want to thank both Ken Barlow for his enthusiasm for the project and Kim Walker for taking it to its completion.

Finally and personally I would like to thank Perys, Daisy, Rosa and in particular my one love and soulmate Sammi for being there for me at all times.

Introduction: Morbid Symptoms

The financial crisis of 2007–2008 was always likely to lead to instability and unrest and to a sustained period where existing norms and practices were questioned and contested. The post-cold war neoliberal order that emerged out of the collapse of the Soviet Union and the wider push for greater global integration around a free market form of capitalism had found itself in structural crisis. The subsequent decade has seen a succession of policies linked to forms of 'austerity' utilised as an attempt to maintain the principles of the prevailing order and subsequently of continuing the presiding governing logic of neoliberalism (McBride and Evans, 2017; Cahill and Konings, 2017). Yet a decade on from the crisis, these attempts of renewal and continuity have coincided with the emergence of new political movements that have sought to contest the management of the manner in which such a continuity might progress.

Whilst much has been made of the politics of resistance brought about by civil groups (Bailey et al., 2017; Seymour, 2014; Bieler, 2014; della Porta, 2015), politically left parties have fared quite badly since the crisis. The left in Portugal, as well as – in more limited ways – Syriza in Greece have had electoral success and the campaigns of Jeremy Corbyn in the UK and Bernie Sanders in the US have sought to redefine what a radical politics from the left might look like, but in general these have been few in number (Panitch and Gindin, 2018). Indeed, even where the left had been successful in South America, electoral defeats in recent years have seen many suggest that the era of the so-called 'pink tide' is on the wane (Webber, 2017). Instead, the emergence of a right-wing turn within the contours of international politics has been more profound. Parties that were considered on the 'radical right' of politics have gained significantly in the last decade and parties that had previously not existed have moved quickly into prominence. More substantially, it has not merely been in electoral politics and in votes where we have witnessed a substantial shift towards the right. Right-wing narratives and arguments that were nurtured in previously marginalised far-right groups have found a way to figure in mainstream debates. With the election of Donald Trump in 2016 this took on even more significance. The utilisation of populist themes such as anti-immigration, American nationalism and anti-globalism during the Trump campaign has seen the world's largest super power elect a president that fully engages with such narratives (Kellner, 2016).

As a result, questions have been raised about how the contemporary neoliberal world order might sustain itself in light of Trump's administration. Certainly those in more conventional streams of international relations (IR) who write on international order have suggested that the post-war cold war order is indeed in great danger of being dismantled (Jervis et al., 2018; Ikenberry, 2018; Mead, 2018). Yet, those state-centric and geopolitical commentators from the conservative and liberal traditions within the discipline of IR have made this claim many times before. Most notably, in the aftermath of the Bush administration and in the war in Iraq, many suggested that the form of globalised world that emerged in the 1990s would become dismantled by the less institutional approaches to international affairs that were favoured by the so-called 'Neo-Cons' of the Bush administrations (Worth, 2017a). Yet, within studies of what we can tentatively call 'Critical

IPE',[1] the effect that this recent right turn will have on wider processes of neoliberalism within the ordering and the shaping of the global political economy has been considered less. Also, the wider structural effects that this right turn might have more generally on the nature and sustainability of capitalism itself need to be assessed in greater depth.

This introduction sets out to tentatively explore the role that the contemporary far-right has within the neoliberal order. In doing so it looks to touch upon the major questions that will be answered by critically examining the nature of the far-right throughout the book. In particular it asks whether the far-right represent a form of structural opposition to neoliberalism or whether it might complement it to a degree that would sustain its existence, albeit in a different form. It asks whether, even if the far-right does not necessarily represent a hegemonic challenge to the contours of free market capitalism, it reveals a world order that might be suffering from morbid symptoms and unravelling towards terminal crisis.

Neoliberalism and the Far-Right

As the governing ideological principle of the post-cold war, the concept and meaning of neoliberalism is one that has been debated in depth over the last decade. Since the financial crisis there are those that have suggested that the era of neoliberal governance is either in terminal decline or in deep crisis (Kotz, 2015; Dumenil and Levy, 2011; Overbeek and van Apeldoorn, 2012). At the same time others have suggested that neoliberalism has risen from the ashes of the crisis to continue as the main ideological driver of the global economy (Cahill, 2014; Mirowski, 2013; Crouch, 2011). Certainly, whilst bank bailouts became a feature of the post-crisis environment, many at the time logically concluded that a new regulatory framework at the heart of the international financial system would develop. Instead, stringent economic policy in Euro Zone countries that appeared based upon the World Bank Structural Adjustment Policies, saw the politics of debt management and austerity adopted, which re-asserted neoliberalism as the central focus of the post-crisis environment.

The ambiguity behind the content and sustainability of 'neoliberalism' has led certain commentators to question its validity at all in contemporary debates around political economy. Some for example have suggested that the term has become so vague and overused that is has become meaningless (Eriksen et al., 2015; Dunn, 2017). They argue that neoliberalism has been used in a manner whereby it can 'explain all things to all people' and as a result limits the analysis of very real events and political behaviour by reducing them to being a part of the wider 'neoliberal' process. Yet, as recent collections demonstrate in depth, neoliberalism has remained the overriding ideological focus of the contemporary political order (Springer, Birch and MacLeavy, 2016; Cahill et al., 2018). The main driving principles whereby politics becomes subjected to economic domination so that it appears almost as a form of 'inverted totalitarianism' remain intact (Kiely, 2018). In this sense, politics remains constrained by the need to be economically competitive as a state, to become attractive towards investments and consequently to appear to 'internationalise' in order to develop (Picciotto, 1991). As a result of this, tax reductions, privatisation and financialisation have become commonplace as states seek to respond to the pressures of the global market. Indeed, as the decade of austerity measures have led to the trimming of state expenditure amidst the importance of 'debt management', it could be suggested that this 'inverted totalitarianism' has been strengthened from the crisis (Kiely, 2018).

In this sense, the contemporary post-crisis world order is one that remains characterised by its neoliberal hegemony.

However, whilst neoliberalism might have maintained its ideological grip on the workings of the global political economy, the political reactions that have emerged post-crisis have also shown up its contradictions. They have provided avenues of political protest and polarisation to levels that dwarfed the pre-crisis era. In this way, the very essence of the logistics behind neoliberalism have been challenged. The so-called taken-for-granted accumulation of 'knowledge' that binds its very fabric together, or what Antonio Gramsci understood as the 'common-sense' of a particular order (Crehan, 2016: 43–44; Gramsci, 1971: 325–327), has thus come under greater scrutiny. Yet, despite the criticisms, it has been the left which has failed to build on this discontent and has, to an extent, allowed far-right narratives to develop. Conversely, the far-right has forged a critique not around the economy or indeed upon many of the key assumptions within the fabric of the neoliberal order, but instead on what they understand to be their social consequences. As a result, processes such as globalisation, multiculturalism, immigration and the erosion of national culture have been their main targets of resentment. As the social fallout of the crisis began to take effect, anger directed towards immigration and the perception of 'over-population' has become prevalent across Europe and the US. Added to this has been the growth of an Islamophobia that has escalated since the attacks on the World Trade Center on 11 September 2001.

These issues have not emerged without an economic content. Economic nationalism has had a long tradition in opposing free market principles. As many economic and world order historians have commented, it was indeed the return to the international arena of forms of economic nationalism that was to ultimately see the unravelling of the 19th-century liberal order (Hobsbawm, 1987; Cox, 1987). The further unravelling saw the tragedy of the First World War played out as a result of competing imperial European powers and the subsequent post-war emergence of fascism that was to prove the ultimate expression of economic nationalism. The beginnings of such an economic nationalism as a reaction to neoliberalism was noted by some well before the economic crisis, as movements emerged in the 1990s such as the American Patriot movement, the anti-NAFTA movement and the campaigns of individuals such as Pat Buchanan and Ross Perot who opposed the idea of a post-cold war economic order (Rupert, 2000; Worth, 2002). As a form of opposition, economic nationalism is seen through the endorsement of policies such as protectionism, a rejection of free trade and through a form of nativism in the labour force that favours indigenous workers. In this instance, the economic logistics of neoliberalism are explicitly challenged.

It would be wrong, however, to assume that when the economy is discussed within far-right discourses it reverts to a form of economic nationalism as a default position. Far from it. There have also been many accounts that suggest that the far-right do not appear in opposition to neoliberalism at all, but instead are part of its process. Rather than following the historical precedence of 1880–1945 which saw market liberalism attacked by nationalist forces that supported a return to protectionism, the far-right can also be seen to aid neoliberalism continuity. Terms such as 'neoliberal populism', 'neoliberal nationalism' and 'authoritarian neoliberalism' have all been discussed in recent years and all stress that far-right discourses are actually compatible to neoliberalism and can provide a basis for its sustainability and legitimacy.

Neoliberal populism refers to parties that place campaigns such as anti-immigration and anti-multiculturalism alongside ones that seek to reduce taxes and the role of the state in society (Betz, 1994). The populism is not just geared around nativist traits but also upon forms of 'welfare chauvinism', where recipients of the welfare states are categorised as 'lazy', 'unwilling to work' and of living off the taxes of those in employment. Here therefore, a spirit of economic individuality is placed alongside the prejudices that are commonly associated with the right-wing. It should be noted, that this combination long pre-dates the post-cold war era of 'globalisation' and was associated with a new right that quickly became the mainstream in the 1980s with Reaganomics in the US and Thatcherism in the UK. Indeed, as the late pioneer of Cultural Studies, Stuart Hall demonstrated in the 1980s, forms of populism and nationalism were integral to the very mobilisation of neoliberalism (Hall, 1988).

'Neoliberal nationalism' was a term used by Adam Harmes to denote the fact that neoliberalism was not just compatible to nationalism but in some instances depended upon national-ist discourses in order to function adequately (Harmes, 2012). Harmes distinguishes between conservative populism or 'paleo conservativism', that tends to favour forms of protectionism, and what he calls neoliberal nationalism (2012: 73). He suggests that whilst the former has been associated with traditional forms of European nationalism, the latter is more akin to an American tra-dition that complemented the Thatcher–Reagan form of market populism of the 1980s (2012: 74–77). Neoliberal nationalism is categorised as one where free market ideals are upheld best not at the international level through global institutions but at the level of the nation-state. Certainly, the libertarian traditions inherent within the rise of the Tea Party in the US and the Eurosceptical appeal that led to the Brexit vote in the UK seem to combine the forces of economic libertarianism with popular nationalism. The problems with engaging with both forces, however, is that the contradictions of the two become more and more apparent as they gain prominence, resulting in more reactionary expressions of nationalism.

Finally, 'authoritarian neoliberalism' draws from this to a degree but largely refers to the turn towards strong leadership alongside state coercion in the wake of the financial crisis. Rather than attempt to forge forms of consent in order to sustain neoliberal continuity, states and institutions have tended to resort to hard-line measures. Whether they be from the so-called troika of the European Commission, European Central Bank (ECB) and International Monetary Fund (IMF) that enforced debt measurements as a result of the Euro crisis or from the emergence of popular authoritarian leaders who look to use instruments of the state to marginalise opposition, the emphasis in maintaining the market system has been one that has been managed 'from above' rather than through the forging of consensus (Bruff, 2014; Tansel, 2017). The success of Trump has thus added to the success of leaders such as Putin, Erodogan and Modi in establishing a populist form of nationalism in order to sustain neoliberal continuity (Bruff, 2017; Chacko and Jayasuriya, 2017). Whilst this post-crisis categorisation has been well articulated (particularly by Ian Bruff), this is again, not a new phenomenon. Not only had the architects of the neoliberal doctrines themselves – particularly Hayek – welcomed the authoritarianism inherent within Pinochet's Chile, which is often seen as the first experiment of neoliberalism, but Hall's own understanding of the rise of Thatcher was very much understood in the same manner (Peck, 2010; Hall, 1988).

These three positions thus suggest that neoliberalism is compatible with reactionary campaigns associated with the far-right and at times thrives when engaged with them. Despite this, the historical precedent and the very content of populism and nationalism that we have recently seen from the far-right suggest that even if some of the populist and nationalist rhetoric does show a dimension that has always existed in the fabric of neoliberalism, they allow a set of forces to be unleashed that are geared towards its ideological contestation. Subsequently, another way of understanding this relationship is by viewing it through a wider historical lens and the role the far-right plays in the *longue-durée* (Saull et al., 2014; Saull, 2014). Here, rather than appearing as a form of opposition per se, far-right positions and movements have been absorbed into the fabric of a specific historical order through a process of co-option and absorption (Anievas and Saull, 2019; Davidson and Saull, 2017; Kiely, 2017). Yet, due to the contradictions inherent between right-wing populist positions and the wider logistics within capitalism, the appeal of far-right ideas appear more prominent during times of crisis. It is during these times that such ideas cease to be co-opted and emerge more prominently from the margins. At the same time, it is also during times of crisis that the far-right appears as a form of 'alternative' to the status quo. In this instance, it can appear as both a facilitator and a potential resistor of a prevailing order, which can go some way to address the riddle of the question of neoliberal/far-right compatibility.

Taking this further, at the wider international level, capitalism is characterised by a competitivism and an inequality that is marked by an even deeper contradiction. As capitalism developed, fractions of capital become internationalised through the formation of transnational classes that become increasingly prominent over time (Jessop and Overbeek, 2018). Due to the uneven development of capitalism, class interests express themselves in different forms across the realm of international production, utilising different forms of control strategically (Bieler and Morton, 2018). The social utilisation of populist nationalism associated with the far-right can be used as a vehicle where class interests can be maintained. Yet, whilst these might be employed in a manner that appears consistent within the dominant forms of (neoliberal) capital, they also bring about a series of measures that serve to contradict or constrain such interests. As a result, they can lead to wider ruptures to the content and reproduction of international capital as a whole (Panitch and Albo, 2015). Here we can see how the role of the far-right in the *longue-durée* plays out in terms of the historically fashioned world order and its transformation.

Wars of Position

If we are to perceive that the far-right provides a significant threat to the future character of the neoliberal world order, we should see how such an order can be challenged or transformed. Before doing this, it should first be acknowledged that the enormity of different positions taken by what we might call the far-right or populist right make any wider claims on the durability of the world order hard to make. Thus, whilst we might talk about the 'far' or 'radical' right in the form of a singular global actor, the multifaceted nature of all the different parts that make up this new wider phenomenon need to be looked at more closely in order to make such conclusions.

One of the problems with many recent commentaries on the far-right has been in terms of both its definition and in its overall strategy. As we have already seen, the different interpretations given to their engagement with neoliberalism show that understanding and conceptualising its wider significance is both problematic and open to wide scrutiny. To begin with the categorisation of what might be considered as the far-right becomes difficult. For many in the field of comparative politics for example, the term 'radical right' appears to be the preferred title as it accounts for parties that are critical of the political establishment but do not look to overthrow the democratic system (Rydgren, 2017). Terms such as 'right-wing' and 'far-right' tend to be used interchangeably to include a wide range of groups, individuals and movements that have emerged in the neoliberal age and espouse a wide range of campaigns associated with populism, nationalism, nativism and xenophobia (Vieten and Poynting, 2016). Whilst the 'alternative right' at first referred to those that put forward an alternative position to those of the 'mainstream' right, they have subsequently been associated with the 'alt-right' in the US. This has tended to represent forms of extreme and often fringe versions of the radical/far-right that also are more likely to engage with white supremacy, neo-fascism and extreme conspiracy cultism (Hawley, 2017).

This study is not concerned as such with definition and uses the terms right-wing, radical, populist and far-right interchangeably throughout, accepting the general confines of these wide categories, but the objectives of such groups should come under scrutiny when examining their wider significance. For example, can we understand the far-right as a 'global' process at all and if so, is there any form of coherence for such a process to have a material effect on the global political and economic system? Whilst this in itself sounds like not just a comprehensive task but one that can only be subjective and speculative, it is useful to look at Gramsci's idea of a war of position in order to assess its relevance as a potential source of opposition.

One of the many areas of interest within the notebooks written by Gramsci when in a fascist prison in the 1920s and 1930s,[2] was his understanding of how to mount an effective form of opposition to a prevailing hegemonic order. He argued that for a challenge to an order to be successful it needed to be applied through both a war of 'movement' and a war of 'position'. A war of movement or manoeuvre represents a frontal assault on the state and its institutions of power. This might enviably look towards a 'total victory' in a revolutionary process of the sort that Trotsky envisioned for the Soviet Union, but it also can refer to the process of the mass strike suggested much earlier by Rosa Luxemburg, where she outlined how a strategic attack on the forces of production during a period of crisis can lead to revolutionary transformation (Gramsci, 1971: 233–234; Gramsci, 2007: 209). In contrast, a war of position refers to the battle of the 'hearts and minds' in society and where the key assumptions, principles and 'common-sense' of a particular order are contested, challenged and ultimately replaced (Gramsci, 1971: 229–230). For Gramsci the war of position was the more difficult to sustain as it required the building of a different form of hegemonic order so that a new set of values could be developed. This required time and could take many stages and forms.

The war of position thus can be seen as a process where the basis of an alternative hegemonic project is presented within civil and political society at large. It is also here where a prolonged historical struggle can occur in order for norms and ideas to be built, challenged and debated. For Gramsci, the war of position was an important process in the building of socialism and one that both Bolshevik and other socialist leaders have often underestimated in their own perception of revolutionary strategy. Hence, any success of a socialist society depended upon the building of a hegemonic project that could win the 'hearts and minds' of the public at large through a prolonged war of position (Brodkin and Strathmann, 2004).

Gramsci saw the various types of passive revolutions[3] that occurred throughout Europe in the 19th and 20th centuries as ones that took on different characteristics and forms during their wider wars of position and movement. The struggle of social forces in 19th-century Europe resulted in the success of the bourgeois European nation-state, but this would later suffer crises which allowed for new alternatives to develop. As Gramsci argues:

> In Europe from 1789 to 1870 there was a (political) war of
> movement in the French Revolution and a long war of position
> from 1815 to 1870. In the present epoch, the war of movement
> took place politically from March 1917 to March 1921; this
> was followed by a war of position whose representative – both
> practical (for Italy) and ideological (for Europe) – is fascism.
> (Gramsci, 1971: 120)

Thus, at his time of writing, the forces of fascism had seemingly emerged out of the various crises which appeared from the ashes of the Great War and had gained significant momentum in the war of position.

We can take parallels from this with the growth of the far-right today. Whilst, the far-right cannot be seen as a single entity with a single ideology, it nevertheless represents a reaction to an order that has thrived during the period of economic crisis. Therefore, one way of looking at the relevance of the far-right in terms of its wider significance would be to see it as a form of a war of position looking to gain the same significance as fascism during Gramsci's own era. In an earlier study, I used the notion of the war of position to assess the progress of three oppositional or counter-hegemonic challenges to the post-crisis neoliberal order. These were what I tentatively called 'progressive inter-nationalism', 'national populism' and 'religious fundamentalism' (Worth, 2013: 42–46). I argued that these provided a basis for a war of position and as such a hegemonic challenge to neoliberal-ism, but each suffered from contradictions and a distinct lack of unity within them (Worth, 2013: 47–49). I also suggested that the 'national-populist' group which embodies the far-right did provide greater clarity with a potential protectionist alternative to the others. Yet, as outlined above, due to its ambiguity to neo-liberalism, the idea of the far-right as a form of economic opposi-tion becomes more questionable (Worth, 2013: 90–91).

This book will look to question whether the global far-right has indeed the necessary components to embark upon a successful war of position. It is also aware of the ability of neoliberalism to co-opt particular forms of resistance or potential opposition to it by subsuming them into its wider hegemonic sphere. Gramsci himself referred to this process as *trasform-ismo*, whereby challenges are fended off and absorbed back into a passive form (Gramsci, 1971: 58–59). Indeed, in terms of class relations, this is particularly pertinent. For whilst the many far-right discourses might seem to contradict international capitalism – especially in terms of limiting freedom of movement, through anti-immigration measures, thus limiting the growth of capital – these are often played out in the realm of existing class relations (Davidson, 2014).

Morbid Symptoms

The war of position provides us with ways in which we can understand how far-right discourses are challenging the key assumptions of a specific order. In addition to this we can also borrow from Gramsci to use a different yet complementary synopsis for the present time. He talks of the world environment of 1930 as one which contains morbid symptoms, whereby one social order appears to be 'dying' but a new one is yet to emerge (Gramsci, 1971: 276). As a wider quoted piece that appears as passage number 30 in his third notebook, he also questions whether the use of force and coercion can be used in order to block a new order from developing and instead to lead to an alternative 'arrangement'. To quote the piece in full:

> The crisis consists precisely because the old is dying and
> the new cannot be born; in this interregnum a great deal of
> morbid symptoms appear[4] … a problem caused by the 'crisis of

authority' of the old generations in power, and by the mechanical impediment that has been imposed on those who could exercise hegemony, which prevents them from carrying out their mission.

The problem is the following: can a rift between popular masses and ruling ideologies as serious as that which emerged after the war be 'cured' by the simple exercise of force, preventing the new ideologies from imposing themselves? Will the interregnum, the crisis whose historically normal solution is blocked in this way, necessarily be resolved in favour of the old? Given the character of the ideologies, that can be ruled out – yet not in an absolute sense. Meanwhile physical depression will lead in the long run to a widespread scepticism, and a new 'arrangement' will be found. (Gramsci, 1971: 275–276)

There are a number of dynamics we can draw from this in order to understand the contemporary order. We should, however, also put this in its context. As has been suggested by Gilber Achcar, his use of 'morbid symptoms' is not entirely associated here with the rise of fascism. The very fact that the Italian Communist Party (PCI) had followed an internationalist ultra-left position that believed that the defeat of fascism was inevitable, rejecting the idea that the Party needed to engage with civil society to contest fascism ideals, was consistent with his understanding of hegemony and the strategy of the war of positon (Achcar, 2018).

Yet, the idea of a crisis of authority, coupled with periods of coercion, competing hegemonic projects and the possibility of a 'new arrangement' are all realities of where we find ourselves today. Coercion – whether understood as 'authoritarian', 'nationalist' or 'populist' – has been increasingly used by leaders such as Putin, Modi and Duterte as a means of maintaining popular support. To a degree they are all reminiscent of Marx's classical understanding of Bonapartism and with Gramsci's own understanding of Caesarism, whereby competing social forces conflict with each other resulting in a strong leader who looks to forcefully bring them together (Gramsci, 1971: 219–223; Marx, 1967). However, these have also been popular terms within political science for a long time when accounting for the emergence of strong leaders in places that have not developed a mature democratic system of governance and are in no way solely related to post-crisis society (Alavi, 1972). Indeed, certainly with Putin, the idea of Caesarism has long been applied to account for his rise and consolidation of power (Kagarlitsky, 2008; Worth, 2009; Simon, 2010).

It is therefore not necessarily the retreat towards coercion that is prevalent here but the crisis of hegemony itself and of the unknown that might appear. Morbid symptoms emerge out of such a hegemonic crisis and where the old leadership and form/ character of hegemony finds it difficult to maintain legitimacy. It is there when either a new arrangement between the old and competing forces can be built, or whether a set of opposing forces can emerge to construct a 'new' order. Such an interpretation of the condition of post-crisis malaise can also provide ways of thinking about the contemporary order and the role that right-wing oppositional forces might play. Whilst for the left, the emergence of reactionary populism amidst a backlash against globalisation might appear to contact morbid symptoms by their very nature, the relevance of the term appears to be one that takes on a more poignant meaning when considered structurally. The very fact that the fabric of the current order has been placed under threat by a number of forces – of which the far-right represent one and perhaps the most significant – leaves a sense that it is the order itself that is experiencing such morbid symptoms.

In terms of what we see in this book, the electoral rise of parties that have embodied right-wing rhetoric, the Brexit phenomena and the success of the Trump campaign are all indicative that the contemporary neoliberal order is suffering from morbid symptoms. The fact that this has occurred relatively quickly in each of these cases is another sign of this. For example, as we shall see in Chapter 3, the emergence of parties that have appeared from outside the political mainstream has shaken the foundations of European politics to its core. Traditional political parties on the centre left and centre right that had politically managed the post-cold war era have quickly come under electoral pressure from populist right-wing parties. The Brexit campaign in the UK saw the accumulation of a set of reactionary positions and populist assertions that have not been witnessed in modern political British history (Gough, 2017). The result of this has seen a series of Conservative-led governments looking to act upon these sentiments in their pursuit of Brexit. Similarly, the Trump presidential campaign allowed for the legitimacy of groups associated with the 'alt-right' in order to gain popular support (Lyons, 2017). As with Brexit, when Trump let the genie out of the bottle of the alt-right, his administration looked at ways in which it could co-opt its general rhetoric whilst holding its extreme elements at bay.

These can all be viewed as potential morbid symptoms that have become inherent within the post-war neoliberal order. Whilst these might not serve – and indeed in many instances do not seek – to bring an end to its overall character, they all have led to a deepening of its instability. The question for us is then to ask whether the far-right might appear as an architect of the 'new' and put forward a war of position that could blossom into successfully challenging the current order or whether this might lead to a position whereby a new arrangement is put forward that retains much of the general characteristics of the contemporary neoliberal order.

The Fallacy of Market Society

Whilst Gramsci's unique brand of Marxism allows us to understand how and why the contemporary order is in a state of crisis and how far-right discourses might look to position themselves within such a crisis, it is also of interest to look at Karl Polanyi's account of the fallacy of market society. This is especially relevant when added to the idea of the morbid symptoms of neoliberalism. Karl Polanyi's *Great Transformation* has long attracted attention within political economy as being the antithesis to Hayek's *Road to Serfdom*, which remains the most influential text in support of a self-regulating market society (Filip, 2012). Indeed, Polanyi's *magnum opus* has attracted so many different interpretations that it is nigh on impossible to find agreement on where his main criticisms were directed in the book (Dale, 2010).

Central to Polanyi's narrative in the *Great Transformation* was that the market society on which the 19th century was built had collapsed and the reasons behind this were contained in the fallacies inherent within the idea of the self-regulated market (Polanyi, 1944: 3–21, 71–81). He then moves between the very fabric and notion of market society through the perpetration of a self-regulated market and the history of its inception within England in the early part of the 19th century. His main critique of this self-regulated movement was that it was characterised by a 'double-movement' whereby whenever the market economy expanded it was met by a counter-movement that looked to check its expansion and protect society from its excesses (Polanyi, 1944: 136). The realities within British society were that after winning the battle of the importance of the self-regulated market through the 1830s and 1840s, the period of 'golden age liberalism' followed from 1846 to the 1860s,[5] whereby the laissez-faire economic system became prominent but was nevertheless controlled by regulatory banking acts passed by parliament. As Polanyi then shows, by the time the British were importing the Gold Standard as the benchmark for international finance, a backlash had occurred within society whereby the new industrial working classes demanded the vote (Polanyi, 1944: 234–235). This led to a period where the laissez-faire system was highly compromised domestically, as welfarism and nationalism became increasingly commonplace, yet internationally the Gold Standard remained unchallenged (Cox, 1987).

As a result, the world order in the late 19th century saw a renewal of inter-state rivalry and the eventual unravelling of the whole liberal system in a slow demise. Whilst many in international political economy (IPE) have provided a synopsis for this, in terms of a decline in hegemony (Keohane, 1984; Cox, 1987), there is another important consideration. For whilst British influence at the time might have waned, the liberal international system continued to persist through the international financial system and the workings of the Gold Standard. Polanyi argued that the belief in the Gold Standard became so sacrosanct that figures from all traditions 'from Bismarck and Lassalle, John Stuart Mill and Henry George, Philip Snowden and Calvin Coolidge, Mises and Trotsky' accepted it as an unchallengeable institution (Polanyi, 1944: 26). To this extent, Germany adopted the Gold Standard and then seemingly used it for protectionist measures by the end of the 19th century adding to the contradiction of the liberal state. The collection of counter-movements within society provided national protection that halted the move towards free trade (Polanyi, 1944: 19).

The parallels with the contemporary order are striking. There are many studies that illustrate how counter-movements have emerged to challenge contemporary market relations in the neo-liberal era, which have appeared in a number of different guises (for example, Chin and Mittelman, 2000; Silver and Arrighi, 2003;

Birchfield, 2005; Munck, 2007; Hyman, 2015). Yet, with all the social movements and labour groups that have challenged the ideology of market neoliberalism, the turn to nationalism that occurred towards the end of the 20th century has been less discussed. Whilst the liberal system might have collapsed by the 1920s, it began to unravel and display morbid symptoms by the turn of the century. Indeed, the first signs of these were noted by Karl Marx as he classically accounted for the crises in the 1850s and 1860s in his third volume of *Capital*, suggesting the wider unsustainability of capitalism (Marx, 1981). Yet the long depression of 1873–1896 saw the undermining of the market system further amidst a backdrop of nationalism and rival imperialism. We can tentatively understand today's growth of the far-right and its growing influence on political discourse in a similar vein. For just as the Gold Standard-inspired market system of the 19th century stumbled on in the aftermath of crises, so has the neoliberal system of the 21st century.

Rather than looking at the rise of the right as a sign that the world is moving to the politics of the 1930s as many a popular commentary has suggested (Stephens, 2016; Mason, 2016), it might be more accurate to perhaps see the rise of the national right as a symptom of the result of an accumulation of countermovements in the same vein that was beginning to emerge by the end of the 19th century. Like then, as now, the market-based system looked for continuity in the aftermath of crisis. As the Gold Standard was maintained throughout the 19th century and well into the next century, then the neoliberal system, characterised through its marketisation logistics and managed through its working principles of floating exchange rates also continued in spite of crisis. Similarly, the moves to nationalism in their various forms, from the rise of populist right-wing parties in Europe, to the realisation of Brexit and the move towards tariffs brought in by the Trump administration, see the contemporary economic system come under greater strains amidst growing contradictions.

The right-wing movements discussed in this book could thus potentially be seen as being indicative of a wider collection of counter-movements that might point to a prolonged unravelling of the neoliberal market system. This also resonates with Gramsci's metaphoric understanding of morbid symptoms. Whilst Gramsci was, of course, writing from the position of witnessing the total collapse of a system in the 1930s, his sentiments of morbid symptoms within the legitimacy of an order can also be given to understand the more drawn-out unravelling of a wider global system. The book will look to see whether these new right-wing movements have made such a significant impact on the wider global order that we can suggest that morbid symptoms have indeed become profound. It will look at whether far-right social forces are in the process of a war of position and whether this will lead to a different 'arrangement' or configuration of neoliberal capitalism or to a crucial stage of hegemonic crisis and subsequently class struggle.

Outline of the Book

The book will move on from this introduction to look firstly at the origins of the far-right prior to the 2001 attacks on the World Trade Center. The new world neoliberal order that emerged in the early 1990s might have attracted a certain response that was unique to the post-cold war environment, but the reactionary nationalist discourses that emerged were drawn from an array of nationally specific movements that were already fully developed. The first chapter looks at the remaking of the far-right after the end of the cold war and how the focus of conspiracy – that has always been a feature of the right-wing narratives, transformed around the significance of the 'New World Order'.

In terms of watershed moments, many in electoral studies would point to the financial crisis as a trigger for success (Mudde, 2016). Certainly, this was the case with the emergence of the Tea Party and in the marked increase in radical right support in Europe. However, in terms of moments that shaped what form new right-wing movements would take, the twin-towers attack would be monumental. It was from here that Islamophobia took a far more central role within the reactionary right and a form of crusade against Islam began to surface (Sheridan, 2006). Chapter 2 looks at how this new populist right took shape after 9/11 and then post-crisis began to emerge as a serious collection of parties, movements and networks across global society. It looks at whether these assortments of social forces have a coherence that could be regarded as a hegemonic challenge to the neoliberal order, especially in light of the financial order

The next three chapters build on this question by looking at the specific cases of the far-right's development. Chapter 3 looks at the growth and electoral success of radical right parties across Europe and at the different positions they have taken in regards to neoliberalism. It looks at how certain groups have emerged that have supported protectionism, whilst others have favoured a greater concentration of market economics. Some have also either played down economic ideals as secondary or have been highly contradictory in their understanding of them. It will ask how these inconsistencies would affect the nature of neoliberal continuity in the post-crisis world.

Following on from this, the next two chapters look at the US and the UK. Here, in the so-called heartlands of neoliberalism, two most significant events have taken place that can be attributed to right-wing populism. The election of Donald Trump in the US and Brexit in the UK have unleashed a set of social forces that threaten to re-shape the nature and the direction of the post-crisis neoliberal order. In these chapters I look at the origins behind these social forces and show how they have emerged to the forefront of politics in both countries.

Finally, and following on from this the last chapter looks at how the assumptions taken from far-right discourses have become embedded into mainstream political thought and process. This is particularly significant when looking at questions on the nature of the future of the contemporary world order, as certain norms that were central to the ideological construction formation of the post-cold war order have been challenged and increasingly contested. As a retort to this, the book will conclude by looking at ways in which the right can be countered and what the left can learn from the right's advance. For, as certain media columnists have pointed out, the left does at least know how to construct a critique of neoliberalism on its economic terms (Monbiot, 2016). The problem remains that it appears unable to mount a sustained strategy of post-neoliberalism capable of countering the advances made by the right. The focal point of the book might be to look at right-wing critiques in relation to the wider neoliberal order, but the wider objective still remains, which is how, in the era of neoliberal instability, the left might offer a model as a response which goes beyond the state-centric confines of post-war social democracy.

ONE | Against the New World Order

The end of the cold war was to provide a significant watershed moment in the reconfiguration of politics across the international spectrum. As the neoliberal doctrine began to flourish and a deregulated global economy started to emerge, the right and left began to alter their wider ideological outlook and objectives. Whilst the claims of the death of socialism after the fall of the Berlin Wall and the Soviet Union were to be seen as both exaggerated and ultimately false (see, for example, Fukuyama, 1992; Dahrendorf, 1990), the form of state socialism as epitomised by the USSR and its allies was more universally considered to have been eradicated (Lane, 1997; Cox, 1991). The western form of socialism, prominently identified with the Keynesian inspired national social democracy, also appeared to be in decline. Unable to emerge from its left-nationalist shell and adapt to the rising globalisation of production, left of centre parties began to look towards embracing market-led solutions with ideologies such as the Third Way (Giddens, 1998). These perhaps became associated best with the UK Labour Party under Blair, the Schröder-led SDP and to a lesser extent, with the Clinton administration in the 1990s.

Whilst the left seems to take a step back from the socialism of the 21st century, the end of communism and the 'Russian' threat also had a profound effect on the parties of the right. Not only did the focal point of opposition disappear with the collapse of the

Soviet Union, but the need for a social response to the different forms of socialism suddenly became equally redundant with the onset of globalisation. As a result, traditional forms of Christian Democracy that became dominant during the era that followed the Second World War across Western Europe began to lose their previous meaning (Duncan, 2006). To the right of the post-war consensus, far-right-wing groups were already beginning to re-emerge from their public denunciations in the aftermath of fascism. The 1970s and 1980s saw both the emergence of political parties based upon a renewed expression of nationalism and a number of civil organisations geared to more confrontational forms of expression.

This chapter looks at how the far-right resurgence became part of a wider symptom of fault lines that began to emerge within the post-war European political society in the late 1960s/early 1970s. At this time, new 'post-material' issues and movements became evident in politics which seemed to break from the traditional political divisions such as class, age and occupation (Inglehart, 1971). As a result, issues that emerged from the so-called 'counter-culture' discourse in the 1960s, which included values such as racial and sexual equality, environmental issues and humanitarian campaigns, began to be reflected within electoral politics. The inclusion of the far-right into this category appeared more as a reverse post-materialist process. In other words, as such issue-based activism led to the loosening of traditional party cleavages, then the resurgence of neo-nationalism loosened them further, albeit that they often did so in opposition to the very issues that the counter-culture wished to bring to light (Carroll, 2014). As traditional parties began to take heed and respond to the new social movements that emerged from the 1960s, the increased backlash against them allowed a reactionary counter-discourse to grow at the same time.

Emerging from the Abyss

The defeat of fascism in 1945 saw the forces of nationalism on the defensive. In Europe particularly, nationalism was largely placed and contained within a growing political consensus that looked towards co-operation amidst a wider process of de-colonialisation. This was aided by the mixed-economic post-war consensus which saw anti-communism provide a unity on the political right and social democracy a similar accord for the left. The fascist dictatorships which were left in Western Europe, such as those on the Iberian Peninsula survived due to their increasing usefulness to the anti-communist cause. The accession of Portugal to NATO and the strong relationship Franco had with the west was aided by their technical neutrality during the Second World War and their eagerness to reform economically in order to survive in the post-war environment.

Right-wing nationalism was thus generally contained at least in Europe in the initial post-war period as the revulsion of fascism, coupled with the long process of war crimes tribunals saw any re-engagement unlikely despite a recognition that the preoccupation with anti-communism had superseded it. In Germany and Austria, the 'de-nazification' programmes looked to ease the potential fear of new fascist resurgences (Taylor, 2011). These included mechanisms and thresholds placed in former fascist states that curtailed the support that ageing figures associated with those regimes were attracting (Backer, 1978). What emerged instead by the late 1950s was a nationalism that became re-awakened as a result of de-colonisation. The establishment of the Organisation Armée Secrète (OAS) in the aftermath of the Algerian war of independence in France was an initial symptom of this. Racial divisions emerging out the Empire also began to surface in Britain. In Britain the Nationalities Act provided freedom of movement for citizens across the Empire and saw an influx of immigration to the UK. As the main incentive for this was due to a labour shortage in Britain, a racial hierarchy within the county was quickly established which led to extreme forms of discrimination. Unrest and riots in Nottingham and Notting Hill were to follow which would lead to the establishment of right-wing groups like the Monday Club within the Conservative Party (in 1961) and later to the anti-immigration campaigns of Enoch Powell (Schoen, 1977).

Away from Europe, racial tensions were felt far more prominently in the US. Given that the history of such tensions were steeped in the fabric of American history, it became increasingly problematic for a country to lead programmes against racial discrimination in Europe, whilst continuing to practise them freely at home. As a result, far-right institutions were perhaps quicker to establish themselves in opposition to movements towards great racial equality. Much of this, it has to be stressed, was aided by the hysteria that accompanied anti-communism. Groups such as the John Birch Society, for example, were founded distinctly on the back of the fear of communism and would have a lasting effect on the conspiratorial nature of the far-right in the US. Yet, these fed into the more racial groups and saw a rise in the membership of the Ku Klux Klan and in the establishment of groups such as the American Nazi Party and the National Socialist White People's Party (Cox and Durham, 2000). As the US entered the 1960s the civil liberties movement was already in full swing and the battle-lines between reformers and segregation retentionists was fully developed, with the campaigns of George Wallace and his period as Governor of Alabama – where his attempts to thwart federal laws saw him appear as a symbolic resistance of central government – aiding the growth of a further legacy that would become a hallmark of later American far-right campaigns.

Race and de-colonialisation also saw counter-movements and subsequently the growth of racist regimes in regions where newly formed post-colonial states gained independence. The most notable here being the Ian Smith-led Republic of Rhodesia and the Apartheid system of governance that was to emerge in post-colonial South Africa. Both of these shared support from groups in Europe and the US. In the US, South Africa was admired by right-wing groups that favoured segregation, whilst conservative groups closer to the mainstream argued that their strong anti-communist rhetoric should be recognised and applauded, particularly in light of the fact that Africa appeared to provide ripe pickings for Soviet intervention (Plummer, 2003). Likewise, Ian Smith became something of a symbolic figurehead for the Monday Club, who were keen to support him throughout his period in office and organised annual receptions for him long after his fall from power (Pitchford, 2011). Meanwhile, also in Britain, the SAS forged links with a number of international networks ranging from counter-insurgency units within various remaining European colonies to anti-communism in Latin America (Henissart, 1970). Yet, it was the economic downturns of the 1970s alongside the wider reactions against the new social movements that were emerging in the later 1960s that were to produce the wider environment to allow the far-right to rebuild.

The establishment of the French Front National (FN) in 1972, the development of neo-fascism in Italy that emerged from the Italian Social Movement (MSI)[1] and the establishment of many proto fascist sub-cultures within European civil society saw the radical right move from a position of narrow appeal to one which drew more support from society at large. As a result, the idea of the extreme right was beginning to be recognised within the realms of the study of party politics and sociology. Whilst so-called 'post-materialist' social movements were looking to move civil and political society beyond the post-war discourse of the paternalist catch-all party structure, the emerging far-right sought to rediscover the nationalisms of the past. The new neo-nationalism also gained significant support from the industrial working class and from youth movements. In the same way that the counter-culture of the 1960s and 1970s saw new expressions of socialism and anarchism it also produced similar forms of right-wing nationalism and white supremacism. The punk and 'skinhead' movement, along with forms of leisure identity that were most notable in football and football hooliganism contributed to the re-establishment of the far-right in the decades preceding the end of the cold war (Griffin and Feldman, 2003).

A wider question could be asked: what form did the far-right of the 1970s and 1980s take? The general world-view of such political parties can be explained in some part as the general rejection of modernity in its various recreations. In this sense a common philosophical position could be attributed to far-right positions that could link them from one historical era to the next (Antón Mellón, 2013). In general the far-right was often seen as anything that appeared 'outside' of centre-right conservatism and included elements of nationalism, xenophobia, nativism and neo-fascism. It this case, the far-right was multi-dimensional in form and represented a type of umbrella movement (Art, 2011). Economically, their position, even at this stage, was also unclear. In general, the forms of 'boot-boy' fascism that emerged across European civil society during this time campaigned for renewed forms of National Socialism. Here, movements akin to the political organisations such as the Italian Social Movement located themselves firmly within the fascism economics of 1920s Italy. In contrast, more representative parties such as the FN argued initially for market liberalisation, before moving, by the time the Berlin Wall fell, to a neo-protectionism that was to strengthen as the 1990s proceeded. Where they seemed to unite was in demanding preferential treatment in terms of jobs, pay and welfare for white and indigenous workers (von Beyme, 1988).

The defining principle that united the far-right before the fall of the Berlin Wall was their anti-communism. This included the rejection of the Soviet Union and those within their sphere of influence, but what separated them from the anti-communism of the centre-right (and large elements of the social democratic centre-left) was their own definitions of 'communism'. For example, political groups such as the civil rights movements, the feminist movement and the anti-Apartheid movements were dismissed as being 'communist' in nature. Here, the new right-wing movements in Europe were to express solidarity with those in the US that had opposed anti-segregation and who were quick to condemn as 'communist' those that supported them. In youth and sub-culture, events such as 'rock against communism' appeared for the first time in Leeds in England in 1978 and were to provide the basis for clashes with newly emerged anti-fascist groups that would provide the first parallels with the street altercations of the 1920s and 1930s.

By the time the 'New Right' had emerged in the late 1970s as an intellectual and social 'way out' of the crisis, these neo-nationalist positions became more marginalised, particularly in places such as the US and the UK where Reagan and Thatcher respectively managed to co-opt much of their nationalist appeal within their own wider agenda. By looking to locate the intellectual principles of laissez-faire economics of the classical liberals, the monetarism of Milton Friedman and the social theory of Friedrich von Hayek alongside traditional conservative principles, the far-right became more marginalised. Indeed, Reagan's renewed anti-communist agenda in the US did much to widen an umbrella across the right that contained the development of any potential extremism. Likewise, in the UK, Thatcherism looked to engage with the anti-immigration discourse in a manner that had been previously lacking (Pitchford, 2011). Rather than having the effect of eradicating or neutralising radical groups as such, Thatcher's appeal kept them at the level of a sub-culture rather than one which could find wider support. Likewise, in continental Europe, the appeal of Reagan's anti-communist rhetoric appealed to many on the centre-right and served to curtail the ideological rise of neo-nationalism to an extent.

In France however, the 'left-turn' taken by its first socialist government under Mitterrand saw the FN make considerable electoral gains, often campaigning alongside more moderate right parties in order to provide a counter-weight to socialist advances. In 1986, the momentary shift in the electoral system to proportional representation saw them gain 35 seats in the parliamentary elections. Yet, the success of FN and of its charismatic leader and founder Jean Marie Le Pen in the 1980s was not the anomaly it might first appear. The rise of Jacque Chirac on a Thatcher–Reagan new right platform after that election saw the appeal of Le Pen diminish in line with elsewhere (Hainsworth, 2000). With the fall of the Berlin Wall in 1989 and the so-called triumph of a new right that had constructed the seeds of neoliberal economics that was now to become commonplace, the end of the cold war was to bring new avenues that would lead to a wider development of the far-right.

New Worlds, New Targets

The end of the cold war did not see an immediate change in philosophy for the far-right, nor did it look to change its main focus of attack. Certainly, far-right discourses retained their anti-semitism and the new era of 'global governance' provided ammunition for the retention of the traditional conspiracy of international Jewry that had been a feature from its inception (Hainsworth, 2000; Mudde, 2007). Indeed, parties such as the FN and Austrian Freedom Party (FPÖ) maintained derogatory references to Jewish figures and to Jewish culture throughout certain campaigns (Wodak and Pelinka, 2002). More explicitly, anti-semitism featured centrally in both post-Soviet Slavic accounts of the end of the cold war and right-wing American ones as new narratives were placed to what became known as the 'New World Order'.

The term 'New World Order' became significant in the aftermath of George Bush Sr's speech to Congress in September 1990, where, in light of the Iraqi invasion of Kuwait, he argued for greater integration of major powers in order to embed and empower international institutions (Bush, 1990). Whilst this became symbolic of the changing nature of global politics at the time, it appeared as a highly significant message to many within right-wing organisations. The publication of Pat Robertson's *The New World Order* the following year would provide a reference point for interpretations of the end of the cold war from the mind-set of the far-right. The book argued that the New World Order represented a wider plan to construct a world government that had been devised by elites and secret groups, which had their historical roots in the 18th-century Bavarian society called the Illuminati (Robertson, 1991: 76–80). It drew inspiration form the anti-communist and anti-Semite British author Nesta Webster, who argued in the 1920s that the Bolshevik revolution had been a product of the influence of the Illuminati, which had previously worked alongside a network of well established secret elites which had infiltrated Masonic lodges and influenced the French Revolution (Webster, 1921). Their wider mission was to erode national self-determination and form a one-world government in their own interests. Robertson's own take on this was to add the fact that this held biblical dimensions. For him, the elitist conspiracy is one that is Satanic in its nature and is geared towards destroying American ideals and values that are rooted in Christianity (Robertson, 1991: 10–24, 120–128).

Robertson's book relied on convictions that had already been aired by groups such as the John Birch Society during the hysteria of anti-communism, but the timing of the book was nonetheless poignant. In publishing the book amidst the collapse of the Soviet Union and the communist threat, he looked to show that although we had indeed moved on to a new era of world history, the threat to American liberty appeared more advanced than before. The New World Order thus brought with it a new set of dangers and developments which would lead to the mobilisation of a new type of right-wing politics over the forthcoming decades that confronted new targets which, if not entirely new, were certainly re-packaged. However Robertson's book should not be viewed as a significant literary reference point for those who evolved into the radical right, as it merely reflected a specific religious wing of a specific form of politics within the US. Yet, it certainly has appeared to be a catch-all for conspiracy theory, at least in its content (Wilkey, 2006). Perhaps more significantly, it identified a number of groups and processes that would form the very backbone of future far-right campaigns. These being the ideas of the 'elites', the 'globalists' and the fear of the wider development of a global society (Robertson, 1991: 3–15).

In the US, as the decade developed, the fear of 'big' government became symptomatic within this emerging narrative, providing a dimension that was to be distinctly American in context. As the 1990s progressed, the success of the Ross

Perot campaign in the 1992 election, the Waco assault[2] and the increase in the number of militia was testament of this, as a fear emerged that reflected a belief that there was a need to protect the Constitution from the forces of government. The Oklahoma federal bombing that took place on the second anniversary of the Waco assault, by Timothy McVeigh and Terry Nichols, who were loosely related to the Michigan militia, provided an extreme example of this. The 'Patriot Movement' provided one of the first expressions of contestation to the post-cold world within the US and one which was to underline the fear of a new global order (Castells, 1997). Here the threat of the 'globalists' and of the 'liberal elites' provided a framework where a mistrust of federalist and central government forces – a uniquely American phenomenon that dates back to the Civil War – could be utilised.

Yet, outside the US, the right-wing tradition did not see big government as a problem or indeed as a threat. Indeed, from the very birth of the so-called 'right-wing' from the days of the National Assembly in revolutionary France, its characteristics had been marked by its authoritarianism (Gauchet, 1997). Furthermore the state has been seen as one that is both all-powerful and one that represents a 'natural' form of order (Griffin, 2000; Davies and Lynch, 2002). Certainly in Russia, the initial neo-nationalist explosion which occurred in the aftermath of the collapse of the Soviet Union was geared towards the construction of a stronger state. With the newly formed Yeltsin-led presidency embarking upon a series of liberalisation projects, the nationalist backlash saw a number of newly formed political movements and organisations emerge from the chaos of the new regime, with this reaching a pinnacle in the 1993 parliamentary elections when the newly formed

Ultra Nationalist Party (paradoxically named the Liberal Democratic Party or LDPR) gained 23 per cent of the vote.

Like in the US, the seeds of this nationalist revival were planted prior to the start of the 'New World Order'. In the case of Russia, the *Pamyat* movement emerged from the end of the 1970s upto the mid-1980s as a Soviet sponsored organisation geared to establish cultural and historical networks within the arts (Devlin, 1999). By the time of *glasnost*, it had developed a critique of Marxist-Leninism by accusing it of being a Zionist-Masonic conspiracy in the same manner as those in the west. Yet, the socio-cultural roots of nationalist opposition within Russia have a much longer history. The so-called *derzhavnik* tradition, which dates back to the 19th century, believes that Russia requires a strong and powerful state in order to distinguish the Slavic political tradition from the European one (Neumann, 1996; Buszynski, 1995). The tradition of the *derzhavniki* contrasts from those who see Russia as a western construct (the *zapadniki*),[3] leaving a struggle for cultural identity within the wider political society (Neumann, 1996). By the time that Yeltsin had embarked upon his own form of westernisation, presiding over the disastrous 'shock therapy' liberalisation programme in 1992 and then using force to dissolve the Congress of People's Deputies, the *derzhanik* tradition had seemingly emerged into a wide nationalist opposition towards Russia's future integration into the 'western dominated' international system.

Both cases here show the first signs of a wider mind-set that would become a feature of politics in the decades that followed. The preoccupation with what would later become understood as the 'liberal elites' was all too evident. Whilst in the case of the US, these were big government associates – and paradoxically anti-*libertarianism* – in the case of Russia, they appeared as westernisers. At the same time, the fear of global culture also became apparent. An opposition to globalisation and to multi-culturalism were to develop from this fear and with it attempts to identify the major threats that the so-called 'globalists' at the heart of the major governments in the world were trying to develop. By the time the FPÖ made the first electoral break-through by a far-right political party in Europe, the narrative of globalisation had been developed as one which was highly negative in nature (Mudde, 2007: 186–190). It also fitted into the wider conspiracy that globalisation is a process that has been used and utilised by elites to justify certain practices and objectives (Rupert, 2000).

The process of globalisation is one that does appear through-out this book. As a phenomenon, it reached rapid heights in the areas of the academy, policy and business throughout the 1990s as attempts to account for the changing nature of politics were made (Lechner and Boli, 2000; Kofman and Youngs, 1996). Whilst primarily looking at the development of the global econ-omy, globalisation became a buzzword in the 1990s for govern-ments to develop strategies and policy directions. In particular, leaders such as Clinton, Blair and Schröder all sought to place an engagement with globalisation as a foundation of their respec-tive campaigns. Further afield, leaders in emerging powers such as Jiang Zemin and Fernando Cardoso also stressed the need to place the reality of globalisation at the heart of economic and social development (Cardoso, 2001). Whilst this attracted a whole debate about the essence of globalisation and whether it appeared as anything more than a way of consolidating forms of neoliberal hegemony that had been developing since the 1980s (see below), alternative narratives were being developed by those on the far-right that would understand globalisation in a manner that fits into a wider conspiracy. It is the 'globalist' that has become central to the wider conspiracy theories that have emerged alongside new forms of popular nationalism.

New or Old Conspiracies?

Conspiracy has been a central feature of far-right discourse since the emergence of fascism in the early part of the 20th century. Some accounts suggest that the idea of an external threat formed around a wider conspiracy has been one of the historical traits that serves to define the very nature of the far-right (Saull, 2014), whilst others have suggested that such conspiracies have focused either implicitly or explicitly on 'Jewry' in some form (Jacobs, 2011). The crossover with Marxism and with international Jewry as forms of conspiracy featured prominently in the growth of Nazism and became the hallmark of Hitler's *Mein Kampf*. Indeed, whilst *Mein Kampf* lacks the imagination or historical depth of Nesta Webster's work, it perhaps provides the classical example of conspiracy theory at a global level and one that continues to underpin the obsessional focus on globalists and the idea of a 'global plot' that are inherent within far-right discourses today.

In *Mein Kampf*, Hitler's central focus is on the Jewish race. All external threats that are outlined in the book stem from his pathological hatred of the Jewish race, yet also feed from it. Communism, freemasonry and the dilution of the Aryan race through racial integration all feature heavily, but they are used as strategies for the wider international Jewish conspiracy. Perhaps the most prominent part of this is his illustration of how 'the Jew' appears to attack the fabric of the Germanic and Aryan cultures in a collection of stages (Hitler, 1992: 271–272). He then details these 11 stages, where he argues that the Jews settled in Europe as traders and merchants, before gradually moving to become more influential in the economic, cultural and political activity of society. This appears part of a wider international conspiracy where the Jews seek first to undermine and then to control the fabric of every facet of European life. Using the familiar 'secret society networks' of freemasonry, the plot becomes a wider conspiracy of 'international Jewry', whereby the construction of Marxism serves as a vehicle for the destruction of Aryan society (Hitler, 1992: 280–296). The Jew is furthermore depicted as a sub-human and almost as a type of alien species that appears unresponsive to normal human behaviour.

The extreme, psychotic and contradictory manner in which *Mein Kampf* places a race at the heart of a conspiracy provides us with a specific understanding of the power conspiracy has when taken to effect. Whilst the Communist Party was the natural enemy of the National Socialist movement, *Mein Kampf* suggests that the international Marxist threat was not one that stemmed from an attack on capitalism but was instead a Jewish construction bent upon a wider global plan of destruction. Likewise, international finance was being constructed in a manner which was geared towards obtaining Jewish ownership of the economy. The mutual relationship between international capitalism and Marxism is one that Hitler feels is actually 'logical', as *Kapital* looked to disrupt the national economy in a way that actually played into the hands of international finance and as a result the wider plot of international Jewry (Hitler, 1992: 195). By placing all these contradictions within this wider extreme form of anti-semitism, the conspiracy feeds into a specific narrative.

Mein Kampf provides us with a more useful understanding of how contemporary conspiracies contribute to political discourse than at first might appear. As we shall see in the next chapter, Islamophobia has taken a more central role in far-right discourses than anti-semitism and neither occupy the central role that was implicit within Hitler's world-view, yet *Mein Kampf* still provides us with striking similarities in the manner that conspiracies can be shaped and developed as a counter-discourse. The 'New World Order' conspiracies follow very similar patterns. Each focus on a collection of individuals that appear at the global level and look to endanger the fabric of national culture. Each also stresses the dangers of multiculturalism and believe that it is used as a strategy by conspirators and as a key tool in their wider objectives (Barkun, 2003). Here, the globalists and multiculturalists take on the role that Marxism and international Jewry had for Nazism.

New World Order conspiracies appear to place the 'global elite' as the central form of agency (McAlister, 2003). Yet, it often remains unclear what form this elite actually takes and why. For the John Birch Society the global elite remained part of a wider Marxist plot (Rupert, 2000). For them, the defeat of the Soviet Union and of communism saw 'globalism' provide a new avenue for Marxism to develop. Aided by institutions such as the United Nations, this new Marxism looked to construct a new form of world government that was geared towards the destruction of national determination and civil liberty in the same manner that the Soviet Union was attempting to do (John Birch Society, 1996). From here, further theories were developed around the citing of black helicopters near UN buildings, which became a particular favourite for the US militia movement. Here, such black helicopters were being employed on behalf of globalists within the UN to prepare for a takeover of the US (Keith, 1995). Yet, the identity of such individuals was still unclear, other than to assume they were part of a secret network that worked within global institutions and had infiltrated American federal governmental bodies.

Others have sought to identify at least the main players within the New World Order. For example, many have suggested that international finance has been controlled by certain elitist families and groups which are at the heart of the conspiracy. As a result, the Rothschilds and Rockefellers along with other traditional banking families have been responsible for the global development of finance to serve their own ends (Rupert, 2000: 98–99). Yet, these figureheads are not really original in any study of contemporary capitalism. Indeed, some of the most sophisticated analysis of class within the traditional confines of Marxist historical materialism have shown how families such as these were figureheads within the development of transnational capitalist classes (van der Pijl, 1998; Sklair, 2001). The conspiratorial alternative thus provides another context. Whilst these family-originated banking companies are seen as pioneers of the development of capitalism, here they are presented as ringleaders of a global plot that looked to regulate the economy in the same manner as socialism.

If the emergence of a New World Order would lead to an array of such conspiracy theories, then the growth of the information age and of what Manual Castells defined as the 'Network Society' allowed their potential to flourish. For as the process of globalisation led to the expansion of communications and information flows across the world, it also allowed fresh space for the development of such narratives (Castells, 1996). The depth of conspiracies seemed to further complicate questions on the actual composition of conspirators besides historical banking families. The most extreme have seen the main conspirators as 'reptilian lizards' that emerged from another planet to control Earth by taking on human form (Icke, 2001). Here, we see further similarities with the absurdities from *Mein Kampf*. Whilst in *Mein Kampf*, Hitler depicted Jews in a way that presented them as alien beings and sub-human, this takes the idea literally. The post-cold war era thus provided an opportunity for conspiracy theory to develop, which provided a basis for right-wing politics to develop a narrative that could oppose the development of the so-called neoliberal New World Order (Worth, 2002).

As we shall see in future chapters, the New World Order conspiracies and in particular the idea of an elite at the global level is one that has gained attraction, with the resurgence of many right-wing movements across global society. The origins of such conspiracies remain within the US. To some, conspiracy theories are a uniquely American phenomenon which has a certain appeal to the American public (Uscinski and Parent, 2014). Conspiracies are thus by no means merely associated with the political right but are also used within leftist discourse and are indicative of American diversity within civil society. Whilst for example claims have been made that up to 12 million believe in the reptilian theory,[4] many have suggested that it is unlikely that sections of the public actually believe in them but accept certain aspects of their conspiratorial narrative (Dentith, 2014). As a result, they do serve to provide a platform where hegemonic practices can be questioned and alternative narratives put forward. The same can be said of the influence of such conspiracies on far-right movements in Europe. The lower levels of enthusiasm for conspiracy theories in the 1990s on the other side of the Atlantic were reflected by the reception given to one of the pioneers of reptilian theory, David Icke. Icke, an Englishman, previously known in Britain for his reporting on minor sports for the BBC, was ridiculed in the UK, before gaining support in the US. However, as far-right discourse became increasingly mainstream over the next two decades, conspiratorial language over 'elites' and 'globalists' became far more commonplace. Therefore, it is useful to look back at how the roots of these took hold before and after the cold war and indeed how much of the conspiratorial mind-set is still retained.

Multiculturalism

If conspiracy provided the basis for the post-cold war right-wing reactionary world-view, then multiculturalism became its initial target. Certainly with the ethnic explosions in both Russia and Yugoslavia in the early 1990s, ethnic nationalism had re-appeared to replace what could be understood as the ideologically-driven multiculturalism that was indicative within state socialism (Hainsworth, 2000). This re-thinking of ethnicity – or 'ethnic revivalism' – has occurred alongside the changing dynamic of global conflict that has seen a so-called transformation of traditional great power rivalry with a new environment of global politics (Kaldor, 1999; Kennedy, 1993). The realities of post-war global society have resulted in a stark increase in the levels of migration due to the greater fluidity of movement in the last three decades. Even if the levels of migration have not resulted in rapid population changes in countries where the perception of levels are high, there has been a marked increase in the numbers of residents born outside their country of resistance in the large majority of the advanced and emerging economies (World Bank Group, 2016). To some, it has been a fear of the effect the processes of multiculturalism have on the national fabric of their respective countries that has been the main driving force behind the success of far-right mobilisation in Western Europe (Prowe, 1994).

Multiculturalism plays into the myth of an elite driving a project against the will of the people very well and also into the broader context of globalism or globalisation. It is also here where the understanding of what is meant by globalisation fundamentally differs politically on the left and right. Whilst the former points to the neoliberal economic project and the inequalities that stem from it in their understanding of the problems with globalisation, the right places identity and culture at its heart (Rupert, 2000; Worth, 2002; Mudde, 2000; Steger, 2005). Multiculturalism thus appears to the right in the same manner as neoliberalism does to the left – as the overriding ideological process that is at the heart of everything wrong with society. This was indeed a point made by Flemish nationalist and prominent member of Vlaams Blok/Vlaams Belang,[5] Filip Dewinter, who argued in the light of right-wing resurgence in Europe that old ideological con-flicts of the cold war were being replaced by ones based upon multiculturalism vs identity and belonging (Dewinter, 2002). Furthermore it was this latter sense of identity and belonging that offered the basis for a populist alternative against abstract and academic constructs that seemingly appeared 'from above' (Betz and Johnson, 2004).

Multiculturalism has also been associated with the politics of regionalism – in Europe the association of the European Union (EU) with multiculturalism, specifically with the freedom of movement associated with the European Economic Areas (EEA)/Single Market and the Schengen Agreement. To a lesser extent, the popular-nationalist attack on the North American Free Trade Association (NAFTA) was seen in the same man-ner, although this focused exclusively on Mexican immigra-tion to the US (see Chapter 4). As a result, there is a constant correlation between scepticism of regional organisations and attacks on multiculturalism. As Cas Mudde also suggests, how-ever, state societies within regional bodies can also use them for a modicum of support in instances where further outsiders threaten the combined culture of that particular region (Mudde, 2007: 158–182). This is particularly the case in Europe where immigration from outside the continent appears as the most endangering aspect of multiculturalism and one that threatens European culture. As suggested earlier, the nationalist fervour in Russia and that which was inherent within figures such as Slobodan Milosevic was geared around protecting a Slavic culture alien both within Europe and beyond. Therefore, whilst wider regional integration might appear to be seen as a method for multiculturalism to be levered, opposition to it from radical right positions is more complex and contradictory than it might first appear.

As the 1990s progressed, political movements began to gain from utilising this anti-multicultural position, especially in the light of the Third Way rhetoric that was on the ascendency at the time. Regional parties such as Vlaams Blok and Lega Nord embraced a rejection of multiculturalism in order to illustrate how their region had been let down by an inclusive constitution within their wider nation-state that is geared towards penalising them in favour of other more unproductive regions. Across Eastern Europe, the fear of multiculturalism was also central to new nationalist organisations as a means of gaining support. In Hungary, István Csurka explicitly attacked multiculturalism as a basis for the founding of the Hungarian Justice and Life Party (MIEP), which gained support throughout the 1990s, peaking with the gaining of 14 seats at the 1998 general election. Similarly in Slovakia, the Slovak National Party (SNS) used a similar platform to sustain themselves as a key player within domestic politics. Finally, in Scandinavia, the emergence of a number of conservative populist parties also targeted multiculturalism and immigration as being harmful to the Nordic culture (Bergmann, 2017). Both the Swedish Democrats (founded in 1988) and the Danish People's Party (founded in 1995) emerged as significant forces by the turn of the millennium.

It was the FPÖ's big electoral breakthrough in 1999 coupled with the consolidation of the FN in French politics that character-ised the most significant developments of the far-right during the 1990s. The FN directed significant effort towards opposing multi-cultural endeavours by adopting a 'national preference' agenda, whereby French citizens, or more poignantly the 'indigenous' French, would gain preference for housing, jobs, welfare etc. over 'outsiders' (Bastow, 1997). This was to complement their economic shift away from a belief in market economics to that of a protectionist stance that looked to spearhead a new era of national-first economics by opposing the setting up of the World Trade Organisation (WTO) and the influx of foreign capital into France (see Chapter 3). The FN would find appeal with these positions throughout the decade, with their popularity halted in the late 1990s not by the waning of the position on multicultural-ism but by splits in the party.

Likewise, in Austria, the FPÖ set themselves up in the 1990s as a party which stood against the virtues of immigration, inte-gration and multiculturalism. Previously, it had appeared as a conservative post-war party that looked to find a position where it could oppose both dominant elements of Christian Democracy and Social Democracy. Despite emerging as a party which 'housed' former members that had previously been in the Nazi Party, it did not take a far-right position until Jörg Haider took over as leader in 1986. Even then, it was not until the 1990s when Haider steered it to adopt an anti-immigration/anti-multicultural line. In 1999 the Party sent the first significant shock-waves through the European political environment by taking 26.1 per cent of the vote to take its place as a junior partner within a broader right-wing government.

The turn towards resisting multiculturalism allowed parties in Europe to uphold principles associated with the far-right and moved them in a way that made them popular with voters. This became particularly noticeable as the 1990s developed, as they looked to contest the consensus that was seemingly emerging around a political and economic neoliberalism that was committed towards global and European integration. By the turn of the century, the realisation that multiculturalism was becoming a contested issue and as far-right movements and radical right parties began to make further inroads in the following decades, mainstream parties began to re-think the concept themselves as a means of reducing their potential popularity (Han, 2015). Here, we see evidence of the beginnings of the political mainstreaming of ideas that were aired initially as a right-wing reaction against a specific aspect of the post-cold war order in Europe.

Conclusion: Contesting Neoliberalism?

If an alternative narrative emerged from the ashes of the cold war that drew upon forms of popular nationalism, how far did it appear to establish a coherent 'counter-hegemonic' position to the emerging form of neoliberalism? As questioned in the Introduction, in what way can these new parties and organisations provide us with a strategist form of opposition that can be seen as a war of position. To revisit Gramsci's observations on the nature of contestation and resistance (from the Introduction), for a war of position to gain momentum from a specific ideological standpoint it requires a conscious grand strategy in how it wishes to replace and/or transform a prevailing order (Gramsci, 1971: 235–237). We have seen in this chapter how the far-right have re-invented themselves as a form of opposition to the post-cold war neoliberal era, which they have labelled (prompted by George Bush Sr) as the 'New World Order'. Yet, whilst this emerged in the 1990s, the idea that it appeared as an alternative is less convincing.

The far-right's relationship with neoliberalism is one that has been increasingly debated recently and one that appears more complex and problematic (Worth, 2014; Davidson and Saull, 2017; Saull, 2018). It is, as also expressed in the Introduction, one that is a constant feature within this book, whether indeed, the move towards the emergence of these alternative right parties in the 1990s appears as a distinct ideological challenge to free market capitalism or whether they look to embed its core principles within its realm or further. In the 1990s, the most significant development that suggested the former was the shift by the FN to the protectionist stance. Here we see a distinct attempt to present an economic alternative to the post-cold war era of globalisation. More importantly, it places the so-called New World Order within an economic framework and understands that framework as being one where market economics is both harmful and inadequate.

At the same time, however, a trend was emerging which saw the economy as one which complemented neoliberalism. Indeed a body of scholars, particularly within Germany, were to suggest that big business and the far-right are not only compatible but indeed go hand in hand. They reinforce the logistics of the free market (Kitschelt, 2004). Of considerable interest here is the work of Hans-Georg Betz, who used the term 'neoliberal populism' to describe the emergence of such parties in the early 1990s (Betz, 1993; 1994; 1999). The first sign might have indicated that indeed this might be the position after the cold war. Certainly, the campaigns of Ross Perot and the libertarian movement in the US suggested that the idea of less 'big government' was of paramount importance to any alternative (see Chapter 4). However, it also attacked the influence of big transnational business and of any institutional attempts to internationalise the free market. As the decade progressed, the idea of a 'neoliberal populism' was certainly not indicative or explicit within any populist right party or movement. Whilst the FN and later groups like the British

National Party were to explicitly endorse nativist protectionism, no significant political organisation did likewise with neoliberalism. The FPÖ and later parties such as the Swiss People's Party might have pointed to greater liberalisation of markets, particularly with relevance to their stance of 'welfare chauvinism' – a position that attacked the notion that state funding should go to the unemployed and 'lazy' in society – but this was by no means explicit.

Another suggestion is that the economy is of secondary interest to radical right groups. Certainly Cas Mudde, who is perhaps seen as the most significant commentator on comparative rightwing political parties, infers that the economy has never featured highly in the majority of their campaigns or indeed in their voters (Mudde, 2007: 132–137). These are valid points. The populist appeals that surround immigration, multiculturalism and the fear around regional and global integration have provided the obvious impetus for voters. Yet, their rise in importance has been as a consequence of the wider materialist project of free market capitalism that has developed since the end of the cold war. As was pointed out in the Introduction, Karl Polanyi observed that market-based societies lead to a variety of reactions as society looks to protect itself from the potential dangers of an unregulated market. His illustration of 19th-century market liberalism showed how such 'counter-movements' gathered momentum by the end of the century and eventually led to its collapse (Polanyi, 1944). As we shall see in next chapter, whilst the 1990s might have seen the beginnings of such movements emerge in the shape of a new era of far-right ideas, campaigns and parties, the 21st century would show how systemic crisis led to an increase in support for them. That said, it must be stressed that the different positions taken on the economy and in relation to the market system provided an ambiguity that were already evident in the 1990s with the so-called emergence of what was deemed the new 'radical right' (Art, 2011). Indeed, as this chapter has also shown, these positions did not just appear as a result of the end of the cold war but were part of a continuity of sorts that began to emerge once the spectre of fascism had seemingly been laid to rest in post-war Europe and America. Therefore, in terms of its wider emergence as a hegemonic challenger to neoliberalism, it has always appeared contradictory.

To summarise, the 1990s did see the emergence of a new genre of political party which attracted great interest within the study of European comparative politics. Beyond party politics, it also saw the re-emergence of an ideology of populist nationalism that surfaced within civil society and seemed to challenge the emerging norms of globalisation. Immigration, sovereignty and national culture appeared as the key issues that united the different movements contained within this genre. Consistently, these were also found in their main attack. Also united amongst this emerging post-cold war 'radical right' grouping was their opposition to the notion of multiculturalism, which they claimed was being 'engineered' from above by 'globalist elites'. Whilst ambiguity was evident over their wider economic objective to transform or contest neoliberalism, their emergence certainly asked questions about the nature of world order. The events of 11 September 2001 and the global financial crisis of 2008 in the first decade of the 21st century would see support for this renewed nationalism intensify.

TWO | Gathering Momentum: The Fallout from 9/11 and the Global Financial Crisis

In the 1990s the beginnings of a resurgence of a radical right saw a new form of discontent with the post-cold war order. The first decade of the 21st century saw such movements develop and emerge as a more recognised force within global politics. The events of 11 September 2001 followed by George W. Bush's 'War on Terror' unleashed a collection of anti-Islamic forces that would serve as the foundations for the building of a network of right-wing movements that would yield electoral success in the following years. The so-called 'clash' of extremism resulting in the growth of terrorist Islamic activities within western societies, alongside far-right revivalism (in its many guises) has placed greater strains on the legitimacy of multiculturalism and the post-cold war embrace of a global society (Steger, 2005).

This chapter shows how the politics of Islamophobia provided a unifying area for new forms of right-wing groups to mobilise. In Europe and in North America, but also, through implication, South Asia and the Middle East, Islamophobia provided a platform where a form of 'cultural war' could be imagined, as groups argued that they were looking to defend western or human civilisation from attack. Popularised academically in the 1990s by the works of Benjamin Barber and Samuel Huntington who argued that a clash between different belief systems was inevitable in the 21st century (Barber, 1996; Huntington, 1996), anti-Islamic sentiment has been central to the development and indeed the mobilisation of an alternative right agenda. This crusade against Islam has also been utilised in a manner that complements existing concerns over multiculturalism and immigration that have formed a large part of the backbone of their emergence. Indeed, the ability to infuse anti-Islamism with the wider concerns of immigration provided a backdrop for populist appeal.

Whilst the events that followed 9/11 provided a catalyst for reactionary populism, the global financial crisis provided an environment where this could flourish and make considerable inroads into the political mainstream. One of the tell-tale signs of the aftermath of the global financial crisis was that contrary to assurances made by politicians, the neoliberal financial system was not reformed, but seemed to move to a position where periods of 'crisis' were seen as 'natural' features of a market capitalism system where periods of 'austerity' occur (Blyth, 2013; Major, 2014; Schiavone, 2016). As a result, neoliberalism as an ideology seemingly went from a position where it was under great strain to one that seemed to re-emerge with new purpose in the years following the crisis (Crouch, 2011; Worth, 2015; Cahill and Konings, 2017).[1] Yet, the emergence of protest parties and movements from both the left and the right have shown that this process has not provided stability or reduced oppositional groups from emerging out of such instability.

It has also been an environment where alternative right-wing parties have thrived. As the instabilities produced by the crisis led to instances of austerity which saw an increase in poverty, inequality and social fallout, such parties and movements have managed to successfully exploit the politics of anti-immigration and use wider narratives of anti-globalism to build upon the discourses that were outlined in the last chapter. The result has seen the building of a substantial collective of groups that had previously resided on the margins of politics, or in the case of certain specific political parties had not existed at all. It also saw a collection of movements emerge that were to make significant impressions on the very fabric of global politics. Thus, it could be stated that it was the first decade of the 21st century which really saw an alternative right agenda emerge, grow and develop.

From Anti-Semitism to Islamophobia

Islamophobia has appeared in various forms for centuries without necessarily becoming a significant feature within wider international society. The growth of Christendom, followed by the crusades and subsequent 'enlightenment' in Europe did much to create a narrative of Islam as the 'other' in terms of civilisation (Seton-Watson, 1985). As Edward Said eminently suggested, this was to continue during the process of colonialisation as this 'otherness' became embedded within wider western-centric international thought (Said, 1978). Following from this, post-colonial episodes such as the Iranian Revolution were similarly decried and depicted in an anti-western, anti-civilised 'barbaric' manner as any form of deviation from contemporary post-war trends – in this case capitalism or state socialism – were seen as backwards (Halliday, 1999).

Despite the historical roots and indeed the historical prejudices of Islam, Islamophobia did not develop as a significant phenomenon until after the end of the cold war. Due to the prominence of anti-semitism within nationalist and right-wing discourses of the 19th and 20th centuries, along with the anti-communist rhetoric that followed throughout the existence of the Soviet Union, Islam was not seen as a systematic threat, even in light of the Iranian Revolution and the growth of groups such as Hezbollah and Fatah in conflict areas such as Lebanon and Palestine respectively. Indeed, for large parts of the cold war, Islamic states were seen in the west as significant allies in the war against communism.

Admittedly, much of the American discourse of the time seemed to prefer the idea of 'good Muslim, bad Muslim' when looking at the nature of the respective regimes' more prominent enemies. Those who seemed more provocatively anti-western (such as Iran) were presented as 'threats', whilst those who saw the Soviet Union as a bigger enemy (such as the Mujahedeen) were seen as 'friends' and 'allies' (Mamdani, 2005).

As stated above, the end of the cold war saw recognition that Islam was emerging as a threat with conservative warnings from scholars such as Huntington and Barber gaining immediate recognition. Yet it was a British government report published by the Runnymede Trust that popularised the term Islamophobia. In this, Islamophobia was understood as being a term that reflected a worldview which has both a fear and a dislike of Muslims and the wider religion (Runnymede Trust, 1997). It was furthermore practised through a wide range of prejudices in everyday social and political life that were becoming widespread by the time of the report. Yet, despite recognition as a phenomenon, Islamophobic literature from groups associated with the far-right was less forthcoming. In general, the old mantle of anti-semitic narratives were still used by right-wing parties in the initial stages of the post-cold war era (Hainsworth, 2000). This is not to say that anti-Islamic sentiment within society did not lead to gains from far-right parties as initial resurgences in Britain, France and Holland (amongst others) were in areas with a high Islamic populations. The move from a position of anti-semitism to Islamophobia within far-right discourse was thus a gradual shift over time.

The catalyst for the increase in Islamophobia was, unsurprisingly, the events of 11 September 2001. The immediate aftermath saw both heightened attacks on Islamic communities but also the emergence, almost within months of the event, of a number of parties, a result of the very fear that the attacks on the Twin

Towers had on western communities (Sheridan, 2006). In the Netherlands, the sudden rise in popularity of Pym Fortuyn, campaigning on an explicitly anti-Islamic platform, sent shock waves through the Dutch political system. This was brought into even greater focus as the Netherlands had previously prided itself as a society that lacked any history of a right-wing party, a factor that was particular notable due to its quite concentrated proportional representation system (Mudde and Van Holsteyn, 2000).

The story of Pim Fortuyn was a unique one in terms of the development of the radical right and provided some indication of what was to develop later in terms of the form and content of new Islamophobia groups. Fortuyn was a sociologist who was a supporter of 'liberal' values and freedoms regarding sexual equality. He argued that Islam and Islamic immigration to the Netherlands was threatening these freedoms which the Dutch state and Dutch civil society had spent decades developing (Fortuyn, 1997; 2002). His outspoken attacks on multiculturalism, immigration and the position of Islam with Dutch society whilst leader of the short-lived Leefbaar Nederland party[2] saw him removed from his position, but at the same time brought him certain appeal amongst the public. He won the subsequent municipal elections in Rotterdam in March and founded his own party, List, for the forthcoming May elections, where his speeches and anti-Islamic rhetoric were gaining significant support and notoriety. Nine days before the election Fortuyn was assassinated by environmentalist activist Volkert van der Graaf, leaving his supporters quick to point to his death as being the first assassination in modern Dutch political history, appropriating to him almost martyr status (Margry, 2003). As a result, Pim Fortuyn's List gained 17 per cent of the vote and were propelled to second party status (26 seats).

Pim Fortuyn's List project did not have longevity. It entered a new right coalition as a junior partner to the ruling Christian

Democrats but suffered splits that led to a fresh election that following year. The party's vote fell to just over 5 per cent and it subsequently faded from public support and was dissolved in 2008. List had all the hallmarks of the type of radical right phenomenon that would become a feature within the 21st century. Firstly it was shaped by national specificities – in this case the fear that the legacy of 'Dutch liberalism' was in danger due to the Islamification of Dutch civil society, 'unique' to Pim Fortuyn's List. Secondly, short-lived experience coupled with infighting within the ranks has become standard with similar right-wing parties that have since emerged across Europe. In the case of Pim Fortuyn's List, it would be the forerunner to Geert Wilder and the Partij Voor de Vrijheid (PVV) (de Lange, 2011).

The move from anti-semitism to Islamophobia is also reflected in the shift in international allegiances. Many of the new radical right parties that have become prominent across Europe since 9/11 have tended to favour Israel, with some such as the Alternative für Deutschland (AfD) actively supporting the Israeli state in its hard-line approach to Palestine. The AfD have not been in any way alone in their support for Israel. Many of the new populist parties and indeed individuals within the mass media commonly associated with far-right sentiment have also taken positions that have been favourable – in different degrees – towards the Israeli government, yet due to the history of right-wing nationalism in Germany, it has been its own endorsements that have caught the eye. This has added to the idea that Islam has taken on all the characteristics that 'international Jewry' had presented to right-wing discourses in the 20th century (Døving, 2010). In doing so, one could suggest that the 'external enemy' situation has changed from a position that Zionism – which for generations formed the conspiratorial cornerstone behind right-wing nationalism – suddenly faded into insignificance to be replaced by a similar narrative on Islam and *jihad*. Yet, this trend should also not be overestimated. Anti-semitism has made an indelible mark on the very nature of far-right politics that we cannot merely assume has suddenly become irrelevant or side-lined. Indeed, many of the conspiracies behind 'globalism' still focus on the same transnational business elites of Jewish origin (Rupert, 2000; Worth, 2013).

At the same time, the move taken to praise Israel within the ranks of the AfD has been met with similar scepticism. In early 2017 for example, prominent party founder Björn Höcke suggested that Germany needed to rethink its attitude towards holocaust memorial, a move which was internationally condemned. It was also discussed within the hierarchy of the party itself before a consensus was reached where it was deemed that Höcke's statement was inappropriate. Further afield, the claim that anti-semitism is no longer a feature of the contemporary far-right due to the emergence of Islam is also rather dubious. For example, Marine Le Pen looked to appeal to the Israeli state, the French Jewish community and commentators within the Israeli media for wider support, but the historical shadow of the party as an anti-semitic party which played down the holocaust has led to a mixed response from those respective groups.[3] In the US, the origins behind the history of the alt-right were not rooted in fresh anti-Islamic fervour, amidst a new admiration for Zionism, but built upon a white nationalism in which anti-semitism played a central role (Hawley, 2017).

Whilst, therefore, it can be said that Islamophobia has appeared at the forefront of contemporary campaigns and equally that anti-semitism has taken more of a back seat, it would be folly to suggest that it had disappeared altogether alongside a fresh admiration for the increasing hard-line taken by the Israeli state. Indeed, in many cases, Islam appears as the new 'number one' enemy from a wide collection of foes in which 'international Jewry' remains a member. Within the far-right discourse, the importance of hate and fear are such that one such group can gain greater prominence at any one time and can see their prominence alter and change in reaction to specific events. Whilst this might provide great contradictions in terms of providing a consistent logical argument, it has not hindered or undermined its support. In the contemporary environment, Islam has thus taken the role that was previously reserved for communism and international Jewry, in that more support can be gained from its prominence as a belief system that seeks to threaten the fabric of everyday national life. It also provides a suitable ally for the twin processes of immigration and multiculturalism.

The Post-Crisis Environment

As 9/11 provided an environment where radical right discourses could gain support from the fear of Islamification, then the global financial crisis would – inadvertently – see the support of such discourses increase further. In addition, whilst we can see that 9/11 might have seen the beginnings of an Islamophobic right-wing breakdown, it has been the financial crisis that has provided the real environment for its development and rise. The initial aftermath of the crisis saw a collection of world leaders call for a tightening of the regulatory mechanisms of the global economy and an overhaul in the way that the neoliberal economic system operated. In the 2008 G20 summit George W. Bush, Gordon Brown and Nicolas Sarkozy all made calls to suggest that a type of Bretton-Woods II system was required in order to avoid the volatility of the global market, whilst Alan Greenspan, Chairman of the American Federal Reserve until 2016, admitted that the unfettered free market philosophy practised under his tenancy was flawed. In light of this and after the Obama victory in 2008, parties on the left might have looked to build upon the moment and seek to forge new alternatives to a neoliberal capitalism that was seemingly in crisis.

Yet, as with the financial crash in 1929, the left failed to capitalise on the fallout from the crisis and through the logistics of austerity, the market system has looked to gain renewed legitimacy (Crouch, 2011; Mirowski, 2013). As a result, the social consequences that emerged from the crisis played into the hands of the emerging right wing. Issues such as immigration gained greater significance as radical right figures and parties were quick to blame the effects of austerity cuts on raising immigration. In addition, parties such as Jobbik (in Hungary), UKIP (in Britain) and more recently, the AfD have urged for the discontinuation or reduction of state spending on international aid, whilst in Sweden and Finland respectively, the Swedish Democrats (SD) and the True Finns have sought to gain support in opposition to the political consensus within the Nordic countries that commit towards accepting a quota of refugees. In both of these cases, the premise has been that additional spending on non-indigenous and/or non-native individuals and projects is being prioritised ahead of the welfare of indigenous citizens, who have suffered cuts and job losses. Therefore, rather than attack the practices and principles of austerity, scapegoating has been used for nationalist and reactionary ends. It has indeed been the social hardships caused by the economic downtown that has seen the anti-immigration sentiment grow, particularly in industrial/post-industrial working-class areas that have been hardest hit by the austerity measures.

At the same time, certain nationalist groups have looked to be more explicit when attacking austerity. For example, Greece's Golden Dawn and Bulgaria's Ataka – one from within the Eurozone and one from a country committed to stringency for ERM membership – have looked to challenge the very fabric of the austerity perused by the European Central Bank (ECB) and EU by favouring a nationalist-protectionist alternative. Whilst both have faded in significance as political forces, they nevertheless gained significant support in the aftermath of the crisis and throughout the sovereign debt crisis (see Chapter 3). The explicit pursuit of nationalist forms of economic protectionism follows those responses against the crisis that were seen in Europe in the 1930s. Yet, other right-wing responses have not come from an opposition to austerity but from an endorsement of it. The Tea Party had a multitude of contrasting agendas in its origins, but at its heart it remains committed towards both a concentrated free market platform and an anti-statist agenda (Lowndes, 2012; Skocpol and Williamson, 2016). This provides an entirely different response to the financial crisis and turns the notion that it emerged from a deregulated market system on its head.

For the Tea Party, the crisis occurred not because of too little regulation but because of too much. The libertarian argument that was epitomised by the 'Godfather' of the Tea Party, Ron Paul in his various books written in the immediate aftermath of the financial crisis, outline arguments borrowed from von Mises and the Austrian school of economists decades before him, that state and regulatory interference in the economy artificially inflate the market and do not allow it to find an equilibrium (von Mises, 1934; Paul, 2008; 2009). As a result, the Obama administration's endorsement of fiscal stimulation and quantitative easing was criticised as being indicative of such an interference. As a consequence, the Tea Party remains committed to the radical overhaul of the economic process through debt reduction and the diminishment of federal state power (Tea Party, 2015).

The importance of the Tea Party cannot be understated when evaluating the wider development and form of the global radical right. The fusion of nationalism with libertarianism was to appeal to similar organisations across the Atlantic. The Swiss People's Party was to endorse many features of the Tea Party, particularly in the manner in which they presented themselves (Carroll, 2014). Similarly, in Britain, UKIP looked to position themselves as the 'British Tea Party' in an attempt to firmly distinguish themselves from the British National Party (BNP), who were, at the time of the rise of the Tea Party, competing for votes and support (UKIP, 2010). It also allowed parties such as the FPÖ to strengthen their ideological position on welfare chauvinism, which was outlined in the previous chapter.

The ambiguity between this new confrontational, oppositional right and neoliberalism, which was outlined in the Introduction, was seen evidently in light of the crisis. There were those who looked to explicitly take on the nature of the free market neoliberal economy by re-asserting states' control over the economy and endorsing a traditional form of nationalism on the one hand alongside those who believed that the economy needs even less intervention in order to work efficiently on the other (Worth, 2014; Davidson and Saull, 2017). In addition, there have been those who have tended to focus solely on areas such as immigration as a means of utilising a scapegoat for the problems that have arisen as a result of the crisis. These see the economy as a position of secondary importance and, as Cas Mudde is quick to remind us, as the standard position for new parties of the right (Mudde, 2007; 2016). Here, whilst the financial crisis has provided an environment where they have been able to gather support, they have done so without forwarding any alternative economic plan. Yet, by utilising populist rhetoric they have used the economic crisis as a means to depict themselves as 'anti-elitist'. Despite being the catalyst for the upsurge in their support, neither the financial crisis nor the post-crisis austerity measures are used in their rhetoric. Instead, radical right movements have managed to appear as 'outsiders' to elite politicians who are intent on maintaining high levels of immigration and on constructing a multiculturalism that appears against the will of the people.

Yet, as the following chapters will show, these different takes on the economy play a highly significant role in understanding how far-right discourses will develop over time. Both those that have favoured a protectionist alternative and those that have favoured a more concentrated free market approach have been compromised by the nationalist and populist campaigns that appeal more. For example, as we shall see, the distinct Austrian school idealism behind *some* figures within the Tea Party movement quickly became undermined by the surge in patriotism and nationalism (Zeskind, 2012). Likewise, the campaigns around immigration, EU membership, Islamification and multiculturalism have for the most part negated any viable attempt to sustain a nationalist form of economic alternative to neoliberalism. In both cases, these shortcomings have, to a degree, allowed the neoliberal model to continue its post-crisis revival (Cahill and Konings, 2017). Thus, it can be suggested that whilst a populist right-wing alternative has appeared in the decade that has followed firstly 9/11 and secondly the global financial crisis, its contradictions have also become just as apparent.

The Defence of Masculinity

Another significant development of the far-right has been in its gendered dimension. The rejection of 'feminism' by radical right parties and movements has become a recent feature in the same manner that Islamophobia, anti-multiculturalism and international elites have. In fact, feminism has become regarded as taking a significant role within the globalist agenda as it has appeared to attack the fabric of the traditional family that serves as the basis for western national culture (Peto, 2016).

Feminism and feminists thus join the ranks of Marxists, liberals, international organisations, bankers and multinationals in contributing towards the wider attack on traditional everyday life. Yet, to add irony to these positions, the far-right has attracted much significant female representation within its different national movements, both as formal leaders of political parties or as significant commentators within popular culture.

To understand this from a wider level it is useful to consider Raewyn Connell's work on hegemonic masculinity and globalisation. Connell has long argued that the practices of neoliberalism have been forged through a gendered dynamic based around masculinist norms. Therefore, the very foundations of neoliberal governance are based upon a 'gendered world order' whereby the practices of global capitalism have been constructed in a manner that reflect a male-dominated culture and draw on traditional forms of masculinity (Connell, 2005). This form is central to its hegemonic character. Individuals who thus participate within the confines of the global political economy adhere to these principles, regardless of their gender. Within global society, these forces are reflected at different levels within the state-societal structure that provides us with different examples of how the gendered dynamic of neoliberal hegemony plays out across different societies across the international arena (Beasley, 2008).

Gendered critiques of hegemonic masculinity allow us to see how opposition forces look to contest certain elements within masculinist narratives that allow space for contestation and resistance. Ultimately, this provides us ways in which we can imagine emancipatory strategies (Fischer and Tepe, 2011). At the same time, it also provides us a framework where we can position the far-right and understand reasons why woman might front such groups. For whilst these critiques allow for space to contest these constructed narratives of masculinity, the far-right look to do the reverse. Not only do they look to defend such narratives but they aim to strongly reinforce them by condemning all forms of feminism as being part of a larger globalised attack on national and traditional cultures. For example, the Austrian Freedom Party firmly endorsed family values and the return to traditional and distinct gender roles in society (Olteanu, 2017). The evangelical movements in the US also targeted feminism, with Pat Robertson infamously suggesting through his Christian Coalition that the feminist movement 'encourages women to leave their husbands, kill their children, practice witchcraft, destroy capitalism and become lesbians' (Robertson, 1992). As the 1990s and the 2000s progressed such sentiments became mainstream across right-wing media outlets within the US, with the term 'Feminazi', which was initially coined by conservative radio host Russ Limbaugh, being increasingly used by the radical right as a means of attack against women's groups and welfare groups that focus on the eradication of domestic violence.

This has not discouraged women from actively engaging in far-right discourses or indeed contrasting their own narratives on women's rights. Pim Fortuyn made great attempts to demonstrate his protection of women's rights in opposition to Islamic practices – a position that is reflected in many radical right positions on banning the burka and Marine Le Pen's own protest when refusing to wear a headscarf during a meeting with the Grand Mufti, Lebanon's Sunni leader in Beirut. In addition, the presence of the 'strong' woman that has been portrayed by Marine Le Pen and Frauke Petry but also by Ivanka Trump has laid out another avenue for women to progress as prominent actors within the far-right. The increasing number of anti-feminist women's groups have looked (aided by social media) to reinforce the idea that feminism is a singular ideology relying on 'brainwashing' and 'destruction' in a similar manner to international Marxism and socialism (see, for example, Women Against Feminism, 2017). In addition, the myth of the 'white, western working male' as an oppressed figure has also been one that the far-right have sought to uphold. The recent growth of certain men's rights groups, that have run counter to welfare groups, has also fuelled this myth, with studies showing distinct links between them and far-right groups (Träbert, 2017). These have all looked to reinforce masculinist discourses and to take a more extreme interpretation to those fashioned through the development of neoliberal capitalism. As a result, a growing distinction is increasingly made between those who embark upon addressing gender inequalities within the workplace and society at largely and who seem to form the mainstay of the 'contemporary establishment' that is pushing the feminist agenda, and 'anti-establishment strong women' who appear as anti-feminist women within the radical right movement (Williams, 2015). It is from this departure point that we can understand the increasing prominence of women as leaders and actors within such reactionary movements.

Within politics, many woman have taken this 'anti-feminist strong woman' stance and assumed leadership positions within right-wing parties. The most obvious here being Marine Le Pen, but also Frauke Petry and Alice Weidel in the AfD, Siv Jensen and more recently Pia Kjaersgaard in Norway have all assumed significant positions within far-right parties. In addition, the hard-line right-wing Unionist Northern Ireland party, the Democratic Unionist Party, elected their first woman Arlene Foster as leader, who has maintained their party's commitment towards a set of social, cultural and moral principles that represent a water-tight example of a radical right party (Mudde, 2007). Outside Europe, Pauline Hanson became one of the first female leaders of a far-right, anti-immigration and pro-protectionist One

Nation Party in 1997 and promptly dominated the fabric of the party since then. The prominence of Sarah Palin and Michelle Bachmann as leading figureheads of the Tea Party masked the sheer number of woman that were active at various levels within the movement through the country. Nikki Haley, another significant member, was to reflect Trump's brand of masculinist populism with her confrontational style as the US representative at the UN (Deckman, 2016).

Away from the confines of traditional party politics, women have also appeared as activists within more adversarial forms of street politics. For example, as deputy/joint leader of the confrontational political group Britain First, Jayda Fransen has appeared as the image and new media star of the group. Young, brash and antagonistic, Fransen has led marches against Islam, organised occupations of Mosques and confronted alleged homeless immigrants; actions which have all been introduced and recorded online (Fransen, 2017). Fransen's arrest and subsequent imprisonment in 2018 for racial hate crimes (see Chapter 5) brought to a conclusion a set of activities that represented a more hostile form of masculinity within far-right undertakings.

Women have also been prominent as right-wing popular media figures, particularly in developing the anti-feminist rhetoric. Ann Coulter and Laura Ingraham, who have long been stalwarts of the popular conservative media, have both embraced the Trump era with a gusto that has included a collection of attacks on 'feminisms' and 'feminists', especially in light on the many incidents of misogyny (Coulter, 2017). Others such as British 'writer' Katie Hopkins, a staunch Brexit and Trump supporter and recent proponent of the new far-right anti-Islamic splinter group For Britain (led by another woman, Ann Marie Waters, who is also paradoxically, Irish born) has been keen to explicitly utilise Limbaugh's term 'feminazi' for full effect (for example, Hopkins, 2018).

In each of these examples, traditional leaders have thus joined with the organic intellectuals from popular and social media to construct a collection of narratives that have looked to strengthen forms of masculinity. In positing all forms of what are considered to be 'feminist' as 'dangerous' the far-right has looked to construct a distinct gendered dimension that in the post-crisis environment has become increasingly prevalent. Traditional gendered roles have thus been vigorously re-emphasised in a manner that is consistent with the re-invention of nationalist traditions. Women's rights and liberties are defended and also appear opportunist when attacking Islamic gendered traditions. It has been here where the growing number of prominent women within right-wing movements have been effective. For, whilst the role of the 'strong woman' within western society is applauded and increasingly takes a significant position within the mind-set of right-wing movements, feminism is seen as dangerous. The fact that so many women have risen within their ranks to condemn feminism as part of the wider 'globalist' conspiracy has added weight to this mind-set.

The Global Spread of the Far-Right

Whilst certain characteristics have served to define the post-crisis far-right within Europe and North America, the spatial scope of such a movement leads us to another question. The claim that the new populist right has reached global significance is one that has been discussed in academic circles within the differing fields of international relations, political science and political psychology (Inglehart and Norris, 2017; Moffitt, 2016; Aydin-Duzgit and Keyman, 2017; Kaltwasser and Mudde, 2017; Aytac and Onis, 2014; Worth, 2017a). Yet, in light of Brexit, the Trump ascendency and the success of new populist right parties in elections across Europe, this has become a feature within various mainstream media outlets. *The Economist*, *Washington Post*, *Time Magazine* and ABC in Australia have all led with features declaring the global scope of the populist right. In these cases, Trump is depicted alongside Nigel Farage and Marine Le Pen to form the triumvirate at the centre of such a global push, yet they are often joined by notable additions. Putin is often included as an addition to the ranks of such leaders, particular in light of the alleged funding links to both Trump and the Brexit campaigns (*The Economist*, 2016).

The assumptions taken from this is that a form of right-wing populism is emerging at the very heart of global politics. Furthermore it tends to suggest that such a trend is geared towards challenging the geo-politics of international relations in some form through the contestation of the post-cold war order (*Time*, 2017; *The Washington Post*, 2018). The actual manner in which such a contestation is imagined in such publications is not forthcoming, but the very fact that such popular media outlets have proclaimed such a development leads us to suggest that wider structural processes might be occurring that are indeed global in nature. In which case, two questions need to be asked. Firstly, if such a challenge is forthcoming then how and in what way would such forces appear to transform the contemporary order and secondly, whether indeed this is actually a global process or just one that is confined to certain areas of Europe and the (post-Trump) US.

In considering the first of these, this book is primarily geared towards ascertaining whether a global far-right project has the clarity to offer an alternative to the form of neoliberal hegemony that has been prominent in the last few decades and this will largely be assessed throughout the following chapters. It is also from here – at least from a (neo-)Gramscian understanding of hegemony and world order – that we can make sense of the potential altercations that might occur. The second provides more relevance to us in this chapter. If we have seen a snowballing of the appeal of the radical right, then just how widespread has this been? Outside of the advanced economic areas of Europe and the US, have similar trends been forthcoming? Or is the phenomenon solely Eurocentric in nature and one that is reflective of the neo-colonial attributes of many of the far-rights themselves. Indeed, both the right-wing traditions in France and the UK speak fondly of their associations with their previous empires and have adopted ideas for future relations with their former colonies that could certainly be considered as being staunchly neo-colonial in nature (Namusoke, 2016).

Whilst it could be argued that there has been a lack of far-right ideology in less developed countries, at least in the form of those in Europe and North America, it could be argued that many neo-conservative ideologies do exist which both can complement and conflict with them. In particular, the relevance of religion has made a significant impact on the developing world (Mandaville, 2007; Haynes, 2007). These ideologies have contributed towards a rejection of modernity and of the processes of globalisation that might conflict with the forces of western consumerism as Benjamin Barber has pointed out (1996), but also have contributed towards contesting the fabric of the contemporary world order (Butko, 2004; Evans, 2011).

In more advanced developing nations, leaders have emerged that have embodied forms of authoritarian populism that have striking similarities with the radical right. Rodrigo Duterte in the Philippines and Recep Tayyip Erdoğan in Turkey have, along with Putin, strong characteristics of the nationalism inherent in the core areas of Europe and the US. Apart from Russia, regional hegemons such as Nigeria and Indonesia as well as the counties of the BRICS[4] have seen certain elements of populism appear that could be interpreted as having likeminded reactionary tendency. The most obvious case here is within India, where a populist form of Hindu nationalism has been constructed that threatens to bubble to the surface (Vanaik, 2017). A closer look at these tendencies might allow us to see how they relate to those occurring within the 'core' countries in global society to fully ascertain the 'global' scope of this new right.

The Semi-Periphery

The term semi-periphery refers to states that have economic and social characteristics of both advanced core economies and peripheral developing ones. As a result, they generally appear very uneven and unstable in nature and have often appeared as being at the forefront of resistance and change (Chase-Dunn, 1990). They have also traditionally suffered from state fragility and authoritarianism. Geographically, regions that are regarded are being 'semi-peripheral' include Latin America, Russia, the Middle East and parts of East Asia (Chase-Dunn, Kawano and Brewer, 2000), although the definitions can be extended to include states that provide specific services to core countries such as tax havens or as rentier states (Vlcek, 2009; Simon, 2009). Semi-peripheral states have also had a history of populist movements from both the right and the left and of distinct forms of nationalism. This characterisation would fit with some of the dialogue that has been generated by the populist right discourse in the advanced nations.

In Latin America, where the seeds of populism were rife for the right during the various military dictatorships of the 1970s and 1980s, in the 2000s a series of left-populist governments were formed which made a considerable impact across the larger American continent as a whole. This 'pink tide' coupled with the rejection of US development in the region led to the rise of popular leaders such as Hugo Chavez in Venezuela, Evo Morales in Bolivia, Lula in Brazil and Rafael Correa in Ecuador (Castaneda, 2006; Panizza and Miorelli, 2009; Remmer, 2012; Chodor, 2015). In recent years, an opposition trend from the centre-right has seemingly countered this position and has opened up potential for right-wing forms of populism to re-surface (Muggah and Winter, 2017). Election victories for the right in Chile and Argentina has seen an increase in right-wing populist rhetoric from such governments, with figures both in and close to governmental circles embarking upon the types of anti-immigration rhetoric that have been evident in Europe and North America (Encarnacion, 2018). However, it was the election of Jair Messias Bolsonaro in the Brazilian presidential election in 2018 that overshadowed anything that preceded it.

Styling himself on Donald Trump, Bolsonaro made a name in politics firstly as a Federal Deputy for Rio de Janeiro fighting, in his own words, the 'socialist' cause. This included attacks on homosexuality, abortion, secularisation and drug liberalisation. He gained further controversy by dismissing the military dicta-torship of the 1970s and 1980s as 'democratic' and praising the work of the intelligence police at the time, which has led to sug-gestions that a new wave of such populism is emerging (Schipani, 2017). His 2018 presidential campaign was aided in part by the imprisonment of Lula, yet his resounding victory made a sig-nificant impact around the continent as a whole. Bolsonaro's commitments include tax reduction, a shake-up of Mercosur by re-orientating its principles so that it favours more engage-ment with the US, a reduction in indigenous rights, a loosen-ing of the laws on gun control and a number of authoritarian measures against civil liberties. Rather than appear to adopt the protectionist or neo-mercantilist measures of previous right-wing governments during the era of military dictatorship, some have suggested that he seems to have more in common with the Pinochet style of authoritarianism mixed with free market economics (Finchelstein, 2018).

The effect that Bolsonaro will have on Latin America is unclear at present, but the tone of populism on the continent appears one that is shifting back from left to right. Bolsonaro is certainly not the first Trump-style leader to emerge in the 'south'. Rodrigo Duterte in the Philippines was dubbed the 'Trump of East Asia' and became a kindred spirit during Trump's presidential campaign (Curato, 2017). Having gained notoriety as a Major of Davao, where he was accused of organising a set of death squads to carry out summary extrajudicial killings of drug users and petty criminals, Duterte won the 2016 presidential election with nearly 40 per cent of the vote six months before Trump's success in the US. His campaign was largely based on extending these principles of summary justice to the country at large and suggested that the Philippines would leave the United Nations to form a new organisation, if criticism was forthcoming. Still with Trump's election, both he and Duterte have been presented as kindred spirts, embarking upon similar ideological missions, yet beyond the vigilante approach to law and order, there was little further substance to this political position. Whilst, therefore, Duterte can be considered to embark upon a similar form of populism to that of Trump, it is still largely indicative of the country's own specific populist history (Teehankee, 2016). It could also be said that it fits loosely with the character of a wider semi-peripheral regime and does not represent anything novel in these terms.

Putin and Erdoğan can also be seen as being indicative of a semi-peripherality. Whilst Putin's international outlook certainly provides the potential for collaboration with those that seek to bring the nation-state back in to challenge the premise of an inter-connected world and indeed has won praise from a whole host of radical and far-right parties and individuals, his style of governance has followed one that has been marked by Russia's prolonged position on the fringes of Europe and within the semi-periphery of the global economy (Neumann, 1996; Simon, 2009; Robinson, 2012). The same might be said of Erdoğan. Like Putin, Erdoğan has looked to forge a general form of national continuity by stamping out any form of opposition that had previously been evident in Turkey's emerging civil society. What has emerged since has been an attempt to maintain a functional market economy whilst adopting a rigid authoritarian structure at the centre (Somer, 2016; Esen and Gumuscu, 2016). In both cases, the regimes have not emerged from popular opposition in the way that the implosion of the radical right has done in the west, but from a monopolisation and a tightening of authoritarian power.

India

If there is an example of a semi-peripheral state which provides confirmation that the populist right goes beyond the western-centric world it might be India. To a degree, it might also be said that with the rise of the Bharatiya Janata Party (BJP), Narendra Modi appears as the forerunner to Trump. The BJP emerged out of a discourse of Hindu nationalism that was commonly referred to as Sangh Parivar, an umbrella group that represented its construction within Indian civil society (Berglund, 2011). The BJP traditionally associated itself with social conservatism and with an economic nationalism that opposed the economic liberalisation processes that were developed from the early 1990s onwards (Flåten, 2016). Whilst the BJP had topped the parliamentary poll and had indeed led coalitions previously, the general election result was unprecedented. The centre-right coalition that the BJP led swept to power taking well over 300 of the

545 seats contested. Not only did this mean that the coalition could go into government on its own, but with the BJP being the overwhelming largest party in the coalition (over 280 of the seats), it had a free rein to pursue its own agenda. This huge endorsement continued up through to the 2019 election re-writing the nature of Indian political leadership as it did.

There are a number of accounts given to the form of nationalism that the BJP seeks to develop. Some suggest that it represents a nationalism that could only really be comparable to that of the European fascism of the 1930s, with the distinction being that it was geared towards religion as opposed to racial superiority (Jaffrelot, 2016). Others have suggested that the real essence of the BJP revolves around the construction of a form of Hindu authoritarianism where a narrow inclusive nationalism is forged that views other religious and political traditions as 'foreign' or 'colonial' (Vanaik, 2017; Anderson, 1991). Yet, Modi's own style often appears to contradict these assumptions. Like Trump and Farage, he often appears to look for effect more than substance. His appetite for social media also pre-dates the others, with his 2014 and subsequent leadership style being marked by a direct personal tone (Schroeder, 2018). This cult of leadership was maintained throughout the 2019 general election campaign which seemed to endorse the necessity of continuity.

Yet, as a leader, he does not appear to necessarily challenge the confines of the contemporary world order. Indeed, his backing of neoliberal reforms and the internationalisation of the Indian economy was evident in the coalition in the 1998–2004 governments and his position has not shifted since. Therefore whilst Modi has embarked upon a form of nationalism that has all the hallmarks of the current wave of right-wing populism, it has also been used as a means to contribute to and enhance the norms of the global political economy. Therefore, as with other forms of the semi-periphery, India has continued to articulate its nationalism in a manner that fully coincides with its role as a key contributor to the workings and the mechanisms of the global economy (Downes, 2009). In this sense, for all Modi's nationalist inclinations, he does not appear to stand against the wider world order. Economically, Modi has not looked to engage with the national-protectionism that was ingrained within the BJP's traditions, nor has he looked to offer a fresh economic alternative. Modi thus has the attributes of the type of leader that is being fashioned elsewhere, but appears more of an articulator than an ideologist. This does not mean that Modi does not provide a useful ally for those right-wing actors in the west, or indeed would not support a wider project of some kind. It also remains interesting how he manages to contain this form of Hindu populism and sustain his own brand of leadership at the same time, particularly when the forces of anti-neoliberalism and protectionism remain bubbling under the surface.

Political Islam

Political Islam might be understood as the natural enemy of new far-right organisations (see above), but its emergence has been pivotal to a contestation of modernity in the developing world. Since the Iranian Revolution in 1979, a collection of Islamic narratives have been developed that have emerged to challenge the very nature of secular civil society. At the end of the cold war a variety of Sunni organisations appeared that were useful allies to the US against the Soviet Union and Shia Iran's attacks on western secularism (Thomas, 2005). By the time of the events of 9/11, transnational organisations developed upon the principles of Salafist Jihadism had grown to significant prominence that forged a specific critique of the processes of neoliberal global society (Worth, 2013). Through the stringent conservativism of specific readings of the Koran, political Islam shared some of the social concerns that are implicit within the radical right (Abbas, 2017). Whilst the centrality of Islamophobia means that the two will never form a partnership as such, their mutual dislike for one another has potential wider implications when looking at challenges to the neoliberal world order.

The disruption caused by extremist forms of political Islam also contributes to the potential for change. As far-right discourses play into a narrative that looks to constrain the practices of a globalised world, then so does radical political Islam in the developing world. It has a distinct set of criticisms of the contemporary world order that look to explicitly alter and change the way the world functions and operates (Mandaville, 2007; Hroub, 2011). In a strange twist of logic, the neo-conservatism of radical political Islam compliments the conservativism inherent within the radical right as they both serve to contest the prevailing norms that have been developed within international organisation. As such, they both reject the logistics behind international human rights, international law and wider global practices. This is not indicative of a Barber (1996) or a Huntingdon (1996) 'clash of civilisations' argument as the notion of 'western liberal civilisation' is contested by both groups. Instead, it illustrates that as both look to attack the fabrics of the world order from their different positions, the order itself naturally becomes more strained.

Yet, this is perhaps where the comparison ends. The centrality of Islamophobia to the development of the far-right has developed precisely as a result of the emergence of such radical groups. The only way they can be seen therefore as a form of right-wing response themselves is through a shared contempt of the nature of the prevailing world order. As indeed I have argued elsewhere, 'religious-fundamentalist' opposition to neoliberalism makes up its own distinct critique and should be distinguished as such (Worth, 2013: 45–46). The very fact that radical political Islam is geared towards a world view that looks to oppose nation-states suggests that their respective expressions of neo-conservatism come from entirely different departure points. For whilst the notion of an Islamic 'state' might have emerged in the 20th century from places such as Iran, Pakistan and the Kingdom of Saudi Arabia, the ideology behind transnational groups such as Al-Qaida, Boko Haram and the (rather misleading in this case) Islamic State or Daesh is one that is geared towards the fight for global *jihad* (Turner, 2014).

It can be said then that if the far-right and popular forms of nationalism have emerged as a response to the form of the post-cold war order in the so-called advanced societies of Europe and North America, then political Islam has appealed to some areas of the developing world. Whilst there have been many documented accounts of the radicalisation of citizens from western states into Islamic terrorist movements, particularly as a means to carry out attacks in their native countries, the terrain where such movements have flourished remains in unstable weak developing states (Hafez and Mullins, 2015).

Conclusion: Building a Hegemonic Challenge?

At the end of the last chapter, I questioned whether the emergence of a collection of far-right narratives in light of the end of the cold war could be seen as a challenge to the emerging hegemony of neoliberal economic globalisation. The two decades that followed the events of 11 September 2001 and the financial crisis have seen this collection of narratives grow and expand to new dimensions. In particular, the notion of Islamophobia and the need to save national cultures from this perceived threat has become a unifying theme that has grown since 9/11. In addition to this, the financial crisis has seen some of the concerns that had been given to the consequences of globalisation take on greater significance. In particular, anti-immigration movements that were gaining support on the back of Islamophobia saw their support increase as a result of the financial crisis. In terms of its wider focus, the attacks on globalism, multiculturalism and political elitism that were introduced last chapter as key characteristics of right-wing criticisms of the post-cold war environment in the 1990s have been fully incorporated into new parties and organisations that have emerged this century. Indeed, as the next three chapters show, these key characteristics have remained the cornerstone of the new radical right movements that have gained such prominence recently. To this extent the ideas that were being forwarded by far-right new world order conspirators in the years after the end of the cold war have emerged into mainstream debate.

It can therefore be acknowledged that the development of Islamophobia and the anti-immigration agenda has complemented these foundations of critique and allowed them to expand into the realm of practical politics. This leaves us with two questions to pose before looking more closely at the rise of such politics. Firstly, in what way has this movement reached global dimensions and secondly, are the inconsistencies that were highlighted in Chapter 1 more or less apparent since these ideologies have emerged into political realisation?

In answer to the first question, whilst radical right movements are often seen to have primarily been a feature of western, advanced states, there have also been cases particularly within the semi-periphery and in the so-called emerging powers of similar developments. South America has traditionally been a breeding ground for populist politics yet it has been the left that has had made such advancements here in recent years in a way that has gained considerable attention from commentators of global politics. However, the waning of the so-called 'pink tide' seen with the election of certain centre-right governments showed the first signs of this reversal. The watershed victory of Bolsonaro has seen this far more evidently. Following Brazil and before Bolsonaro, it has been in India, with the election of Modi that we have witnessed perhaps the best example of a populist right figure within the semi-periphery. Whilst Russia had a whole collection of nationalist movements emerge from the instability of the cold war, the ascension to power of Putin has both marginalised and co-opted these into his own authoritarian project for Russia. Yet, as argued above, Modi only shares similarities with right-wing populist developments in the west in certain ways. The BJP and Sangh Parivar might have an ideological base for the construction of a movement within civil and political society – a hegemonic project in other words – yet it still remains unclear what the wider purpose of this might be. Certainly under Modi, its main purpose seems to be for India to find a constructive role contributing towards the global political economy, rather than looking to counter, challenge or oppose it.

The ethnic tensions between dominant and minority groups have always been a source of conflict for societies in the developing world that has resulted in the oppression of the majority over the minority (or, in racial cases like South Africa, vice versa – see Enloe, 1973; Premdas, 1992; Haynes, 2002). Yet, the form that this takes bears no resemblance to the nationalism emerging in western democracies. As argued above, if anything, the closest to them can be seen in forms of radical Islam, just as neo-conservative values are upheld in opposition to liberal society. Therefore, it could be suggested that whilst some areas in the semi-periphery have seemed to indicate that the emergence of the far-right has been global in its content, this is highly irregular and as such it remains largely focused upon Europe and the US.

On the second point, has this momentum produced a set of objectives that appear clear enough to mount a specific alternative challenge to the neoliberal order? On one level, it has. The general framework of its opposition represents a liberal elitism which promotes certain transnational business interests – presented as conspiratorial – and is marked by a commitment towards multiculturalism and globalism that ultimately seeks to undermine nationhood. These beliefs have been brought into sharper focus in the last two decades. Whilst they are articulated differently and are argued to different degrees, in general, they are what marks and unites the various strands of the contemporary radical right. Yet, on another level, the ambiguity towards the economic principals remains. Indeed, with the financial crisis and the rise of the Tea Party, the ideas of neoliberal populism that were discussed in the 1990s have taken on greater relevance (Betz, 1994). The sheer fact that the Tea Party actively pursued a radicalisation of the market logic that was indicative within neoliberalism presents an altogether different question. Suddenly, a body of thought looked to critique neoliberalism from a fundamentalist market position. Yet, this remains just one strand of critique within the radical right as a whole. Contained alongside this is one that serves to downplay the economy as insignificant or merely as simply not engaging with it as well as one which reiterates the importance of nationalist economics (Worth, 2014; Davidson and Saull, 2017; Saull, 2018).

It can therefore be assumed that far from constructing economic clarity, far-right parties, campaigns and organisations seem to have merely added to the contradictions and the ambiguities discussed in the last chapter. Yet, if the momentum discussed continues as it has in the last few years, then either an economic alternative convergence might emerge to complement the foundations of opposition that have been developed, or the character of the neoliberal order might adapt to take account of these wider political developments. In order to look at this in more detail, it is necessarily to examine closely how far-right consciousness has developed in detail in both Europe and the US. The next chapter will focus on how in Europe, the far-right have built upon initial successes by the FN and the FPÖ, to achieve great electoral success in both the west and the east, before the two significant achievements that were aided by the wider process of the radical right – Brexit and the election of Donald Trump – are considered in Chapters 4 and 5. This should provide a clearer picture for us to understand whether a serious hegemonic challenge is being levelled in a manner that threatens and transforms the fabric of the post-cold war world order.

THREE | The Far-Right in Europe

The entry of far-right parties into the mainstream of European politics was to be part of a wider evolving political earthquake that has seen centrist established parties come under great scrutiny. The 2017 French presidential election perhaps summed up the atmosphere of upheaval more than anything else. Here, the final round of the run-off was between two candidates that represented parties that had not previously featured in government. In this instance, it was the centrist pro-European, Emmanuel Macron that ultimately triumphed with his party, La République En Marche, which two years previously had just emerged on social media, taking 310 seats out of 577 in the subsequent National Assembly election (Evans and Ivaldi, 2018). The environment for anti-establishment parties thus appeared from across the political spectrum, with the potential for parties that favour the broad status quo looking to supersede traditional parties in the same manner as those which have emerged as oppositional forces (De Sio and Paparo, 2018).

As it was, Marine Le Pen's campaign as Macron's main challenger saw the Front National gain its highest share of the vote on the first ballot. This was the second time the FN had managed to reach the final round. The shock defeat of socialist Lionel Jospin in the first round of the 2002 presidential election saw Jean-Marie Le Pen make the final round, resulting in a landslide for the residing president, Jacque Chirac as Le Pen could only muster just over 17 per cent of the vote. Marine Le Pen managed nearly double (33.9 per cent) that of her father, yet still fell well short of any meaningful challenge to Macron. Unlike 2002, however, when the Front National was routinely criticised by all but a small number of fringe parties,[1] Marine Le Pen garnered support from many of the anti-establishment right that had emerged within both politics and the media across global society in the years between. Donald Trump also showed support for Le Pen, even if he did stop short of officially endorsing her campaign (Quigley, 2017).

The events in France might have provided a 'showcase' for how established party politics can be altered within a short time span, but the FN themselves have – as we have explored – been perhaps the most established and certainly the most well known radical right party in Europe. Indeed, the FN has managed to avoid the terminal splits and feuds that have led to the short time span of comparative parties.[2] The emergence of other radical right parties to prominence in other parts of Europe has shown their real significance as an opposition force. The success of the AfD in Germany has provided an apt example of this. Emerging in 2013, it narrowly missed the 5 per cent representation threshold in the Bundestag election within months of its formation. By the time of the subsequent 2017 elections it had already gained seven MEPs and made significant gains in the state elections. Yet, its performance in 2017 saw the AfD take 94 seats becoming the third party in parliament. Other examples of the rapid rise of far-right parties can be seen across Europe, with some – such as the Nationalist Alliance in Latvia and Kotleba in Slovakia – emerging as new parties that have shot to prominence, whilst others – such as the Swedish Democrats (Sverigedemokraterna) or Golden Dawn in Greece – existed previously, but with little previous success.

Yet, as we shall see in this chapter, the various parties on the populist right have adopted both different styles and different strategies (Fieltz and Laloire, 2016). In addition and perhaps more significant has been the contrasting economic positions they have adopted. As indicated last chapter, parties have tended to favour either a protectionist form of nationalism, which has the effect of explicitly challenging the neoliberal order, or a free market position, which looks to reinforce it. Positions have also been adopted that have remained ambiguous in their economic outlook. Here, the economy has either taken an insignificant role in the programme of a specific movement, or it appears highly contradictory in its nature. In this instance we can tentatively locate and outline which specific parties have emerged to articulate these different economic positions.

Protectionists

Economic protectionism in the context of right-wing groups can appear as a mind-set within more confrontational forms of neo-fascism or in a more sophisticated form which draws from the mercantilist tradition. They can also appear as rather vague or as a developed set of principles that have very real objectives. Strong traditions of protectionism can be found across Europe and North America. Whilst Thomas Mun might have looked to utilise protectionism for aggressive forms of colonial expansion as a means to develop a positive balance of trade (Mun, 1628/2017), both Hamilton in the US and Friedrich List saw it as a necessary strategic form of economic development in a state's evolution (Hamilton, 1791/2016; List, 2005). Whilst List might have argued that protectionism served a specific purpose in a state's development and should not be regarded as a permanent or universal economic blueprint, he nevertheless became very influential in the first half of the 20th century and was regarded by some to be influential to the economic strategies within the fascist movement (Tribe, 2010). Certainly industrialists such as

Walther Funk and Gustav Krupp looked to play down the ideas of Gottfried Feder, who was seen as the economic theoretician of National Socialism, in order to stress the importance of national competition. At the same time in Italy, the free market principles of Mussolini's first finance minister, Alberto De Stefani, were met with an opposition that would lead to the form of corporatism with which Italian fascism became synonymous. The ideas thus arrived to a degree – however unintentionally – from List's model of the national economy.

Protectionism was also quick to emerge as a response to the 'new world order' of the 1990s. As outlined in Chapter 1, the Patriot Movements and the campaigns of Pat Buchanan were all derived from what he defined as 'economic nationalism' whilst the post-communist explosion in Russia and Eastern Europe saw the emergence of a nationalist opposition that was drawn from traditional forms of protectionism. Yet it was the Front National who emerged as the most significant representation of protectionism. The turn by Jean-Marie Le Pen might have moved the party towards the embrace of protectionism but this appeared very much as a convenient move in light of the end of the cold war, especially after his own appreciation of Reagan a decade earlier (Hainsworth, 2004). Marine Le Pen looked to nurture the idea of protectionism by developing a narrative that complements the economic position far more. In particular, by developing a deeper critique of the process of *mondialisme*, she has built upon the conviction that the real opposition to nationalism is globalism, which is developed through bankers, international organisations and deregulated market economics (Eltchaninoff, 2017). Through this, the campaigns against immigration and multiculturalism are strengthened as the FN is presented as a crusade against a globalisation that has been elitist and un-democratic in its appearance.

Keen to draw from the intellectual tradition of protectionism, Le Pen coined the term 'intelligent protectionism' and suggested in her campaign that she could maintain a 2.5 per cent growth in the economy by utilising strategic forms of tariff and constructing a national preference system (Le Pen, 2017). This was to be complemented by the re-establishment of the Franc in favour of the Euro and the re-negotiation of the EU Treaties. Whilst Le Pen has looked to engage with protectionism in a way to make it appear as a rational and logical response to the shortfalls of economics, it was nonetheless condemned by the national press as well as by financial and international onlookers. The attempts to somehow 'normalise' the principles of protectionism and free them from the assumption that they appear outdated and inappropriate for the rigours of the global market might not have succeeded with the establishment, but its framing as a viable alternative certainly gained recognition.

The attempt to frame economic nationalism as an intellectual project was something that the FN might have copied from the American post-cold war revival in economic nationalist discourses that were initially seen in the success of the Ross Perot's presidential campaign in 1992 and developed by individuals such as Buchanan, but also from additional and often unlikely sources. For example, Nick Griffin, the leader of the British National Party (BNP), looked to provide 'intellectual guidance' to the French FN in contributing to the development of the discourse of economic nationalism (see Chapter 5). In these instances, an attempt is thus made to construct both a coherent framework for an economic alternative as well as an accompaniment for a popular movement. Other political parties in Europe that have seemed to adopt the ideas of protectionism include, amongst others, the True Finns and the Swedish Democrats in Scandinavia, Jobbik and to a lesser extent Fidesz in Hungary and the Slovak Nationalist Party in Slovakia. In each of these, protectionism has emerged more as a result of populism rather than as any part of a viable plan or attempt to deepen an intellectual tradition. Nativist slogans thus urge potential supporters to favour national businesses and industries (Bergmann, 2017; Bar-On, 2018).

Away from the powerhouses of Europe, the place where right-wing parties have been most explicit in terms of protectionism has been in Bulgaria. Ataka was formed by Volen Siderov in 2005 and pledged to nationalise industry previously privatised post 1989 and set up a national economic system that would look to build domestic industrial competition protected from the global market by the state. The emphasis on social protection for nationals and the tendency to appraise the social protectionism of the Soviet Union has led some to suggest that Ataka engaged in both left-wing and right-wing discourses in the same manner as the red–black alliance in Russia in the early 1990s (Ghodsee, 2008). Ataka's own brand of protectionism has tended to follow a traditional mercantilist outlook on the one hand, yet was not explicitly against their integration into the European Union, instead favouring a form of a loose intergovernmental partnership that was both ambiguous and implausible in reality (Sygkelos, 2015). Indeed, other nativist parties that have favoured economic nationalism but have not been as forthcoming as Ataka in underlining their economic outlook, such as the Swedish Democrats or the True Finns, have also been rather unclear and inconsistent when looking at the wider question of European integration.

Ataka's star began to decline after the 2009 Bulgarian parliamentary elections where it approached 10 per cent of the vote. Its recent alliance with the Bulgarian National Movement (IMRO) and the National Front for the Salvation of Bulgaria (NFSB), endorsing Krasimir Karakachanov for president in 2016, saw the establishment of a wider umbrella group called the United Patriots which saw them take 27 seats and third place in the 2017 elections at their first attempt. Whilst Ataka's economic plans have taken more of a back seat in the new alliance, the commitment towards economic nationalism remains a key objective, even if election material seemed to place it further down the alliance's pledges (United Patriots of Bulgaria, 2017). Furthermore, the alliance's agreement to enter and form part of the government has seen these ideals further compromised as they look to reinvent themselves as a governing party rather than an opposition umbrella (Kutiyski, 2016).

For the more confrontational forms of the far-right, protectionism is generally assumed through aggressive forms of slogans and campaigning. For those who appropriate the term 'neo-fascism', protectionism appears as a logical equaliser of the wider racial politics that are central to their objectives. For example in Greece, Golden Dawn's brand of violence, which has included attacks on immigrants, ethnic minorities, political opponents and the LGBT community, has been at the forefront of their political strategy. The relative parliamentary success of Golden Dawn, seen in the gaining of 20 seats in the 2012 election and in the retention of this level of representation in subsequent elections, has allowed the party to forge firm policy commitments. In terms of its wider philosophy, Golden Dawn claims it is a movement that embraces the ideology most rooted in the 'history of people' – that of nationalism. This, they argue, is fundamentally opposed to the twin ideologies of 'communist internationalism' and 'universalism-liberalism' (Golden Dawn, 2018). This commitment is extended to the right of each state to build its own national community and claim to believe in respect between the 'spiritual, ethnic and racial difference of men' in order to 'build a society with egalitarian laws' (Golden Dawn, 2018). Here, the violence and confrontational forms of ethnic nationalism that have been endemic in its rise are glossed over in an attempt to characterise themselves as a moderate force (Eilinas, 2013).

Golden Dawn's economic plan was one that was also drawn up after limited parliamentary successes. The first indications of this appeared in 2015 in light of Syriza's emergence as a main player in government. Here, they commit towards an increase in agricultural and manufacturing productivity, the re-establishment of national territorial waters and Greece's economic exclusion zone, the exploitation of Greece's national resources, free trade deals with Iran and Russia, the nationalisation of banks and tax breaks for companies that employ only Greek nationals (Golden Dawn, 2015). Whilst these policies do not explicitly mention economic tariffs or withdrawal from the European Union, the implications of enacting such policies would in reality mean exactly that.

The tendency for groups that emerge as 'neo-fascist' to look to reinvent a more moderate form of nationalism when they begin to gain popularity has been endemic to right-wing groups in recent years. In some cases, such as with the National Democratic Party (NDP or Nationaldemokratische Partei Deutschlands) in Germany, they have managed to retain their ultra-nationalist rhetoric and have not had to distinguish themselves from their links to neo-Nazi ideology, more subversive underground groups linked to violence or from their anti-semitism. The rise in recent years of the AfD, with a seemingly more 'acceptable' form of nationalism (and indeed the rejection of anti-semitism, but the advancement of Islamophobia) has seen them reduce any 'normalisation' of the NDP by claiming their potential electoral vote (Marcks, 2016). In other cases, the transformation has been more apparent. Indeed, both FN (successfully) and the BNP (unsuccessfully) had made strides to distance themselves from sub-cultures and strains of fascism in order to present themselves as 'normal' parties.

Another example of this, albeit from a less extreme position to the example of Golden Dawn, can be seen with Jobbik in Hungary. Both have espoused ultra-nationalist positions and have also certain links to subversive groups in civil society (Kyriazi, 2016). Jobbik emerged as a political force from 2006 but first made significant electoral advancements at the 2009 European elections and the 2010 general elections. Despite reports to the contrary[3] Jobbik always rejected any claims that they had neo-fascist roots, instead arguing that they emerged as a form of nationalist opposition to the workings of global capitalism (Jobbik, 2010). As such, this suggests a traditional nationalist-protectionist response to neoliberalism along the same lines as seen with the FN. Yet, Jobbik's association with anti-semitism as well as its anti-Romani sentiments and its association with the disbanded paramilitary group Magyar Gárda Mozgalom has made it difficult to look at the group in this manner.

Yet, Jobbik and indeed the wider events in Hungary shows us just how quickly far-right parties can indeed reinvent themselves. For, with the rise of Fidesz, Jobbik has appealed to move to the centre-ground. With both Jobbik and Fidesz operating within the same political sphere, Jobbik has looked to reinvent itself more as a big-tent conservative party and distance itself from explicitly racist and xenophobic campaigns. Recent literature from the party has shown that this moderation is continuing as Jobbik seeks to become a party of moderation compared with Fidesz, which has replaced it as the new powerhouse for the Hungarian far-right. This is reflected in the party's new approach to Hungarian economic development. Whilst, the emphasis on sovereignty is maintained, previous hostility to multinational corporations has been replaced by a commitment to 'retaining the partnership with those international corporations that play a key role in the Hungarian economy', in what appears increasingly synonymous with a strategy that resembles the third-way centrism inherent in the 1990s, rather than any form of economic nationalism (Jobbik, 2018).

This brings us to Fidesz themselves. In the increasingly eccentric world of Hungarian politics, Fidesz seems to start off as a centre-right party before moving further and further to embrace far-right campaigns. Fidesz was largely a vehicle for Viktor Orbán, who was Prime Minister between 1998 and 2002 and more recently since 2010. Orbán spent his first term looking to cut taxes, reduce fiscal spending and gain entry to the Euro Zone. In the initial stages of his second term, he implemented a low flat tax rate for personal income, both of these in direct opposition to Jobbik at the time. Orbán's move to reactionary populism has seemingly mirrored Jobbik's move towards moderation, with the two appearing to wear each other's ideological clothes. Whilst the Fidesz-led government has seen Hungary slide increasingly towards an attack on democracy and pluralism and has been forthright in its anti-immigration campaigns, its economic philosophy remains rather ambiguous (Agh, 2016). Whilst Jobbik appeared to endorse a protectionist form of economic nationalism prior to its 'modernisation', Orbán and Fidesz have not as such provided any distinct shift in their ideological approach to the economy. They seem to favour some form of intervention against 'foreign ownership' of the economy, and no decisive plan of action has emerged of the type of 'national preference' that Jobbik had endorsed. In their successful election campaign of 2018, where they won 133 of the 199 seats (incidentally Jobbik finished second with 26), these slogans were used alongside the populist campaigns that targeted immigration, multiculturalism the European Union and globalism, which was often understood within the context of 'foreign meddling'. Yet, they appeared to be used as a way of generating such support for a wider populist campaign that suited the nationalist and reactionary position that Fidesz had adopted.

Traditionally, economic protectionism remains the natural home for far-right movements. Not only has it a long historical tradition, but it is geared towards a systematic attack on the principles and workings of globalisation. However, with the rise of socialism and post-war social democracy, economic intervention of any type became associated primarily with the left. In addition, the premise of anti-communism, which took a significant position within the politics of the right, combined with the appeal of the Thatcher–Reagan 'new right' in the 1980s saw right-wing initiatives emerge that endorsed a completely different economic world view to the protectionists.

Libertarians

The 'libertarian' position on the economy might owe much to the market 'revolutions' of Thatcher and Reagan but draws as much from the conviction that international organisations seek to constrain national economic freedom. For whilst the Reagan–Thatcher doctrine might have provided the ideological foundation for the growth of the contemporary global market, the results for libertarians have provided a set of financial organisations run by 'globalists' whose main objective is to regulate and control national liberties in order to enhance their own individual gains. The emergence of the Tea Party in the US might be seen as the water-tight example, yet the history of right-wing groups which favour a laissez-faire approach to the economy is a long one. Victorian England saw the birth of liberal economics alongside a state which was to harbour imperial expansion, empire and the belief in cultural superiority. As we shall see in Chapter 5, these values and ideals have been significant in the nationalist revival in contemporary England, although the freedom of labour required in the Victorian era is forgotten when measured alongside anti-immigration campaigns. Both in the US and across Europe, the anti-communist rhetoric was drawn to anti-state intervention in the economy and this in turn was to feed into conspiracy theories around globalisation and global governance.

The libertarian position also goes far beyond the idea of 'authoritarian neoliberalism' that has recently been popular to describe recent reactionary post-crisis trends identified in the Introduction (Bruff, 2014). Certainly, figures such as Putin, Erdogan and Duterte can be seen in this mould and arguably those that seek to downplay economic factors in favour of populist rhetoric can be seen to contribute to this process (see below), yet those that adopt a concentrated market economic strategy do so from a position that looks to criticise the contemporary neoliberal system. For them, the global market system has been consistently dominated by international organisations and by global financers, who have created a form of 'crony capitalism' that has not allowed the market to operate freely.

Whilst the economic philosophy might have emerged from von Mises in terms of his arguments that financial institutions that interfere in the market by artificially intervening in interest rates negate the role of the market to freely regulate itself (von Mises, 1934), the main concerns for right-wing parties following these principles lay close to home. The first, which has been highly significant is that which can be defined as welfare chauvinism.

Welfare chauvinism is the belief that certain groups in society should be able to access services more than others (Anderson and Bjørklund, 1990). These can refer to nativist forms of chauvinism where welfare benefits should be restricted to those that are indigenous to a specific country. Indeed, one of the initial campaigns of Jorg Haider was to argue that a welfare state should be primarily served by those that were indigenous citizens and had shown patriotism in some way to the state. Immigration thus puts external pressure on the fabric of such a welfare system (Ennser-Jedenastik, 2016).

Yet, the way that welfare chauvinism meets a free market approach to the economy is through the belief that the welfare state itself is fundamentally flawed as it creates a system of dependency. In the same manner that the Whig-inspired governments of the 1830s in Britain looked to minimise poor relief,[4] then contemporary welfare chauvinists look to do the same. The main targets are thus those receiving welfare benefits such as the unemployed, the incapacitated, immigrants and refugees who 'drain' the system. Thus, support for reduced taxes, the rolling back of the state from social and economic life and for 'individual liberty' provide a foundation for forms of nationalist populism to be built upon. This libertarian mind-set also provides a similar platform for the European Union. By identifying the European Union as a bureaucratic machine that interferes in the functions of social and economic life, a mix of populist nationalism alongside an endorsement of market ideology results in what Betz identified in the early 1990s as neoliberal populism (Betz, 1994; see Chapter 1).

As we shall see in Chapter 5, one of the arch-typical examples of this ideological approach is UKIP, who, increasingly alongside elements of the British Conservative Party, have looked to draw on the British superiority of the Victorian era in order to critique the contemporary British state. However, in mainland Europe there have been a number of parties that have looked to embody this form of right-wing populist movement. In parts of Europe where the post-war consensus was largely made up of social and Christian democracy, this form of radical market populism provides an alternative to the status quo. Certainly (as we have seen) the appeal of the FPÖ was that it appeared to break such a consensus and Haider's initial attacks on the nature and accessibility of the post-war welfare state appealed as a form of protest politics (Riedlsperger, 1998). In Italy, Lega Nord has been regarded by some as embodying such a 'far-right neoliberalism' (Perlmutter, 2015). In the case of Lega Nord this goes beyond traditional nationalism as they ultimately emerged if not entirely out of a separatist movement, certainly out of one that is primarily seeking greater regional autonomy for more advanced areas. Welfare chauvinism, lower taxes and less state spending, particular in deprived areas in the south, were thus ways in which Lega Nord could maximise popular support. Placed alongside other campaigns such as anti-immigration, Euroscepticism and anti-globalisation, Lega Nord have established a party that seeks to 'speak' for the indigenous, 'productive' citizens of northern Italy.

Perhaps the most successful example of 'populist neoliberals' has been seen in Switzerland. As the spiritual home of confederalism, Switzerland has long been regarded as a constitutional utopia for those that preach anti-statist conservatism, with those from the libertarian tradition in the US in particular paying considerable attention to the Swiss Canton system (Tarr and Benenson, 2013; Paul, 2016). The success of the Swiss People's Party (Schweizerische Volkspartei, SVP) also perhaps best reflects the attack on the two-party social/Christian democracy consensus in continental Europe. As with the FPÖ in neighbouring Austria, the SVP looked to exploit such a relationship. The SVP were able to build on initial gains made by the Swiss Freedom Party, who looked to Thatcher's rhetoric of the rolling back of the state in order to appeal to sections of the Swiss electorate (Betz, 1999). The SVP were to build firmly on these principles but place them more centrally in the aims of a party that was already gaining significance in the German-speaking part of the country in the broader area of Swiss nationalism (Skenderovic, 2009).

The 21st century has seen the party's ideology evolve into one that has managed to utilise free market philosophy alongside a collection of campaigns that have engaged in Islamophobia and an increasing scepticism of the EU. This has seen the party top the poll in the federal elections, establishing themselves as the leading political party in the country. Due to the nature of the Swiss system, the SVP have not managed to enact some of the rhetoric that they espouse. Nor have they managed to influence the political system in a manner that would see some of their policy recommendations realised at a national level. Here lies an interesting paradox of the sort that is endemic to libertarian forms of far-right populism. On the one hand, they look to devolve power to levels that appear to dismantle the centrality of the state, but by doing this, their overall objectives at a national level are (naturally) limited by this structural reality (Skenderovic, 2007; Ivadi and Mazzoleni, 2017). However, in terms of its success, the SVP have been the one party associated with the far-right and certainly with this brand of 'neoliberal populism' that has managed to top the poll at the national level.

In recent years, others that have followed this pro-market position have included the Flemish nationalist group Vlaams Belang. Indeed, whilst the FN in France altered their economic position from free market to protectionist, the Flemish nationalist tradition has in general gone the other way. The emergence of Vlaams Blok in the 1980s and 1990s saw a prominent form of Flemish nationalism develop that – like the Lega Nord – looked to illustrate how their particular region or nation far out produced their counterparts within the state. Vlaams Blok used this form of indigenous supremacy as a departure point for both wider drives against immigration and in particular Islamophobia, where, in the post-cold war environment, they were one of the first parties to publicly condemn the 'ideology of Islam' (Swyngedouw, 2000; Mudde, 2000). They appeared at the time to favour forms of economic nationalism which looked to give preferential treatment to Flemish businesses and produce. In 2004, Vlaams Blok, who had just emerged as the second party within the Flemish parliament, was dissolved as it was found to have breached Belgium's anti-racist laws.[5] Vlaams Belang, which replaced them, maintained their general principles but did alter their economic ideology.

Vlaams Belang looked towards continuing the legacy of Vlaams Blok, but to tone down some of its rhetoric, particularly in light of the fate of Vlaams Blok. The only noted change in Vlaams Belang's platform was indeed in its economic ideas. As commentators remarked at the time of the inception of the new party, the idea of national solidarity[6] and conservative collectivism, which has its roots in Italian fascism and which formed the basis of the economic ideals of Vlaams Blok, were replaced by a model dedicated to free market economics and neoliberalism (Erk, 2005). This position is reflected in the party literature not only in terms of its commitment to reducing taxation and economic regulations, but also in the way that standard forms of welfare chauvinism are expressed. The belief that Flanders is kept back in a 'straight jacket' due to the other parts of Belgium is confirmed, with its own dynamism undermined by those reliant on welfare and subsidies from outside Flanders (Vlaams Belang, 2018).

This has allowed Vlaams Belang to develop a narrative on welfare chauvinism similar to other radical right parties that favour a free market approach to the economy. Not only do they claim that Flemish social security is undermined by other less productive groups within the Belgium state, but also by the fear of immigration and the further costs of welfarism.

Other right-wing populist parties have given certain endorsements to the general principles of market economics, but cannot really be classified as being explicitly geared towards embodying a mind-set that believes that contemporary economic problems have ultimately emerged from the over-regulation of the economy. The Norwegian Progress Party (Fremskrittspartiet), the Danish People's Party (Dansk Folkeparti, DF), Poland's Law and Justice Party (Prawo i Sprawiedliwość) and more recently the AfD have all endorsed market-based systems at different times and indeed have all shown signs of welfare chauvinism in their approaches. Yet, all of these have also been rather vague in such endorsements and have often been seen to contradict themselves, especially when campaigns for national-first strategies imply degrees of economic nationalism and degrees of intervention in the market by their very nature. These might espouse a general commitment to the workings of market capitalism, but their own programmes generally tend to either downplay or overlook the economy and their relationship to the wider global neoliberal economic system.

What unites all these parties is their understanding of the EU and why they oppose it. Whilst right-wing parties of all guises are united in their belief that the EU erodes national sovereignty, those that are pro-market also believe that it serves to restrain the workings of the market. For example, the party literature from Vlaams Belang, the SVP and Lega Nord have all made reference to the notion that the EU has served to place great constraints on the national and local economies, which in turn has limited the ability of the market to maximise greater productivity and competition (Vlaams Belang, 2018; SVP, 2015; Zaslove, 2011). Taking the juxtaposition to those on the left that see the EU as a neoliberal construction, here we see an attack on the EU from the entirely opposite position – that it exists as a body that regulates and interferes in the economy in a manner that could only be understood as being highly interventionist in nature.

Economic Ambiguity

Whilst we can distinguish between those that economically favour forms of protectionism from those that believe in a more concentrated form of market economics, the reality, which has been made by the vast majority of studies within comparative politics, is that the economy is more often than not of secondary importance to radical right parties (Ignazi, 2003; Swank and Betz, 2003; Roy, 1998; Rydgren, 2017). As we established in the first two chapters, Cas Mudde's dismissal of economic affairs can be seen in his own statement that 'It's Not the Economy Stupid!' (Mudde, 2007: 119). What this displays at a wider level is also of interest, with those which are economically minded being at ideological loggerheads over their position on the wider workings of the global economy, whilst those that lack an economic mandate at all just contribute to a further blurring across Europe of any form of wider oppositional cohesion the radical right might have. Without this economic mandate they can merely appear as pawns within a wider system that they are not able or interested in changing. It is indeed here where those that talk of authoritarian neoliberalism or of neoliberal nationalism (Harmes, 2012) hold some relevance. For, if reactionary campaigns are placed within an environment that sees the overriding material conditions as irrelevant, then they would be contained and operate within prevailing conditions. We are reminded of Polanyi's world in the *Great Transformation*, in the decades prior to the market collapse that I mentioned in the Introduction. Here, nationalist movements emerged that led to renewed geopolitical rivalry and the growth of European national supremacy amidst nation-building, yet at the same time, these looked to adhere to the general principles of the Gold Standard and the international structure of liberal capitalism (Polanyi, 1944). This might have ultimately led to the collapse of the system eventually and indeed with the rise of a nationalism in the 1930s that was far more conscious of its economic objectives, but the late 19th-century forms, which Eric Hobsbawm termed as 'national flag waving' (Hobsbawm, 1987), operated within its parameters.

Parties that have genuinely been rather ambiguous about their economic strategy include those that I have mentioned above, such as Fidesz and Prawo i Sprawiedliwość, but other examples include Brothers of Italy (Fratelli d'Italia), the Bulgarian National Movement and their recent partners National Front for Salvation (which split from Ataka), the Conservative People's Party of Estonia (Eesti Konservatiivne Rahvaerakond) and the Party of Order and Justice in Lithuania (Partija tvarka ir teisingumas, PTT). In addition, trans-European groups such as Periga (an acronym from Patriotic European Against the Islamisation of the West or Patriotische Europäer gegen die Islamisierung des Abendlandes), which was founded as an anti-Islamic movement in German, but has added many of the campaigns associated with the far-right (such as anti-immigration, anti-multiculturalism, the erosion of European national culture etc.) and has branches in Norway, the Netherlands, Ireland and the UK, also did not have a coherent economic direction.

Yet, perhaps the most obvious has been Geert Wilders' Party of Freedom (Partij voor de Vrijheid, PVV) in the Netherlands.

Whilst looking to build on the success of Pim Fortuyn, Wilders has not chosen to follow his generally favourable view on market economics. Instead, he has adopted a number of contrasting economic positions that whilst hard to map, place them on a broadly centrist position, between the free market on one axis and intervention (in its different ideological varieties) on the other (Krouwel, 2012). Partly, this has been because of the PVV's attachment to causes that appeal to potential voters rather than ones that form the basis of a specific meaningful ideology. For example, in an attempt to appeal to increase their support within the older generation, the PVV has looked to uphold the age of retirement (PVV, 2010). This commitment towards welfarism is then compromised by the reduction in a whole variety of taxes, including carbon taxes and taxes on petroleum, which in turn are then compromised by a blanket attack on businesses that appear to be ecologically unfriendly.

In the case of PVV, apart from the central attack on Islam, Geert Wilders has seemingly endorsed a form of anything-goes populism, with a tendency to support a number of campaigns that often come from contrasting positions in order to gain more electoral support. As a result, whilst their attack on Islam proposed a whole set of draconian authoritarian measures to restrict religious freedoms or to deport immigrants for 'anti-social' behaviour, they also look to uphold and extend certain liberties that the indigenous – or, more correctly, those from the 'Judeo-Christian western current' – population enjoy (Vossen, 2016). Whilst Fortuyn did look to build a movement that protected the social liberal tradition that had emerged from post-war Dutch civil society as a vehicle against the social conservatism of Islam, thus building an ideologically distinct project, Wilders seems to lack this consistency. His voter base is one that is defined through education levels more than comparable parties, with those with a lower level of education more likely to vote for the PVV. Their supporters are also generally younger than the majority of radical right party support across Europe, where success has been found in attracting support from older generations (Ehrenberg-Shannon and Wisniewska, 2017). Thus, those financial attractions offered to those at pensionable age are another sign of the party engaging in isolated populist campaigns in order to enhance popularity.

Less obvious in such ambiguity has been the emergence of the AfD. As mentioned, they appear to favour a free market position and certainly one geared towards tax reduction, yet downplay these to significant levels. Indeed, the AfD, in their short history and in the small number of campaigns they have as yet been involved with, certainly support the notion of the economy being an after-thought and secondary (AfD, 2017). It is also possible that as the AfD develops, a free market approach might emerge more prominently. Some have indeed pointed out that the AfD was initially constructed by the economist Bernd Lucke, who, along with other like-minded economists founded the party as a free market critique of the politics of the Merkel/SDP coalition, which they saw as too interventionist (Gabriel, 2016). Despite this, the party quickly became populated by social conservatives and then enshrined anti-immigration and Islamophobia as its main tenets, resulting in the founder and many of his associates leaving. Yet, as the right-wing British tabloid the *Daily Mail* proclaimed enthusiastically, the new co-leader of its parliamentary party, Alice Weidel, named Margaret Thatcher as her inspiration and political idol, citing economic reasons rather than populist ones (*Daily Mail*, 2017).

If the background behind the founding of the AfD was concern with the economy and if the aspirations of some of its prominent members might point to a commitment to a freer, more open form of neoliberalism, party manifestos to date do not reflect this reality. The 2017 manifesto saw a mixed approach to the economy that endorsed certain tax reforms, reduced certain regulations in the labour market, yet also put restrictions on privatisation processes and pledged vast increases for financial incentives to families (AfD, 2017). Whilst less inconsistent that the PVV, the economic platform of AfD is at present mixed and cannot be seen as radical or as one that offers an alternative in either direction.

The economic ambiguity of such parties has also seemingly allowed for anti-immigration and anti-Islamic campaigns to develop at a level that has been felt both within sub-cultures and within different strands of civil society (Fielitz and Laloire, 2016). Yet, without a coherent hegemonic alternative that would arrive from an economic plan that is rooted in an ideological position, they appear as campaigns which can be utilised in different ways by political parties (including those on the far-right) at the centre. This again sees the potential for forms of authoritarianism or the emergence of a type of Caesarism within the workings of politics (Short, 2014). Yet, as we see from the case of Poland, there has been a build up of parties which appear on the one hand to endorse free market forms of neoliberalism, yet on the other utilise forms of nationalism in such a manner that they look equally like countering and opposing the same principles (Shields, 2007; 2014).

The sheer intensity of right-wing nationalist parties in Poland that have emerged both within the realms of party politics and, more recently, in government have made it increasingly difficult to maintain a participatory parliamentary democracy (as opposed to strong centrist authoritarian catch-all 'leaders' or 'Caesars' such as Putin or Erdoğan). In Poland, the success of Prawo i Sprawiedliwość can be seen in the same vein as Fidesz in Hungary.

Like Fidesz, Prawo i Sprawiedliwość favoured market economics at first, but moved increasingly towards more populist forms of intervention as their vote increased and in response to the emergence of other right-wing parties. The presence of Solidarity Poland (Solidarna Polska), the National-Catholic Movement and the National Movement – who are inclined towards popular nationalism and protectionist politics – and the Congress of the New Right, the Right Wing of the Republic and Liberty or Wolność – who are geared towards forms of free market economics – as well as the more traditional moderate conservativism of the Polish People's Party, has made competition for right-wing movements within the Polish political spectrum highly intense and highly competitive. This is especially the case when seeking potential alternatives that look to contest the paradigms of neoliberalism more explicitly (Shields, 2015).

If Poland might find parties looking to open up different alternatives by exploiting the populist space that has grown initially from economic ambiguity, then in Denmark we have seen a recent challenge to the Danish People's Party (DPP) from an ideological perspective. The DPP have long been seen as the traditional populist right party in Denmark. The establishment of Nye Borgerlige was an attempt to challenge the ideological position of the DPP. In line with the presence of women figureheads in far-right movements, Nye Borgerlige was set up by Pernille Vermund and along with her co-leader Peter Seier Christensen looked to offer a more stringent view on immigration and the EU from the DPP. More prominent has been the pledge to abolish corporation tax and adopt a low tax free market system to dismantle the Danish welfare-dependent society (Panagiotopoulos, 2017). Here, a party has emerged to offer a position that addresses the question of economic ambiguity, looking to make a position explicit. Whether there is an actual market for such a position in a country where welfarism is rooted within its political structure is another question. At present, there is no sign that they will experience a rapid rise in the manner of the AfD.

Another question over the economic positioning of the radical right concerns why certain parties choose to adopt a particular economic stance. With some, it is undoubtable that protectionism and market fundamentalism forms a strong backbone of a party's DNA. However, others have fluctuated with time or when certain openings appear appealing. We have seen this with the situation in Hungary with Jobbik and Fidesz altering their economic strategy, seemingly in order to improve their voter target. Yet, if we go back to when the FN moved from a position of supporting free market enterprise to one rooted in protectionism, many were dubious of the claims that Jean-Marie Le Pen made at the time of a change in nationalist philosophy due to far-reaching events (Bastow, 1997). Similarly, whilst the worldview of Marine Le Pen might be one forged against the socio-cultural practices of globalisation, protectionism is perhaps not rooted in her personal philosophy in the manner she claims, but has proved to be useful and tactical with gaining support in light of the financial crisis (Eltchaninoff, 2017). Likewise the opposite could be levelled at parties such as Vlaams Belang, who have looked at the productivity of the Flemish region and concluded that welfare chauvinism, lowering taxes to the extended Belgium state and enhanced market competition make better campaigns for their own nationalist narrative.

Finally, another point that has been frequently made here is about the voters themselves. In general, studies have shown that despite vast differences existing between attitudes across Europe, those who vote for far-right parties tend to be less 'neoliberal' than centrists (Mayer, 2005). This would be in line with historical trends and would also suggest that protectionism would make the most appealing form to construct a wider hegemonic challenge. However, most voters also tend to display huge ambiguities in the ways they see the economy (Mudde, 2007). This is not just in the area of welfare chauvinism, which can suggest an increase in state spending in certain areas to the indigenous population (and also to groups that the voters themselves might be in), but through general logistics as corresponding opposites, such as favouring low taxes alongside greater investment, are often revealed (Norris, 2005). In turn, as we have already seen, these can also be assumed by the parties themselves. As a result, the multitude of ideological ambiguities contained in such parties and their voters lessen any potential for a wider attack on the contemporary neoliberal system.

Conclusion

Far-right parties have not just made significant gains across Europe in the post-crisis era but have also taken positions in government. The FPÖ in Austria and Pim Fortuyn's List in the Netherlands both went into government in the first decade of the 21st century, but at the time these were seen as exceptions and in the case of the latter, short lived. Yet, in the last few years an increasing number of what are considered radical right parties have made their way into government. From Lega Nord's position within the new 'populist' coalition in Italy to the nationalist turns taken in Poland and Hungary, the rise of right-wing parties in government is noticeable. The gains themselves have led to a number of developments that have seen radical right parties in serious contention to top the poll in many European countries.

Despite this noticeable trend, it remains difficult to locate a specific ideological challenge to the wider processes of neoliberalism. There are very definite commonalities that do form the basis of a resistance from a socio-cultural position. The campaigns against immigration, multiculturalism and the varying degrees of Islamophobia are coupled alongside a commitment to reclaim national sovereignty from being eroded by external institutions that the traditional political establishments have created. The EU naturally figures prominently in these attacks. The Brexit referendum result coupled with the succession of refugee crises from 2015 onwards led to a strengthening of the appeal of far-right parties by 2019. Following the general premise of the book, this chapter has illustrated which of these emerging parties have favoured an ideological position closely associated with protectionism and traditional nationalism and which have favoured one which seeks to retain the principles of free market economics – the former being geared towards challenging the wider rhetoric of the neoliberal by looking for the national disintegration of the global economy, whilst the latter maintaining that the principles behind the market doctrine had been tampered with by continued socialist interference (Worth, 2014).

Yet, these categories appear reductionist when looking at the wider content and aspirations of the European far-right. In particular, many campaigns endorsed by such parties on closer inspection contained so many contradictions and are ideologically fraught with inconsistencies that it remains problematic to suggest the various social forces behind the sum of the far-right offer anything more that the potential of a hegemonic challenge to neoliberalism. However, two further points need to be made that leave wider question marks over the stability of the contemporary order. The first is that the campaigns that have been progressed by the various radical right movements have had a significant impact on the nature and expression of global politics and the politics of globalisation. The backlash against the social and cultural practices that have been generated from the advances of the neoliberal global market and realised by technological advancements have left us with very real questions over how these advancements will now develop. Whilst such a backlash might have been considered inevitable due to the instability and fluidity of the neoliberal system itself (Castells, 1996; Rupert, 2000; Steger, 2005; Worth, 2013), the campaigns from right-wing discourses to pick and choose which processes represent a threat to their own national cultures, and as such should be curtailed, leave the future character of the neoliberal system up in the air. This may result in more states looking to tighten up the political system at the centre by reducing plurality within the system and civil liberties within civil society. As we know from a number of classic accounts on various aspects of the nature of the neoliberal state, market economics can function, despite reactionary and populist forces at the centre (Hall, 1988; Gamble, 1996). The rediscovery of these assumptions through terms such as 'authoritarian neoliberalism' is thus apt when looking at potential future forms of expression within global society, where indeed the economic principles of neoliberalism are maintained but the democratic elements that appear to accompany the market development are curtailed (Bruff, 2014). In the same manner, forms of nationalism based upon the premise of neoliberalism have become a growing reality (Harmes, 2012).

The second point is the observation that Polanyi made in his examination of the international market system of the 19th century, which was referred to in the Introduction. That is, that by continuing to engage with the forces of nationalism, the contradictions of free market capitalism become more and more unsustainable. Indeed, by looking to restrict freedom of labour due to immigration controls and by looking to implement certain controls in order to protect various definitions of national sovereignty, the ordering principles of neoliberalism become more difficult to work within. Whilst there remain only a few governments that have contained far-right parties as part of their set-up, as we shall see in the next three chapters, their reactionary and nationalist campaigns have had an effect at the centre of government as governing parties have looked to respond to their increasing popularity with the public at large.

FOUR | The Far-Right in the US

If Europe has seen a collection of radical right parties drawn from a number of contrasting ideological traditions, then the experience in the US has arguably seen the same differing traditions bubble to the surface. The election of Donald Trump as the 45th President of the United States in November 2016 was unique in so many ways for American politics. Not only did his opponent Hillary Clinton win the popular vote by near 3 million votes, but Trump himself won the election having never held political office at any governmental level in the US. His rise to office led to conflicts, within the political establishment, within the Republican Party and – more significantly – within wider civil and political society. The divisions that were created during Trump's campaign left the country divided and polarised. The Trump success can be seen as the result of an accumulation of a number of nationalist, libertarian, neo-conservative and reactionary social forces that had been emerging for some time to challenge what can be understood in Gramscian terms as American 'common-sense' (Rupert, 1997). The novelty of Trump's campaign was that it not only looked to build upon the populism and the grassroots movements that were inherent within the Tea Party and in the subsequent Patriot Movements which became affiliated to it, but it also looked to the more radical, more extremist 'alt-right' for support (Lyons, 2017; Mead, 2018). The use of social media by extremist groups in support of Trump were a significant feature of a campaign that brought out into the open the politics of hate and hostility (Barkun, 2017).

As argued in the first chapter, right-wing nationalist narratives had been developing in the US from the departure point of the synopsis of a 'New World Order'. Essentially, this was the rejection of the belief that the end of the cold war could be seen as a victory of capitalism over communism, but instead belief that a global elite that had previously looked towards communism as a source for world government would turn their attention towards realising this aim through globalisation and institutional integration (Spark, 2000). These seeds of discontent were to grow significantly through the next decade and a half, aided firstly by the internationalism of Bill Clinton and then by the neo-conservative interventionism of George W. Bush. Yet, it was under Obama where these foundations grew. Coinciding with the financial crisis, the Obama administration led to a backlash against big government and the manner in which the state intervened in the economy. In opposition to the growing calls for greater economic regulation in other parts of the world, a populism emerged behind the tradition of economic libertarianism which was endemic in the US. However, whilst certain inspirational leaders within the emerging Tea Party looked to imbed this form of popular libertarianism, the forces of nationalism and American patriotism became difficult to contain (Paul, 2008). As a result, more extremist elements that engaged with forms of economic nationalism, white supremacism and neo-fascism emerged to gain prominence with the rise of Trump.

It is false to suggest that these recent developments have emerged or exploded onto American society. Even the claim that these contemporary movements gradually emerged from the paranoia that a New World Order was emerging after the cold war is one that presupposes some form of explosion in the aftermath of the fall of the Berlin Wall. Instead, the American far-right has a long history that draws intensively from the experiences of the era of anti-communism. Indeed, as recent accounts have argued, the far-right remained highly prominent during the cold war period in the US and were at times heavily drawn upon by governments as a means to reinforce the principles of anti-communism. Yet, they were also largely successfully contained by such governments in a manner that did not allow their rhetoric to gain any ascendency (Saull and Anievas, 2019). Paradoxically, the reverse seems threatening to occur today as narratives once on the fringes appear more frequently within mainstream American political society.

The Foundations of the American Far-Right

Historically, the US has had a long tradition of right-wing civil groups. Racially, the fallout from the Civil War brought in a number of white supremacist groups such as the Red Shirts and the White League that thrived in the second half of the 19th century after the suppression of the first Ku Klux Klan. Yet it was the emergence of the second Ku Klux Klan in 1915 that would symbolically come to represent American racism in the 20th century. Estimates put the number of members of the Klan as high as 5 million in the heyday of the 1920s (Chambers, 1965). Combined with that there has been a succession of anti-semitic, nativist and fundamentalist Christian groups that were rife and prospered during the period of the Great Depression. The far-right in the US has also had a long history of conspiracy theories dating back to the period of Jefferson that have a tradition of conjuring a belief that secret societies and sects are linked with government. Following this, the first Anti-Masonic Party was formed in the 1820s, establishing the roots of a strong obsession that has remained at large ever since.

The idea of such conspiracies according to some has come from the myths and narratives behind the founding of the state itself and in particular the special place that the Constitution has in American political and civil society. Firstly the fear of the outside enemy attacking the fabric of the state came from the British, then the French, then to the notion of secret societies and groups which included the Illuminati and the Freemasons, before finishing with the communists by the time the Second World War ended (Uscinski and Parent, 2014: 3–4). The idea that the Constitution was under attack was to subsequently follow. Within right-wing narratives, the Constitution has taken almost biblical significance in the understanding of the composition of American liberty, with conspiracy theories geared towards the belief that external forces and 'enemies' within government are looking to undermine or destroy its principles.

The combination of reactionary politics and the belief in conspiracy has provided the right with an ethos that has not emerged or grown in stature as such in recent years but has been evident throughout American political history. If there was an explosion as such, it perhaps was more evident in the aftermath of the Second World War than in the New World Order conspiracies of the last few decades. Even then, the many anti-communist groups that grew up in the 1950s and 1960s drew significantly from belief in American isolationism, the paleo-conservativism of the 1920s and the Dixiecrat tradition, which peaked just after the war. What perhaps was significant about the anti-communist movements was that they contributed to the notion that there were forms of international conspiracies geared towards attacking American values and institutions. Most of these were largely geared towards communism, but conservative media outlets such as the newly vamped *American Mercury*, *America's Future* and the *Common-Sense* and *America for Americans* newspapers were quick to point out that bankers, lawyers, the mainstream press and groups such as Carnegie, Rockefeller and Guggenheim were in league with the communists (see, for example, *American Mercury Magazine*, 1953).[1]

It was also in the 1950s and 1960s that the attacks began to develop on the United Nations. The John Birch Society has often been credited with the campaign to 'get the US out of the UN' (John Birch Society, 2009). Yet, the sheer number of groups and organisations that emerged at the time to condemn the UN as a vehicle for either communism or world government (or most of the time for both) was notable. Groups such as the National Council for American Education, the Council on American Relations, Keep America Committee and the National Defence Committee all acted as watchdogs against UN 'activity' (Hoover Institution, 2018: Radical Right Collection: United Nations and World Federalism (Box 44)). They were joined by the Daughters of the American Revolution, who at the height of the cold war contributed to the fears of world government and were also to feature in the anti-NATO movement that emerged at the same time (Daughters of the American Revolution, 1965). The fear that both organisations played a role in the construction of a 'world federation' was one that could be understood through a multitude of conspiratorial involvement. Thus, communism might have been the main target here, but Fabian socialism from Britain, freemasonry, bankers, Zionists, lawyers, educators, anti-Christians of various forms and international Jewry all featured heavily within such conspiracies. Only years after joining the UN, reports that the organisation was secretly plotting to abolish the US emerged (Council on American Relations, 1949). These were to form the basis of endless conspiracies involving internationalism that would develop into the anti-globalism that we see today.

By the 1960s the focus on debt accumulation would take a significant position within right-wing positions (America for Americans, 1969). This was to intensify with the ending of the dollar system in 1971 (which itself was unpopular). Some of this tied in with the emergence of the 'new right' and with Reaganomics. The popularity of Milton Friedman and of the Austrian school of economics was certainly a factor in conservative circles during the 1970s. Alongside this, however, was support for a more nationalist, more inward-looking and conversely more protectionist form of politics, which did favour low taxes and less federal spending, but also favoured anti-immigration measures, economic protectionism for the nation at large and were opposed to wider trade agreements (Hoover Institution, 2018: Radical Right Collection: America for Americans' (Box 104)). As with Trump three and a half decades later, these many positions would come together to back Reagan in the 1980 election, but unlike with Trump, the pursuit of an ideology that would later become known as 'neoliberal' was explicit within Reagan's administration. As such, whilst he managed to co-opt many of the different strands of the conservative right in his wider project, his own form of governance was both internationalist in nature and one that would very much increase the nation's debt.[2]

To a degree these show the difference between the splits of neo-conservativism, paleo-conservativism and anti-federal libertarianism which have long been apparent within the American right (Diamond, 1995). These are indeed the same general types of differences that we illustrated in the last chapter with the case of Europe. Whilst the neo-conservatives favoured internationalism and stressed its importance during the anti-communist 'crusades' during the cold war, the paleo-conservatives were far more defensive in nature (Foley, 2007). Drawing upon the isolationism that pre-dated the Second World War and was popularised by moves such as the US's refusal to join the League of Nations and the Snoot-Hawley tariffs in 1930, paleo-conservatives campaigned to embark upon nativist and protec-tionist campaigns. On the other hand, the libertarian trend on the right looked to facilitate the philosophies of the Austrian economists far more. The setting up of the Libertarian Forum and the Cato Institute by the highly influential economist, Murray Rothbard allowed the libertarian position to engage in debate within right-wing circles. It also seemed to have more in common with the paleo-conservative tradition, especially as Rothbard's own criticisms of Reagan became more promi-nent as he continued in office (Rothbard, 1987). Rothbard himself looked to reach out to the paleo-conservative position and found support in Ron Paul. He also endorsed firstly Pat Buchanan and then Perot in the 1992 presidential elections as he believed them to provide a general libertarian outlook even if their populism would rely on overly nationalist sentiments in reality. This mix would later form the basis for the Tea Party, but before that would give more credence to the rejection of the theory that international communism along with the threat of a world government was over with the fall of the Eastern bloc and the Soviet Union.

By the time of the early 1990s therefore, right-wing opposi-tional narratives were highly developed. The cold war might have brought an anti-communism that thrived on conspiracies based around a belief that an international attack on American liberty existed, but these were built on fears that had their foundations in American history. Likewise, the fear of international institutions such as the UN and NATO was based on an isolationism that had a deep-rooted culture within American society. In the same way, right-wing understandings of globalism and of the New World Order are not new ideas but merely ones that have adapted to recent events to reveal the same conspiratorial fears.

Globalism Reborn

The ending of the cold war thus provided both a form of continuity and an avenue for new interpretations for right-wing thought in the US. The attacks from the right and most notably from Pat Buchanan on the Gulf War set a platform for the interpretation of a new type of internationalism. With Buchanan's support from the libertarians, through the Mises Institute, Paul and Rothbard provided a firm opposition to the war from the right (Diamond Archive, 1991). The New World Order speech of George Bush Sr might, as suggested in Chapters 1 and 2, have gained metaphorical importance in terms of its content, but moves towards establishing a North American Free Trade Association with Mexico and Canada were to prove greater evidence of an external attack (Berlet and Lyons, 2000). Yet, rather than Buchanan, it was Ross Perot who was to become an unlikely beneficiary, taking nearly 19 per cent of the vote in 1992. Running on an independent ticket, Perot largely gained attention due to his opposition to NAFTA, but ran a campaign that also focused on debt accumulation and on big federal bureaucracy without really offering firm solutions for alternatives at the time. He did bring in the notion of globalism, however, referring countless times to NAFTA as a symptom of globalism and to the need to rebuke it as a 'patriot' (Steger, 2005: 96–97). It was perhaps after the election that Perot grew into his role as a potential figurehead for a new right-wing alternative, stepping up his campaigns against NAFTA and establishing the Reform Party (Rupert, 2000: 58–60).

From the years following the 1992 election, both the conspiratorial right and the paleo-conservative tradition found new directions to develop support. At the grassroots level, the militia movements that gathered momentum in the aftermath of the Waco siege and were to gain notoriety with the Oklahoma bombing, took a confrontational opposition to 'big federal' government (Berlet, 1995; Castells, 1997; Berlet and Lyons, 2000; Rupert, 2000). As with many such groups, the militia were to peak in the mid-1990s but seemed to decline during the period of a Republican government (in this case with George W. Bush) before resurging again with the election of Obama as part of the wider umbrella movement that would lead to the Tea Party. Alongside this there was an increase in interest in groups such as the John Birch Society and the Liberty Lobby[3] and an increase in gun ownership pressure groups (Rupert, 2000: 101). The establishment of the Christian Coalition, coupled by Pat Robertson's book *The New World Order*, managed to tie the forces of Christian fundamentalism alongside nationalism and became highly influential in legitimising conspiracies around globalism. As a result, conspiracies developed over the role of Marxists, the Illuminati, homosexuality,[4] Zionists and un-Godly global elites have served to undermine American liberty, which itself derives its inspiration from God (Diamond Archive, 1992–1997).

The paleo-conservatives came to develop a political economy which would look to provide an opposition to the hegemonic development of neoliberalism (Worth, 2002). Perhaps more than anyone it was Pat Buchanan that was synonymous with this. Buchanan's presidential campaign in 1996 placed the premise of economic nationalism at the top of his agenda and openly attacked the premise of globalism. In arguing for an 'American economy for Americans' he called for US withdrawal from the WTO, the dismantlement of NAFTA and the widespread construction of tariffs on US exports (Buchanan, 1996). The position was strengthened by the conviction that the meaning of American liberty was based on limiting federal government and respecting the autonomy of its constituent states alongside the creation of a free market within the nation, which should be highly protected from influences outside. This, Buchanan and his supporters argued, was the America of Washington, Hamilton and Madison (Buchanan, 1998).

The protectionist position was aided by anti-immigration rhetoric, the need to reduce debt and to reform the federal economic institutions in a way that developed an ideological opposition to the Clinton's economic internationalism from a nationalist position (Rupert, 1997). The victory of George W. Bush and the subsequent wars in Afghanistan and Iraq were to see a new form of nationalism, once again built on the premise of internationalism. It also brought with it a wave of Islamophobia which was to become an increasing feature within American far-right discourses. In the same way that Reagan won wider support for his form of anti-communist internationalism, the 'War on Terror' would do the same. Thus, whilst the nationalism developed from the wars brought with it a populism that saw reactionary traits such as Islamophobia thrive, the paleo-conservative and libertarian opposition appeared to be less evident. This was partly to do with Bush's own reluctance to use international bodies. The ignoring of the UN Security Council over the legality of the war in Iraq and the pulling out of the Kyoto Treaty won great appeal for those who had a distrust of and opposition to international organisations and even gained recognition from Buchanan himself (Buchanan, 2002). At the same time, Bush's period in office provided perhaps more ammunition than Clinton's when it came to conspiracy narratives.

The events of 11 September 2001 were to provide the largest single source for the construction of conspiracy theories

(Stempel, Hargrove and Stempel, 2007). The origins of such conspiracies have been widespread and have drawn a number of studies which all show that they cannot be contained within one specific genre or used towards one specific end. The cultural, psychological and indeed political backgrounds behind such conspiracies have been found to be both complex and complicated (Barkun, 2003; Knight, 2008; Bratich, 2009; Olmsted, 2009). Politically, 9/11 conspiracies were certainly not confined to those on the right, with indeed a higher percentage coming from traditional Democrat supporters left of Bush than from those to the right (Uscinski and Parent, 2014: 87–92). However, they have certainly contributed to narratives behind World Order and globalist conspiracies. For example, the 9/11 truth movement has attracted interest from those who wish to build on the conviction that the attacks were a symptom of a wider global plot. In particular, the suggestion that the attack had been organised by Israeli security became popular with anti-semitic groups and those alt-right groups that believe in a Jewish–Zionist plot for world governance, which has been traditionally associated with far-right extremism (ADL, 2003). Another popular belief within some right-wing paleo-conservative circles was the belief that the Twin Towers attacks were symbolic of an attempt by federal government to maintain its dominance over American society by creating an excuse to go to war (Griffin, 2004; Bacevich, 2002). This ties into the wider theme that those at the heart of government were globalists.

9/11 conspiracies also provided the springboard for the broadcasting career of Alex Jones. Jones, who was a member of the truth movement, would fine tune wider conspiracies that the attacks on 9/11 constituted the next stage in the quest for world domination for globalists (Stahl, 2011). Jones founded the website and new media platform *Infowars* in 1999 and started the *Alex Jones*

Radio Show, which broadcasts to national audiences through the Genesis Communications Network. Here, in a raucous style that verges on the hyper-active, Jones outlines conspiratorial comment on the US government and global politics. Jones' reach has been astonishing. The show was attracting far more listeners that other conservative or right-wing national broadcasters by 2011 and *Infowars* was receiving a significant volume of visitors (Ward and Voas, 2011).[5]

It was with the victory of Obama in 2008 that such conspiracies gained greater popularity with the right and put globalist conspiracies firmly back in vogue. Buchanan had already determined that George W. Bush was a 'globalist' back in 2007 (Buchanan, 2007). With Obama's victory, conspiracy theories relating to his birth became popular with polls suggesting that over 40 per cent of Republicans believe that he was born outside of the US (Uscinski and Parent, 2014: 90). With the fallout of the economic crisis, George W. Bush was increasingly seen in the same vein as his Democratic predecessor and successor, along with his father as another 'globalist', a position that he himself has defended in recent attacks on Donald Trump.[6]

The Tea Party

Within weeks of Obama coming into office, the Tea Party began to emerge as an entity within American politics. The two developments that are often regarded as its founding moments are when reporter Rick Santelli called for a 'Chicago Tea Party' whilst commenting on Obama's Homeowners Affordability and Stability Plan from the floor of the Chicago Mercantile Exchange. This was one of the many Obama initiatives that for free market opponents would interfere with the competitive workings of the market. At the same time, the pressure group Americans for Prosperity, which was funded by the Koch Brothers, helped set up, fund and organise groups and rallies for the movement. As a result, the movement snowballed in the years 2009 and 2010 with approximately 1,000 Tea Party groups emerging nation-wide from this time to its peak with 60,000 to 70,000 participating in its first march on Washington in September 2009 (Skocpol and Williamson, 2012: 5–10).

At first the Tea Party appeared to be novel. Whilst individuals, economists, political scholars and parties across Europe were calling for greater regulations on the management of the economy in the immediate aftermath of the financial crisis (see, for example, Gamble, 2009), here we had a movement that suggested the reverse. The Tea Party were to develop a set of campaigns that included the abolition of the Federal Reserve System, the repeal of Obamacare, freedom for Christian education and greater measures to control immigration (Berlet, 2012). These would be joined by gun ownership protection groups, global warming denialists and tax reform groups. All pointed to the US Constitution as the main basis for their protests, suggesting that these campaigns all served to uphold its basic principles that appeared under threat.

The libertarian philosophy behind the Tea Party was one that was rooted in the crisis theory of von Mises. Ron Paul was quick to establish himself as the 'father' of the movement, publishing two books framing the ideas behind the movement (Paul, 2008; 2009). Following a standard line that von Mises promoted on crisis (1912/1934), he argued that the financial crisis was not caused by a lack of regulation but by the state and other regulatory bodies. The logistics of this is that central banks interfere in the economy by adjusting and regulating interest rates which create an artificial credit bubble that does not allow the market to find its natural equilibrium (Paul, 2009). As a result, the abolition of central regulatory mechanisms would allow the economy to float freely and eliminate any state intervention. Paul certainly gained a great deal of support during the early years of the Tea Party and appeared to take the mantle as its main traditional intellectual in the Gramscian sense, by taking the virtues of Austrian school economics and placing them within the confines of the American tradition (Worth, 2013).

Ron Paul was to receive a lot of support and certainly appeared as a popular figure within the movement. Yet he never really moved beyond appearing as a symbolic popular figure. For despite the ideological wishes of Paul, the Tea Party itself appeared as a movement that seem to place libertarian principles alongside populist and religious conservatism in a manner that reflected previous umbrella movements on the American right. Indeed, as the study on the Tea Party by Theda Skocpol and Vanessa Williamson shows, whilst the libertarian philosophy was appreciated by many members, actual agendas that were put forward that reflect such philosophy were not necessarily supported. As they aptly comment on their observations of one particular event:

> A man in his mid-thirties, a regular attendee at Massachusetts Tea Party meetings, brought fliers outlining a plan to get America's financial house in order, beginning with the abolishment of the Federal Reserve – an idea popular with Ron Paul followers. The man was warmly received, but his recommendations did not seem to get incorporated in the main thrust of the Tea Party group's activism, and some of his suggestions – like protesting against Sarah Palin at an upcoming Tea Party Express event – were immediately quashed by meeting organizers. (Skocpol and Williamson, 2012: 38)

To a degree, the Tea Party represented the combination of libertarian and paleo-conservativism that had been long prominent as an opposition within the right to moderate or neo-conservativism. This indeed was reflected in terms of their world view. For example, Walter Mead provided an overview of the Tea Party's understanding of Foreign Policy by proclaiming that it appeared as a mix of Jacksonian neo-isolationism on the one hand and populist interventionism on the other (Mead, 2011). The former (the Ron Paul libertarian position) provided an intellectual basis for isolationism which was welcomed as being honourable but the latter, which was taken on by many Tea Party candidates looking for office at various levels of governance,[7] appeared to garner greater popular appeal, especially as ex-veteran associations featured highly within the movement.

The Tea Party thus appeared as a mix between a hyperliberal attack on the market system and an expression of reactionary nationalism. Yet, the phenomenon was not merely a combination of different right-wing positions but a collection of grassroots organisations that looked to attack the political establishment through unconventional practices. In this sense the Tea Party represented a unique moment in US politics as it appeared as a collection of movements geared towards challenging what was perceived as the mainstream (Rosenthal and Trost, 2012). In particular, it looked to provide a set of narratives or, to borrow from Gramsci, construct a form of common-sense that accounted for the crisis and its aftermath. Comparisons between the Tea Party and Occupy have been made here. Both looked to construct narratives on why the crisis occurred, who was responsible and what action is required going forward, and both appeared at odds with the political establishment and the status quo (Rosenthal and Trost, 2012: 227–229; Crehan, 2016). Yet, as Kate Crehan points out, unlike Occupy, the Tea Party reflects the material interests of capital and whilst they have organised organically through a variety of civil groups, they were still backed by business and supported by a mainstream right-wing media which was epitomised by Rupert Murdoch's Fox News (Crehan, 2016: 144–145).

The central aims of the Tea Party also appeared to reflect the general premise of a more liberal form of free market capitalism, even if some of Paul's more far-reaching campaigns were never seriously taken up. In addition, whilst many informal manifestos made many assertions that the purpose of the Tea Party was to eradicate reckless spending, secure lower taxes and oppose bail-outs and big governments there was never any formal set of policies put forward that would lead to these (Farah, 2010). Likewise, the Tea Party Patriots Movement, which was founded as a non-profit incentive in response to the amount of money being charged for participation at the march on Washington in September 2009 and is the principle sponsor of grassroots movements across the US, bases its support upon the three wide themes of personal freedom, economic freedom and a debt free future. It also pledges to oppose big government, supports tax reform and looks to reform health care, immigration and amendment rights of the Constitution (Tea Party Patriots, 2018). This would again reflect the libertarian foundation of the Tea Party, but the sheer complexity of issues across the umbrella movement has meant that more reactionary campaigns around race and Islamophobia have been evident (Burghart, 2012: 81–82). Here, such groups could be used as vehicles not just for more extreme right campaigns but also for issues that might be locally specific.[8]

The Tea Party appeared at first to have a mixed relationship with Donald Trump as he signalled his intent to run as the Republican nomination for president. Whilst some have seen the Trump campaign as a logical consequence of the action of the Tea Party, many within the movement looked to distance themselves from him (Libby, 2015; Ball, 2016). In part, this was to do with the nominations that the Tea Party Express, the institution within the movement responsible for political endorsements, had put forward. Whilst Ted Cruz, Rand Paul and Marco Rubio were all endorsed by the movement, Donald Trump was not and each of these candidates looked to attack Trump for his 'extremist' views during the campaign. In addition, libertarians attacked his position on tariffs, with both Ron and Rand Paul figuring highly in dismissing his form of protectionist nationalism. Despite this, the appearance of Trump as an outsider appealed to many involved in local groups and as his campaign developed he could present himself as the heir to the Tea Party (Ashbee, 2017: 83–94). Indeed, his appearance as the outsider to those endorsed by the Tea Party Express provided a certain irony. The Tea Party professed to endorse 'anti-elitist' revolution but when Trump emerged with a more concentrated form of unconventionality, those high up in the movement realised that the populism they were keen to unleash became uncontrollable.

Trump and the Alt-Right

If Trump seems to secure support from those engaged with the Tea Party movement, his election campaign gained backing from more explicitly racist forms of groups. From this, it was increasingly difficult to decipher what appeared to the right of the Tea Party – in other words, engaged in conspiratorial forms of nationalism akin to those of the Patriots in the 1990s – and those which went further and explicitly endorsed forms of white supremacy and/or neo-fascism/Nazism (Neiwert, 2017). What was evident was the fact that alt-right groups played a significant role in contributing to the overall flavour of Trump's support. The term 'alternative right' was coined by Richard Spencer in 2008, in order to describe a big tent ideology of different forms of neo-reactionaries who:

> Advocate a return to the an antiquated pseudo-libertarian government that supports 'traditional western civilisation'; 'archeofuturists', those who advocate for a return to 'traditional values' without jettisoning the advances of society and technology; human biodiversity adherents and 'race realists', people who adhere to 'scientific racism'; and other extreme-right ideologies. Alt-right adherents stridently reject egalitarianism and universalism. (Southern Poverty Law Center, 2018)

Spencer himself is openly racist and has been known to quote directly from Nazi propaganda, but fronts the National Policy Institute, which looks to put an intellectual front to his brand of white nationalism by acting as a 'think tank' and a 'forum for research'. Others that have been identified with the alt-right include Don Black, founder of the white supremacist Stormfront website, Jared Taylor, a white nationalist who founded the *American Renaissance* magazine, Andrew Anglin, founder of the neo-Nazi *Daily Stormer*, who is noted for his holocaust denials, paleo-conservative Paul Gottfried, who is seen as one of the biggest influencers of the wider movement,[9] journalist and founder of *Taki's Magazine*, Taki Theodoracopulos and Breitbart contributor Milo Yiannopoulos, who has just recently joined UKIP in his native Britain.

The alt-right can thus be understood as a wide collection of groups which range from radical right ideas on the level that we have seen with European political parties to extremist white supremacist and highly subversive groups. On first glance, this tends to follow the general diversities of the far-right in general.

As suggested in the introduction for example, an alternative right can be used in the same manner as the far or radical right. However to some, the 'alt-right' and particularly the US 'alt-right' can be seen as distinctive. George Hawley, for example, argues that they are indeed distinctive. He suggests that the alt-right should not be seen as having anything in common with the Tea Party or the conservative and libertarian traditions and indeed they have found themselves particularly at odds with the 'morality' contained within all genres of conservativism (Hawley, 2016; 2017: 42–45). Not only are they explicitly opposed to the enlightenment tradition that produced the modern state and capitalism but are also opposed to the Christian dimension that is implicit within many conspiratorial right-wing perspectives (Hawley, 2017: 100–101). The alt-right is also one that has been mobilised largely online, having far more of a fringe element to it.

That said, there have been distinct cross-overs between what might be considered alt-right and other strands of the radical right, leaving the former term difficult to be distinguished on its merits. To a degree, this does indeed reflect those similar developments in Europe. The AfD for example looks to separate itself from neo-Nazi groups and groups such as the National Democratic Party (NDP) and the two distrust each other. The difference here is that with the Trump campaign, the alt-right became legitimised through media platforms such as Breitbart that provided the platform for white nationalist voices alongside other radical right discussion. Furthermore and more important here is the contribution and reinforcement of certain narratives. For example, as journalist David Neiwert points out, the term 'cultural Marxism' was one that was openly used and developed by strains of right-wing conservatism on the one hand and white supremacists on the other (Neiwert, 2017: 224–225). This follows the belief that a conspiracy exists in public life where state institutions are geared towards destroying western culture from within by espousing concepts such as feminism, multiculturalism, same-sex marriages and equality as a means to dilute the forces of patriotism and freedom. This assumption has been utilised as a driving force within the premise of the war of position within US civil society. The Trump surge openly benefited from the results of such convergence.

Figures associated with the alt-right that became involved in Trump's campaign included Steve Bannon and Sebastian Gorka, the former serving first as chief executive of the Trump campaign and then later as his Chief Strategist in the first year and the latter a deputy assistant to the president. Bannon was the former executive chairman of Breitbart News and Gorka was a former advisor to Viktor Orbán and also worked under Bannon at Breitbart. Both have taken extreme positions on Islam and legitimised forms of Islamophobia inherent within the Trump campaign. Bannon is a committed economic nation-alist and has called for a tax on the super-rich, placing him not just at odds with the libertarians but also with many within conservative and business circles (Talev, 2017). His support for isolationism, however, is a stance that is more similar to the paleo-conservatives and is also one considered as less interven-tionist than Trump (Landler, 2017). Brannon's main contribu-tion, however, is that he has been the driving force behind the success of Breitbart.

Breitbart's significance has not just been one which, as Bannon has suggested, has been the platform for the alt-right (Posner, 2016).[10] It has also been symbolic in the rise of alternative news. One of the most significant developments of the Trump campaign was the use of 'alternative' news sources for information. Part of that was due to the rise in social media and in the increasing scepticism of mainstream news. Indeed, this has been aided by the popularity of conspiracy-based narratives that have emerged on media platforms such as *Infowars*. The presidential campaign saw Trump flagrantly add to this conspiracy and appear to adopt a strategy where questioning the validity of mainstream media played to his strength (Guess, Nyhan and Reifler, 2018; Bakir and McStay, 2018). In an Orwellian twist, he used the term 'fake news' to account for mainstream forms of reporting, encouraging potential voters to look towards other – often dubious – sources in order to get their news.

Whilst we might debate the content of and the term 'alt-right', its significance added to the wide collection of far-right discourses that appeared to move centre-stage during Trump's campaign. Part of this indeed developed from the civil opposition that emerged during the Obama era – not just the explosion of Tea Party groups, but the 'return' of the militia and the increase in right-wing groups, which all appeared to be attracted to Trump's style during the presidential race (Neiwert, 2017). In this sense, the alt-right added another dimension to the rag-tag of conspiracy theorists, patriots, religious groups and American nationalists that were always implicit within the contours of American society but became far more visible during Trump's presidential campaign. In the aftermath of this campaign these have been joined by anti-immigration groups and American-first groups committed towards ensuring Trump's twin pledge of ensuring the building of a wall on the Mexican border and re-stimulating American industry. The ambiguity with which Trump responded to the Unite the Right rally at Charlottesville a year into his presidency was another indication that the scope of such a rag-tag is widening.

The Contradictions of Trump

Whilst the emergence of Trump appeared to galvanise a wide right collective, how can we understand this within the wider workings of neoliberalism? On one level, Trump appears to signal a very real danger to neoliberalism within the US and subsequently, to the wider neoliberal order as a whole. Some commentators have indeed declared the end of neoliberal globalisation in light of a new era of popular nationalism (Peter, 2017). In elaboration on this, Nancy Fraser has been quick to show that Trump has been a reaction to the form of 'progressive neoliberalism' which forged a consensus between the right and the left during the 1990s and the first decade of the 20th century (Fraser, 2017). Others have added studies to show this playing out by illustrating the degree of right-wing opposition that has appeared to what we might consider core neoliberal beliefs (Roth, 2018). In response, there have been a number of arguments that suggest that Trump embodies a form of populism that is indicative within the workings of neoliberalism and that this is articulated through class interests that drive the forces of unfettered capitalism (Hallin, 2019; Coles, 2017). Indeed, Trump's background as heir to the Trump Organisation and style of politics embodies every cultural facet of neoliberal-ism and depoliticisation. By looking to run government as if it was a business venture, this politics appears to have been firmly rooted in the embodiment of economics to a degree that seems to have taken neoliberalism to a new level (Schram and Pavlovskaya, 2017). Writing in *The Washington Post*, Daniel Bessner and Matthew Sparke added to this, proclaiming that despite his sym-bolic move on trade protection, his overall agenda remains fixed on a 'pro-market, pro-Wall Street, pro-wealth agenda' (Bessner and Sparke, 2018).

As we saw last chapter, the contradictions between economic nationalism and free market capitalism have remained prominent in nearly all forms of contestation from the right. With the Trump campaigns, however, these contradictions were taken to almost farcical levels. For whilst on first appearance he might seem to bring these traditions together, he instead appears to embody them all at the same time. In attacking Clinton as a 'Progressive Socialist Globalism', Trump's election leaflets were to portray him as the American nationalist alternative that would put up tariffs, protect American workers and dismantle trade agreements, and at the same time reduce regulations and taxes and reinforce free market capitalism (Trump Campaign Poster, 2016). Whilst other forms of the right have looked to establish their politics within either libertarian or protectionist ideology and have looked to clarify their positions when forms of convergence between these positions might arise, Trump seemed to lump contradictory policies together for populist effect. Yet, whilst magazines that pride themselves on being rooted with such traditions, like *National Review*, might have attacked this position as nothing but 'political opportunism seeking a free-floating populism with strong man overtones', it nevertheless was successful in electoral terms (Ashbee, 2017: 22).

In light of such a strategy of empty populism, it is difficult to determine how the Trump administration will play out in relation to the neoliberal order. As we have seen in Chapter 2, leaders have attempted to initiate populism in order to strengthen their own leadership cult to avoid potential crisis. We have indeed seen how terms such as authoritarian neoliberalism have been applied to leaders such as Putin and Erdogan in order to understand how a Caesarist strategy was used to address potential crises that had arisen though instabilities within society at large (Short, 2014). Yet, Trump cannot really be considered as a Caesar, in the mould of a Putin, far from it. Rather than look to avoid instability through strong leadership, Trump appears to encourage instability through his own actions. The standoff with Congress leading to the federal shutdown over funding for the border wall with Mexico in 2018/19 is testament to this. In terms of hegemony, this should widen the potential for contestation and equally widen the potential for developing alternatives. However, Trump has already actively attracted such positions from the right and brought those far more to the core. As a result, a situation has occurred, where these various positions on the right are not necessarily united in a means of facilitating a coherent ideological challenge to the neoliberal system, nor are they being co-opted towards strengthening the existing order. Instead, a pursuit of 'co-ordinated chaos' seems to be the preferred model of governance (Kennedy, 2018).

As we shall see in Chapter 6, Trump's administration has certainly allowed counter-hegemonic narratives to emerge to contest the norms that had been prevalent within US politics since the end of the cold war. In addition, these have led to a re-evaluation of the main foundations of the basic components that make up the hegemonic practices within the American state-societal articulation of the neoliberal order. These have included the fabrics of the institutions of the international liberal system. Trump, or 'Trumpism' itself, however, appears defined by its insecurity (Rojecki, 2017). It contributes towards a war of position, but appears to look to undermine existing norms and forms of common-sense, but does not adequately look to replace them. Instead it entertains a number of contrasting and contradictory ideas which have, certainly on first appearance, led to a deepening of the confrontational nature of contemporary American society. Whether the Trump phenomenon can be considered as being indicative of a wider hegemonic or organic crisis is debatable, but it certainly deepens the growing instabilities that currently exist.

As Trump emerged from the campaign trail to the White House to begin his tenure in office, the sense of chaos and disharmony that he brought as a candidate followed him into his administration. Not only has his style of communication – reflected through his unconventional use of Twitter to attack his opponents and his confrontational press releases – added to the sense of insecurity, but his governmental style and his relationship with Congress has reached depths unknown in modern American history (Nelson, 2018). Amidst the record turnover rate that Trump achieved within his first year of office – noted by the variety of resignations, sackings and general changes in personnel to certain positions – it has been difficult to analyse whether the policies that have emerged can be seen as being indicative of an ideological change of direction or a means of maintaining a neoliberal continuity. Trump was perhaps noted for his persistence with the travel ban legislation that appealed to his 'rag-tag' of populist support (McHugh, 2018). Economically, we once again see stark contradictions. His Tax Cuts and Jobs Act reflected the Republican tradition within contemporary US politics of reversing regulations and taxes that had been placed by the former Democratic administration. Yet, his handling of industry appears to suggest a form of interventionism at odds with the practice of market forces (Mufson and Lynch, 2018). His insistence that manufacturing industries purchase supply chains from other areas of industry within the US that are failing might be seen in Europe as a necessary attempt to kick start a market economy in the form of Ordoliberalism, where the state takes on a necessary role to aid the so-called 'invisible hand' of the market (Bonefeld, 2013). In the US, however, it appears a significant break from the concentrated libertarianism inherent within the Tea Party. It appears paradoxical to the idea of radical tax cuts.

Finally, perhaps the most significant indicator that the neoliberal order might be under threat is from the much publicised tariffs placed on China, the EU, their NAFTA partners and others in 2018 that have been known as the *Trump tariffs*. The retaliatory tariffs that have followed provide us with the first practical signs of a challenge to the longevity to neoliberalism. Whether these token measures can lead to an overhauling of the governance of the vast global and regional trading configuration that has been built up in the neoliberal era is far too premature to determine. Certainly at present, they have been applied alongside a collection of accompanying policies that merely add to the contradictory and chaotic nature of the Trump era.

Conclusion

As the leading state in world politics and the one that has done the most to lead the post-cold war order, the development and significance of right-wing movements within the US is pivotal. As we have seen here, far-right narratives and right-wing political positions have had a long history and have not merely exploded onto the political stage in the last few years in the manner that some might think. The cold war provided a unique breeding ground for the development of conspiracy-based theories as the fear of communism allowed a number of campaigns based upon upholding a version of American liberty and protecting it from international outsiders (Diamond, 1995). At the end of the cold war, communism might have been defeated but the rhetoric was maintained through a renewed fear that a 'New World Order' represented an environment where global elites would push for an agenda that continued to threaten the unique confines of American political and civil society (Rupert, 2000). Alongside this, we have seen a strong tradition of libertarianism and paleo-conservatism which again developed after the Second World War, before re-emerging strongly after 1991.

Under both Ronald Reagan and George W. Bush much of the far-right was contained and co-opted within their own populist forms of neo-conservativism which serve to construct (in the case of the former) and stabilise (in the case of the latter) the contemporary neoliberal order. As an opposition, right-wing forces were always more prominent in the 1990s than later just before Obama took office. With the exception of George Bush Sr, who became a symbolic embodiment of the New World Order, through use of the term when calling for greater international cooperation, it has been with Democratic presidents that such an opposition has become more prominent. The emergence of the Tea Party, in the immediate aftermath of the financial crisis and the rise to office of Obama seemed to put libertarianism on the front foot. The populism of the Tea Party appeared to strongly re-enforce the principles of neoliberalism. Calls for further de-regulation of the economy amidst attacks of governmental bail-outs saw an attack on Obama not come from the protectionist or nationalist right but from an ideological form of market fundamentalism (Worth, 2013: 121–125). Yet, as Polanyi would have no doubt reminded us from his own studies of market society, by utilising forms of populism, new contradictions are created that undermine its credentials. The Tea Party might have appeared libertarian to its ideological supporters, but its form was nationalist. By the time Trump emerged to embark on his 2016 presidential campaign, this nationalism had branched out into a mass of contrasting movements and positions, aided by the alternative media or 'fake news'.

The victory for Trump in 2016 might have reflected this surge to the right, but the chaotic style and his lack of substance make it difficult to ascertain what the wider effects might be in terms of the possible transformation of the neoliberal world order. His own lack of foresight might make it difficult for us to see how a reshaping of the world order might emerge during his own period in office, but it does give us great insight into where the ideological battle-lines are drawn up during a prolonged war of position.

FIVE | The Far-Right in Britain

Up to the turn of the 21st century, Britain has prided itself on the fact that it had never had a far-right movement penetrate the wider political system. Like the US, it has traditionally had a form of two-party system, with the main challenges to this configuration coming from a centrist party and from nationalist parties.[1] As a result, it has managed to keep right-wing oppositional parties at bay at least in terms of parliamentary representation. Indeed, until 1993, a British far-right party did not succeed in any victory at any level in British politics. The first British National Party (BNP) victory in a by-election for the Tower Hamlets Council occurred in 1993 and this sent shock waves through the political establishment at the time. By the time that the Brexit referendum occurred in 2016, the BNP had won and lost a number of seats within local politics across England. It had also gained and subsequently lost representation at the European elections and in the London Assembly. The United Kingdom Independence Party (UKIP) topped this, by winning the highest number of seats in the European Parliament in 2014 and gaining nearly 4 million votes in the 2015 general election. More significantly, unlike American civil society, there had been a general lack of right-wing narratives within British society that could compare with the anti-communist rhetoric developed in the US. However, the success of anti-immigration campaigns by individuals such as Enoch Powell that were orientated against Commonwealth citizens in the 1960s saw that there was an appeal within British society for a form of reactionary British nationalism (Layton-Henry, 1978). As has already been noted, Thatcher's neoliberal revolution also utilised a form of populism that had its foundations in a British nationalism born out of re-imagining the superiority of the days of the empire (Hall, 1988). Whilst, as with Reagan, these were very much contained within the wider pursuit of a neoliberal populism, there remained an appeal for an alternative which moved beyond this. For example, by the 1990s, many media sources noted that there was potential support for a Le Pen style party in the UK (Eatwell, 2000). This was not realised however until the 20th century ended.

This chapter looks at how fringe parties on the right emerged to challenge the post-cold war political consensus in British politics around the themes of anti-immigration, anti-multiculturalism and, in particular, in opposition to the European Union. It will also show how the development of these positions has led to the challenging of key assumptions that had previously been held within British political society. Whilst terms such as 'globalism' and 'liberal elites' have been employed and been developed as a vehicle of critique in the US for a number of years, in British political discourse these are relatively new. The influence of recent events in the US have thus helped to shape right-wing populist rhetoric currently being developed and mobilised in the UK.

Foundations of the British Far-Right

When looking back at the roots of right-wing nationalist movements in Britain, most will point to the British Union of Fascists (BUF), which was formed in 1932 by Oswald Mosely in an attempt to provide a British version of fascism. The BUF gained a number of prominent supporters within the British establishment, including the newspaper tycoon Viscount Rothermere alongside other notable businessmen, aristocrats and several military and well known dignitaries of the day. Rothermere used his most significant newspaper, the *Daily Mail*, which has continued since to be the bastion of right-wing tabloid thought in the UK, to support the BUF and fascism in its heyday in the 1930s (Thurlow, 1998; Pugh, 2006).

The BUF, however, failed to gain any electoral success in Britain. In addition, the BUF rested upon a British form of a tradition that was finding more appeal in other parts of Europe. The British form of exceptionalism seems to gain more support from nostalgia of the British Empire than it does from the form of European right-wing expression from the inter-war years. As we have seen, with certain exceptions, one of the prevailing characteristics of contemporary far-right expressions is the rejection of any form of fascism. Indeed, as with the US, many significant groups in Britain have insisted that fascism is a 'left-wing' movement as opposed to a 'right-wing' movement (UKIP, 2015). The use of the state within economic development and the Nazi Party's identification with 'National Socialism' providing enough evidence to suggest that the right-wing mobilisation that they are engaged with is fundamentally at odds with the fascism or neo-fascism associated with the 20th century (Batten, 2018).[2] The BNP and before that the National Front (NF) might have some very definite connections to forms of neo-fascism, in terms of their explicitly racist and anti-semitic agenda and their consistent flirtation with street violence, no matter how they tried to hide it (Cronin, 1996). Yet, the belief in British exceptionalism and of British superiority, enhanced through empire nostalgia, is not one that has been nurtured through neo-fascist 'boot boys' but through upper-middle-class and establishment resentment of the decline of Britain as a world force.

The Brexit campaign saw the re-emergence of a collection of nostalgic populist movements that looked to utilise the form of British exceptionalism that was rooted in the idea of empire. Individuals such as Nigel Farage, Arron Banks, Boris Johnson and Jacob Rees-Mogg, who are strongly associated with the Leave campaign, all emerged from a background that was descended from 'colonial stock'.[3] Whilst the Thatcher leadership appealed to the sense of the upper-middle-class nationalism of the empire, its origins can be traced back to the aftermath of the Suez Crisis and the opposition to de-colonialisation (Pitchford, 2011: 40–43). The 'wind of change' rhetoric that was brought in by Prime Minster Harold Macmillan, which encouraged the process of independence for British colonies, was challenged by a wing of the Conservative Party in 1961, through the establishment of the Monday Club. The organisation was to feature as a distinct pressure group within the Conservative Party and was to lend support to Apartheid South Africa, Ian Smith's Rhodesia and to the cause of anti-immigration (Seyd, 1972). Whilst at the time, similarities were made between the Monday Club and the John Birch Society, the anti-communist rhetoric was largely silent in comparison to the campaigns against de-colonisation and the emergence of a multicultural Britain (Labour Research Department, 1969).

The Monday Club was to provide a significant launching pad for Enoch Powell. In Powell's infamous 'river of blood speech' he attacked Commonwealth immigration and new Labour Party legislation that made it illegal to discriminate on grounds of race within wider society. Powell gained significant support within working-class Britain and with the National Front party being founded just a year previously, this provided a platform where the Monday Club and the NF could – albeit informally – co-ordinate certain ideas through the production of literature within the two organisations (Pitchford, 2011). The National Front was founded by Arthur Chesterton, who was a veteran from the BUF and who came from the realms of the upper middle classes. The NF, however, was to find working-class support as it developed and gained most of its backing in its heyday in the 1970s from medium-sized towns in industrial decline and from the inner cities in certain areas of England (Whiteley, 1979; Harrop, England and Husbands, 1980). Electorally, the NF managed to gain nearly 200,000 votes in the 1979 election, but they perhaps fared better in 1974, where they stood fewer candidates but averaged a higher vote per constituency.

There were formal interchanges between the Monday Club and the NF in the early 1970s with occasional members of the former standing for the NF at specific elections, yet the Club remained firmly entrenched within the Conservative Party. By the time Thatcher had risen to the leadership of the party, she firmly looked to engage with the Club in order to shape her wider project of populist neoliberalism which appealed to the general outlook of the group. The Falkland's War and Thatcher's refusal to place sanctions on Apartheid South Africa, coupled with her attacks on trade unions and the streamlining of the welfare state all appealed to Monday Club members. The National Front, on the other hand, under the new leadership of John Tyndall, faded as a political force electorally, but became more prominent through its use of violence and direct action on street marches (Fielding, 1981; Copsey, 2008). They would also figure prominently in opposition to Thatcher as they attacked her market-driven 'liberal' policies and her disregard for the indigenous working classes (Jackson, 2016). This turn also suited Thatcher, as she managed to co-opt enough nationalist and anti-immigration fervour within her own project, whilst dismissing the National Front as extremist, violent and dangerous (Hall, 1988).

The roots that were sown before the right-wing genie was unleashed on British political society in the 21st century was thus striking. At one level a group emerged firmly within the British establishment that contested the post-war consensus in British politics concerning multiculturalism, de-colonialisation and also the adoption of Keynesian economics (Pitchford, 2011). When Thatcher gained power, this group endorsed her principles and contributed to supporting the neoliberal plan for the reconstruction of Britain's economy and society. In this sense it gained a certain amount of legitimacy. On the other hand, the National Front, that shared many of the Monday Club's concerns, was founded, but turned to tactics that were more indicative of a form of neo-fascism. As a result, an 'acceptable' 'middle-class' form of right-wing politics that backed a freer form of capital in reply to the advances made by labour during the post-war years found a home within the confines of the Conservative Party, whilst groups that existed outside of this bracket and which appealed more towards working-class support were considered 'extreme' and 'fascist' in origin. Yet, the discourse that these two put together – anti-immigration, empire nostalgia, anti-EEC/EU, anti-multiculturalism – would emerge as different entities in the first decades of the 21st century.

The Rise and Fall of the BNP

In May 2002, The British National Party succeeded where both the National Front and the British Union of Fascists had failed. In the Lancashire town of Burnley they gained three council seats and as such became the first far-right party to gain representation in an election that was decided through protocol and not through a one-off by-election. By the end of the first decade of the 21st century they gained two European MPs, a seat in the London Assembly and had gained councillors in northern England,

East London, the East and West Midlands and in Essex in the south-east of the country. From 2010, the BNP declined almost as quickly as they rose. Tensions within the leadership which led to a number of splits, combined with the emergence of UKIP as a serious political force in UK politics, saw the party rapidly decline as an electoral force. In 2018, its last surviving councillor in Britain stepped down.

The story of the BNP's rapid rise and decline is one that closely illustrates just how the Pandora's Box of British nationalism had been thrown open. Founded initially by Tyndall in 1982, after he abruptly left the NF, the BNP was for its first two decades largely an off-shoot of the NF. Indeed, as more and more followed Tyndall into the party from the NF, it became evident that the BNP was increasingly replacing the NF as a political entity as it declined into concentrating solely on civil disobedience and on violent confrontation (Copsey, 2008). Yet, aside from the one-off by-election victory in Tower Hamlets, it was not until Tyndall was replaced by Cambridge graduate Nick Griffin that the fortunes of the BNP began to grow. For the first time the party had developed a coherent economic and political programme.

Griffin developed a form of nationalism that sought to play down the extreme racism for which the party was renowned and turned it into a legitimate form of opposition. Following the FN in France, he looked to develop an economic agenda that attacked the virtues of free trade, globalisation and the principle of foreign-owned multinational companies. In a series of articles written for the party's newsletters and website, he argued that their emerging brand of nationalism was the only one which would uphold the conservative values of law and order, traditionalism and British protectionism (Worth and Abbott, 2006). In committing the party to economic protectionism, Griffin stated:

> We are utterly opposed to globalisation and the idea that it's
> right for British workers to have to compete with cheap labour
> form oversees … When we set about rebuilding British industry
> behind tariff barriers, we have no intention of subsidising the
> same class of selfish traitors who lived off the sweat of ordinary
> workers for as long as possible, and then set about importing
> cheap non-white labour or exporting their capital and factories
> to the Far East as soon as bad governments gave them the
> opportunity to do so. (Griffin, 2002)

The move towards a sophisticated rationale from which their policies could be derived was accompanied by a commitment to end the move towards the repatriation of 'non-white' or 'non-indigenous' British citizens, to which they had previously adhered (although this was also compelled in part through legal requirements). Griffin also published a collection of pamphlets in which he engaged with the concept of 'globalism', which had been developed at length in the US (as seen in the last chapter). Familiarising readers with the context of the 'New World Order', he suggested that globalism is driven by a collection of transnational business and media moguls intent on the destruction of the nation-state, through a combination of Marxist, liberal and Zionist ideology and a selfish pursuit of greed (Griffin, 2007; 2009).

Nick Griffin and the BNP did look to build upon networks that had been made with the alt-right within the US. The far-right tradition in the UK has indeed long maintained cultural links with groups on the American right and Griffin was quick to oversee the setting up of the American Friends of the BNP as soon as he took office as a means to establish greater ideological connections (Jackson, 2014). As a consequence, Pat Buchanan's understanding of economic nationalism was to heavily influence Griffin, even if Buchanan himself had no formal links to the party.

The new language that the BNP adopted also lent itself to the ideas of 'cultural Marxism' and the 'liberal elite's' form of 'political correctness'. As we have seen from discourses that have emerged in the US, the narrative of 'cultural Marxism' was one that became popular to describe how the left have sought to carry out the 'long march through the institutions' in an attempt to 'brainwash' the masses in their mission to overthrow the nation-state and western civilisation, as they had failed to win the political and economic argument for international socialism (Mayer, 2016). Whilst in the US this had a long history which could be adopted logically to the end of the cold war and the defeat of 'formal' communism, in the UK cultural Marxism took a different turn.

The BNPs usage of the term extended to its 2010 General Election Manifesto where it pledged to abolish the 'political correctness' indoctrination that was inherent within the public sector and end the policy of 'positive discrimination' which they argued was central to the development of multiculturalism (Griffin, 2000; BNP, 2010). This narrative enhanced the direction that the party wanted to go – in terms of creating a counter-oppositional discourse to the status quo and doing so through the use of ideological campaigning as opposed to direct action. The BNP thus promoted themselves as a 'normal' nationalist party that promoted economic and political British nationalism, but distanced itself from the violence of the NF and from the term 'neo-fascism'.

Whilst the BNP made significant inroads in terms of gaining support and representation at the local, regional and European elections, they failed to take a seat at Westminster. The closest they came was in Barking (East London) at the 2005 general election when Richard Barnbrook, who was later elected into the London Assembly, gained 17 per cent of the vote and finished third. The peak of the BNP support perhaps came between the 2005 and 2010 elections and so they might have marginally improved upon this if an election had occurred between these dates, but it was still highly unlikely they would win a seat in the first-past-the-post system. The party also did not succeed in being accepted as a 'respectable' political party. The Conservative Party leader Michael Howard, who was certainly seen as to the right of the Conservative Party in 2004, labelled them a 'bunch of thugs dressed up as a political party' (Tempest, 2004). In addition, right-wing commentators, journalists and media outlets continued to depict them as extremist, racist, violent and neo-fascist in both origin and expression (see, for example, *The Spectator*, 2006). During his one appearance on the BBC's flagship political debating programme *Question Time*, Nick Griffin was vehemently attacked and ridiculed and categorised as a dangerous outsider and the BNP as a threat to British society (*Question Time*, 2009).

Yet, despite this, the influence that emerged from the rhetoric of the BNP cannot be underestimated. The conspiratorial idea of cultural Marxism has been one that has become increasingly mainstream within British society. A multitude of right-wing commentators, mainly associated with the *Daily Mail* have all suggested that a subversive plot, spurred by the public sector and academics, has emerged that is geared towards eradicating traditional values and patriotism as a wider attempt to radicalise society for their own ideological aim. Columnists such as James Delingpole and Richard Littlejohn were some of the front runners here, with the former later expanding these ideas as a leading figure in the London offices of Breitbart (Delingpole, 2011; Littlejohn, 2014). Many point to the *Marxism Today* tradition as an indication of this plot. In the 1980s, many notable academics such as Stuart Hall, Martin Jacques and Eric Hobsbawm wrote for the Communist Party magazine, *Marxism Today* in an attempt to forge a hegemonic response to the advance of Thatcherism. The architects of New Labour and of the Third Way took great inspiration from this, despite that those who were initially involved such as Hall and Jacques distanced themselves and their aims from the New Labour project (Hall, 1998; Jacques, 1998).

Melanie Phillips, a self-promoted 'academic of the right' was in no doubt that the work produced in *Marxism Today* was evidence of a wider plot. Writing in the *Daily Mail*, she outlined how the left-wing Gramscian-inspired plan had successfully attacked the pillars of society and had looked to transform the 'structures and institutions of education, family, law, media and religion'. Ultimately this was geared towards a totalitarian attack on the nation-state (partly led by the European Union), on Christianity and on morality (Phillips, 2009). Despite forwarding this narrative, Phillips and others such as Littlejohn distanced themselves from the campaigns of the BNP. Yet, by building on the conspiratorial notion of cultural Marxism these media figures have added to the construction and indeed the expansion of a far-right counter-narrative. As the century developed into its second decade and as the BNP faded into insignificance, UKIP, the right wing of the Conservative Party and the impetus behind Brexit began to gain momentum. The concept of an elite conspiring to control political and social life began to thrive and became increasingly commonplace. The BNP might have been continually attacked as an entity, but post-financial crisis many of its popular ideas were to gain credibility within organisations deemed acceptable to political consumption.

Nick Griffin's hold on the leadership of the BNP was to play a large role in its downfall. Splits occurred not just due to the direction that Griffin was taking the party, but also due to the dominance he was having on the party. Claims that Griffin was too moderate, too 'intellectual' and too ideological in his outlook all led to his demise (Copsey and Macklin, 2011). The founding of the English Defence League (EDL) by Tommy Robinson in 2009 as a more direct-action protest movement that targeted Islamic groups and the establishment of Britain First in 2011 by BNP members, which looked to do the same as a protest against multiculturalism, saw the NF-style of action return. With the BNP losing funds, suffering legal costs due to racial discrimination charges against them and Griffin himself on the verge of bankruptcy, Griffin was expelled from the party in 2014. Since then, new leader Adam Walker has not been able to stop the decline of the party, leaving it redundant as a political force.

The Road to Brexit

The shift from the BNP to UKIP as an electoral alternative was an obvious one but UKIP were always regarded in a different light to the BNP. In the same way that the Monday Club appeared as the acceptable face of colonial right-wing extremism compared with the actions of the National Front, then UKIP were always seen in the same light. As a body, they did emerge as a single-issue group. UKIP was initially founded in 1991 by LSE historian Alan Sked as a reaction against the emerging Maastricht Treaty, under the name the Anti-Federalist League. Whilst it changed its name in 1993, it was not until the dismantlement of the short-lived Referendum Party[4] that it moved towards embodying a nationalist and a populist posture. The replacement of Sked with Michael Holmes in 1997 provided the platform for this to occur, yet at first it was only really within the European elections that it appeared successful as a protest vote. In 1999, it gained three MEPs and this would increase to 12 in 2004, 13 in 2009 and an unprecedented 24 in the 2014 European elections, which left it as the highest representative UK party in Europe. However, the party fared less well in general elections where it tended to lose heavily and fared worse than the BNP in both 2005 and 2010 in terms of the average percentage of vote in the constituencies that it had contested (British Election Results, 2005; 2010).

UKIPs own philosophy was one that shifted from the single-issue anti-EU position that was geared towards a catch-all form of pressure group, through to a free-market populist party before finally emerging as a sort of hybrid party that looked to prioritise immigration and the fear of loss of British sovereignty and identity ahead of economic materialist ideals. After 1997, it certainly appeared to stress the importance of the de-regulated economy. Within the Conservative Party, Margaret Thatcher's own position as a pro-European and as a pioneer for the establishment of the single-market became compromised in the latter period of her leadership. Indeed, her notorious Bruges speech in 1988 where she criticised the moves to regulate industry at the European level, after she had instigated a decade of de-regulation at home, became seminal in the eyes of free marketers. This produced a mind-set which believed that the EU provided obstacles for a competitive economy to thrive (Worth, 2017b). UKIP began to attract pro-market enthusiasts who had been influential in the genesis of Thatcherism but also those nationalist-traditionalists of the ilk of the Monday Club who had been very much part of the Thatcher offensive in the 1980s. Free market economic think tanks such as the Institute of Economic Affairs as well as the Institute of Directors, which provided the foundations for Thatcherism, forged strong alliances with the Monday Club at the time (King, 2014). With Referendum Party leader James Goldsmith being a former member of the Club, it seemed logical to a degree that UKIP would follow its lead after it folded, attracting significant ex-members such as Graham Webster-Gardiner from the Conservative Party.

The peak of UKIP's free market approach was the 2010 General Election Manifesto under the leadership of Lord Pearson. Here, it endorsed a blanket tax rate, the scrapping of National Insurance, the reduction of welfare and state spending and the promotion of a less-regulated global economy (UKIP, 2010). Indeed, this followed the von Mises/Rothbard reading of the financial crisis that was outlined last chapter. UKIPs fortunes turned, however, when their most charismatic MEP, Nigel Farage, returned as leader after that 2010 election. It was here that Farage looked to make wider networks, adopt populist politics and set the UK on the road to the EU withdrawal referendum. A more significant assault on the practices of immigration, coupled with similar attacks on multiculturalism, political correctness and modernity, where cultural Marxism has featured significantly, was orchestrated (Wilson, 2015; Stone, 2017). In doing so, it turned UKIP into a party that looked to endorse the 'unchallengeable supremacy of the free market' on the one hand and on the other to 'a shift towards rather basic, two-dimensional cultural relations as the principle sphere of social antagonism' (Winlow, Hall and Treadwell, 2017: 44).

The march of UKIP from 2010 substantiated more than just the rise of a populist right-wing party. It instigated a movement that saw the rise of a form of nationalism across the UK that led to both the Brexit result and subsequently a highly divided society. As Farage looked to make significant inroads both in Conservative Party areas and in working-class labour-dominated areas which previously had high support from the BNP, the Euroscepticism about a nationalist dialogue was beginning to attract support across many aspects of the political spectrum. The fear that this would engulf and undermine the Conservative Party-led government was evident.[5] The party had already pulled out of the European People's Party (EPP) to create the anti-federalist European Conservatives and Reformists (ECR) in 2009, but after the 2014 European elections, where UKIP topped the poll, this was even more apparent. In an attempt to maintain Tory support going into the 2015 General Election, David Cameron pledged to offer a referendum on EU membership. Yet, whilst UKIP were polling at over 15 per cent, he underestimated both the extent of the damage that UKIP could do and also the strength of support for the Labour Party, which had been consistently higher than them in the polls during the coalition's last few years in government (UK Polling Report, 2015). As a result, the Conservative Party gained a clear majority in the House of Commons, with UKIP, despite gaining 13 per cent of the vote and over 3 million votes – easily the highest for an 'outsider' party in the history of British politics – only managing to secure one solitary seat.

Farage manged to build upon the foundations of an alternative right narrative in a manner that Griffin and the BNP could never manage. Firstly, UKIP, and Farage himself, always appeared as a party that was acceptable to British society. UKIP was never seen as 'extremist' and for much of the time it appeared solely a Eurosceptic party as opposed to a radical right one (Mudde, 2007). Farage could thus appeal to the 'little Englander' voters from the middle classes, largely based in the south of England and to traditional working-class voters in the north of England and even in some areas of Wales. If there was one demographic that Farage and UKIP seemed to appeal to, it was the older generation. Traditionally, the older generations (60+) have been seen to be the most unlikely to change votes within British politics. However, across all areas of the political divide it was the older generations who had altered their choice of vote in favour of UKIP (Ford and Goodwin, 2014: 160–162). Secondly, UKIP managed to gain a number of backers who would help to build their own support with Eurosceptic sympathisers and this would become especially significant during the Brexit campaign.

One such backer, keen to get on board the UKIP bandwagon, was Arron Banks. A businessman and insurance tycoon who had significant holdings within the southern African diamond mining industry, Banks was a former donor to the Conservative Party but switched his interest and his donations to UKIP in 2014. A Eurosceptic from the neoliberal right, he argued that the EU was 'holding the UK back' and was a 'closed shop for bankrupt countries' and not geared to the promotion of business and enterprise (BBC, 2014). The partnership between Banks and Farage was to prove decisive in the next few years as Banks would fund and back a number of ventures that would provide significant support to the new form of populism that was to engulf the country. Banks' interest in UKIP came just as Breitbart London was being initiated and this was to provide greater collaboration when moving forward to the Brexit campaign and beyond. Despite this, Farage was to resign as party leader for the second time after the relative failure of UKIP at the General Election in 2015. Yet, the momentum behind the new nationalist rhetoric saw him take a wider role in the run up to the Brexit referendum which had been promised by Cameron in his manifesto.

The Referendum

By the time that the referendum had been set in early 2016, Farage and Banks had constructed their own base for running the campaign. Whilst, the official Vote Leave campaign was run by Matthew Elliot, who had previously organised the No to AV referendum, and Dominic Cummings, who had previously advised a number of prominent right-wing members of the Conservative Party, Banks organised the competing Leave.EU. As the campaign progressed, Vote Leave tried to distance themselves from Leave.EU as they believed that the nativist populism that would be peddled by them might serve to undermine the leave vote (Evans and Menon, 2017).

Yet, as the combination of Conservative Party minister Michael Gove and the former Mayor of London, Boris Johnson, joined

Vote Leave on the campaign trail, their own enthusiasm for populist soundbites became more and more prominent. Cummings and Elliot increasingly took on a more confrontational position as the campaign heated up, which saw stunts such as a bus pledging money saved from EU membership to go directly to the NHS, a poster suggesting that Turkey would join the EU and 'flood' Britain through immigration and Gove himself condemning EU 'experts' (*Financial Times*, 2016). Leave.EU responded by issuing their own poster campaigns, that included an anti-immigration one which depicted a mass of people in a crowded queue under the title 'breaking point' and an anti-Islamic poster condemning Islamic insurgency. At times it certainly appeared that the two campaigns seemed to be playing off against each other in an attempt to provide more reactionary claims. Indeed, Banks' own diaries seem to reflect this, with as much antagonism and competitiveness given to the Vote Leave campaign as to the 'remain' campaign (Banks, 2017a).

The wider impacts of the Brexit campaign to British society have been far reaching in terms of post-crisis neoliberal continuity. The intensive focus on immigration and the nativist form of debate that were being aired through various mediums during the referendum have served to open up some of the underlying racial prejudices that had previously long been contained within British society. Whilst many empirical studies on Brexit show that claims of racism and intolerance are overplayed when looking at the Brexit vote (Clarke, Goodwin and Whiteley, 2017), the levels of nationalist discourse that have emerged since the referendum have been significant. Indeed, the vote was certainly seen as being a watershed for the increase in discrimination within wider society as the number of hate crimes involving religious, xenophobic and racial hatred sharply rose after the Brexit vote occurred (Home Office (UK), 2017).

For those who were significant in establishing a populist discourse within the campaign, the result certainly allowed for the building of transnational networks with right-wing populist groups elsewhere. Much has been made of the formal links between the Brexit and the Trump campaigns. Trump invited Farage to share a platform during his election campaign, publicly endorsing his support for Brexit (Wilson, 2017). The main protagonists in Leave. EU were also quick to acknowledge how they drew much inspiration from the Trump team and also joined in on his campaign trail. In the aftermath of the vote, Banks turned to the same form of alternative media sources that had inspired Trump and indeed the Tea Party previously and set up the new media company Westmonster, that would be based on the Breitbart style of right-wing news consumption. Elsewhere, media personality Katie Hopkins, a reality television 'star' turned right-wing columnist,[6] who had produced a stream of columns, tweets and comments attacking globalism, political correctness, feminism, multiculturalism and Islam in the run up to Brexit, also joined Trump on the trail. As a personality presented as the British version of Fox News figures Ann Coulter and Laura Ingraham, she has added to the transatlantic right-wing momentum (Worth, 2018a).

At the end of the Brexit referendum, a collection of right-wing actors were thus emerging who looked to move further than to take Britain out of the EU and to challenge the very nature of its societal function as a country. A collection of alternative media platforms, writers, politicians and groups sought to challenge the 'liberal establishment' through contesting certain norms and practices of British life. Together they have utilised terms such as 'globalism' coupled with the notion of the 'liberal global elite', borrowed from the US and transported them, through the aid of the internet and social life, into British discourse. This transnational movement has not merely been one where British right-wing businessmen, politicians and media figures have made publicly fleeting trips over to the US to 'educate' themselves through conspiracy, Trump and the alt-right, but one that has had a long and more complex relationship (Jackson and Shekhovtsov, 2014). Indeed, as stated in Chapter 1, one of the more extremist conspiracy theorists, David Icke, was British. As was the former 'star' of Breitbart, Milo Yiannopoulos. More recently, the 'home-coming' of Paul Joseph Watson is another case in point here. Born in Sheffield, Watson became influenced by New World Order conspiracies and following others went to the US to work with *Infowars* as one of Alex Jones' trusted assistants. He recently returned to the UK to work with the new UKIP leadership. The next chapter will look into the relevance and form of this transatlantic relationship in more depth.

Brexit has remained the lynchpin of this emerging movement. Symbolically, it attacked the very fabric of the British establishment and subsequently at the heart of the globalists. As Breitbart put it, by voting to leave 'the hated EU', the country chose to 'lead the charge' against globalism (Bokhari and Yiannopoulos, 2016). Post referendum, the form of a post-Brexit society, forged in the aftermath of the government's instigation of Article 50[7] is seen as the new battle line. The push for a Brexit that appears more and more 'clean' in its future relations with the EU has been at the centre of campaigns within Breitbart and Westmonster, amidst a conspiracy that globalists will continue to fight for a Brexit in their own interests. Yet, it still seems unclear what this new anti-globalism right in Britain actually favours. Arron Banks is quite clear in his support for a more concentrated market-led society. During the campaign he endorsed a 'Singapore on acid' model for post-Brexit Britain. One that favours the unilateral abolition of tariffs by the UK that would see a flood of investment coming in, whatever tariffs were put up in response (Banks, 2017a). In this way he is firmly rooted in the hyper-liberal tradition favoured by libertarians such as Ron Paul and in Britain with the economists for Brexit and Thatcherite think tanks such as the Institute of Economic Affairs. However, the paradox of this has been that as Banks and those behind Leave.EU might have favoured a form of free market utopia, the nationalism that they peddled was geared towards stimulating a political economy that looked towards isolationism and protectionism.

After the War: Consensus Destroyed?

Post-referendum Britain has been marred by instabilities and societal conflicts across all levels of class, race, nationality and demography in a manner that could be understood to some extent as signs of a hegemonic crisis. Economic factors might not have played a decisive or conscious role in the actual referendum per se, but the effects that a decade of austerity have had on British society have added to the amount of 'left behinds' that were already endemic within the country at large (Kaufman, 2016; Inglehart and Norris, 2016). This sense of abandonment was symptomatic of a larger process of neoliberal re-structuring and deindustrialisation that had been an ongoing process for the prevailing decades but that became increasingly stark after the financial crisis, with the EU vote becoming a convenient medium for this disillusionment to be aired (Watson, 2017). This just represented the material framework of a national society that had become deeply divided in light of the vote.

The demographic reality of the vote was one that would be continued politically in the years following the vote. Those under the age of 50 voted decisively to remain in the EU and those over voted to leave with the leave percentage increasing the older the voter. Over 70 per cent of voters under the age of 25 voted to remain (YouGov, 2016). In white working-class areas, the high leave vote was also determined by age as there was a huge discrepancy in voting turnout between the ages. In general, in mid-town industrial areas which overwhelmingly voted leave and which were indicative of the profile of 'left behind' areas, those over a certain age tended to vote leave and those under it did not vote (Inglehart and Norris, 2016). The vote was also categorised by race – with ethnic minorities overwhelmingly voting for remain – and by nationality, the latter seeing Scotland and Northern Ireland voting remain, Wales marginally voting leave and England more voting leave with a clearer margin, with the overwhelming remain vote in London inflating its percentage across England as a whole.[8] The claim that it was a vote for English nationalism has been made since, with suggestions this has significant consequences for the wider union – a claim that has been subsequently side-lined by Brexiteers in the pursuit of the expression of Englishness (Henderson et al., 2017).

The divisions between nationhood, ethnicity and demographics were evident within a year of the Brexit vote with the 2017 General Election. In the immediate aftermath of the Brexit vote, David Cameron stepped down as Prime Minister to be replaced by Theresa May, who was a remainer with a small 'r', having not really campaigned strongly during the referendum. May embarked on an ambitious plan for Brexit that looked to leave the EU institutions, end freedom of movement but gain special status as a partner. Riding what she thought was a post-referendum wave, she called a general election in order to drastically increase her majority, which she believed would leave her in good stead during negotiations. This conviction was strengthened by the opinion polls that saw her up to 20 points ahead of Jeremy Corbyn, who was seen to have reached crisis point within his own party (UK Polling Report, 2018). After a disastrous campaign from May, coupled with a successful one from Corbyn, drawing upon an anti-austerity left-wing manifesto, May ended up losing her majority in the House of Commons and needed the support of the ultra-right-wing Democratic Unionist Party (DUP), the only mainstream party in Northern Ireland that backed Brexit (and incidentally also one that had close ties with Banks) in order to remain in office.

The result of the election reflected the instabilities inherent within British political society. To a degree it represented a back-lash against the impetus that was building around Brexit (Mellon et al., 2018). The UKIP vote was wiped out, leaving two parties to soak up support for the divisions that became increasingly evident. Not since 1983 had the manifestos of the two parties differed so much ideologically. Here, the break-down of the post-war order saw one party follow a market alternative and the other favouring a democratic socialist one. The former party prevailed and eventually constructed a fresh neoliberal consensus (Dorey, 1996; Heffernan, 2000). Unlike in 1983, no third party emerged from the centre.[9] Indeed, UKIP's vote collapsed and the Scottish Nationalist Party lost seats from its 2015 dominance, which resulted in the highest percentage of votes for the two major parties since February 1974. These stark ideological divisions are reflected through generational, metropolitan and racial divides, with the additional burdens of a Scotland that is geared towards remaining in Europe, a Northern Ireland divided by the hard-line right-wing of the DUP and a new republicanism and a Wales that has yet to find its identity post referendum but has maintained its hostility with conservatism.

With this stalemate in place, the war of position has taken on significant importance as ideologies from the right and left look to gain advantage out of the instability. Groups and outlets such as Leave.EU, Leave Means Leave, Breitbart London and Westmonster have increasingly aided the far-right discourse.

UKIP's new leader, Gerard Batten, took this further by developing a partnership between the street protest movements of the far-right, such as the EDL and Britain First. Both groups featured prominently in 2018 due to infringement by their respective leaders. March saw the imprisonment of Jayda Fransen and Paul Golding, co-leaders of Britain First, on hate crimes, after their attacks on the Islamic community. After filming for social media on a child grooming case, Tommy Robinson was imprisoned on the charge of contempt of court two months later. Batten had not commented on the first case having just assumed leadership in February, but formally joined the campaign to release Robinson, having previously engaged with Robinson himself in dialogue on social media (Robinson, 2018). UKIP's endorsement of Robinson followed support from Geert Wilders and from Germany's AfD.

Batten appeared to reach out to the more 'unacceptable' side of the nationalist right in a manner that has not occurred before. The combination of this process, alongside UKIPs eagerness to use figures that have been prominent in the US in their campaigning has seen its own persona slot into familiar usages of conspiracy and anti-globalism that have been nurtured in the US. Certainly Batten's own Twitter feed includes a waft of conspiratorial soundbites on the prominence of the global elites (Batten, 2018). Batten himself is not generally regarded as a liability within the party. Indeed, after the publicity-seeking stunts of Farage and the failure of subsequent leaders to put down any other markers within the party, many regard him as a 'safe pair of hands'.[10] In addition, the previous leadership campaign saw Henry Bolton narrowly defeat the former Pegida UK founder and extreme anti-Islam campaigner Ann Marie Waters, who formed her own party, For Britain, as a result. The reality thus being that unless these partnerships are forged, further factions would appear. Yet these attempts by Batten to nurture more extremist elements have also led to problems. His public endorsements of Robinson and his activities led to a number of prominent resignations towards the end of 2018. Long stalwarts of the party such as Patrick O'Flynn, Peter Whittle, Lord Dartmouth and former leader Paul Nuttall all resigned from the party, citing Batten's increasing move towards extremism. In December, Nigel Farage himself resigned, bringing his association with the party that was previously almost entirely associated with his personality to an end.

The formation of Farage's new party, the Brexit Party, appeared to further formalise this split. Formed to endorse a hard Brexit in light of the parliamentary crisis that engulfed the UK in the early months of 2019, the party has succeeded in soaking up the support of many who have subsequently resigned from UKIP under Batten, including financial support (Hope, 2019). More prominently it also attracted the rump of Leave.EU, and quickly overtook UKIP in the opinion polls within weeks of its formation (UK Polling Report, 2019).

Standing as a 'one issue' platform, the Brexit Party duly topped the poll in the European Elections, which only took place due to the suspension of the UK's EU exit. UKIP, it appears, could not contain the ambitions that Leave.EU had developed since the referendum. The collapse of UKIP's own vote has a result led to Batten standing down to make way for a fifth leader since Farage himself resigned after the referendum. To a degree these developments have reflected the same age-old problems of uniting upper-class forms of neo-colonial romanticism with working-class nationalism that was seen previously with the London Club and the National Front. This is without the additional splits that have remained rife throughout the history of the British far-right. At the same time, however, we can also see that in the environment of British civil society post-referendum, never before has there been such support for right-wing reactionary politics.

Conclusion

The story of the British far-right is an interesting one. Contained for large parts of its history through the first-past-the-post system and the reality of parliamentary consensus politics at the heart of government, it has emerged in various forms in the 21st century. Yet, despite the explosion seen with the BNP and then in its more 'respectable' form through UKIP, electorally UKIP only managed to return one MP at their height of popularity in 2015. This can lead us in real terms to conclude that the British political system has once again done its job and effectively shut out any right-wing alternative (Fowlie, 2018). However, the narratives that have emerged from these developments have challenged the fabric of British political society. The logistical opposition that was aired by the BNP a decade ago and which was condemned as being 'extremist' and 'dangerous' have been moved to the centre of political debate. Brexit has appeared as more than merely a debate on the UK's position within regional bodies, it has instead been a seminal moment for the production of far-right narratives. Aided by new media sites, that have progressed from the momentum of the Brexit campaign and encouraged by tabloid columnists, concepts such has immigration, globalisation and global governance through 'elites', cultural Marxist conspiracies, multiculturalism and the purpose of political Islam have been unearthed and dissected in a manner that would have been marginalised and labelled extremist a few years previously. In this case, a very real war of position is occurring within British society. Coupled with the success of Jeremy Corbyn's Labour Party, the very values inherent within civil society are being contested.

Unlike much of Europe, it is becoming increasingly evident in the aftermath of the Brexit referendum that far-right narratives in Britain will not be contained within a specific political party but will be expressed through several instruments across the breadth of political and civil society. The inability of firstly the BNP and secondly – and from a more privileged and more 'respectable' position – UKIP to maintain constant electoral support is partly to do with the British system, although the inability to manage infighting and instabilities within the parties has added to this. UKIP has almost been comical in its management of leadership. Since the resignation of Farage, the party has had five leaders and has been hit by a series of scandals and sensationalism that has harmed it electorally. However, as Arron Banks has suggested, the main objective should be to move focus away from party politics and towards building a form of a 'right-wing version of Momentum' – a grassroots movement that can develop and facilitate these new forms of British right-wing populism in the same manner that Momentum has done with the success of Corbyn on the left (Banks, 2017b). This is particularly important when considering the generational nature of support for Brexit and for UKIP, which relied extensively on the older generation for votes (Ford and Goodwin, 2014: 153). Thus, engaging the disillusioned politically inactive younger generation has become key to its sustainability. The Brexit Party appears as the latest attempt towards realising this aim.

Yet, as with so much recent manoeuvring within the far-right, their economic stance is ambiguous. As with the US, we can position a general free market populist on one side, which stems back to the Monday Club and through to UKIP in its modern day incarnation, and a protectionist form of economic nationalism on the other, that has been favoured by the NF and the BNP. Brexit appears as a comparison to Trump in the manner in which these have been blurred. For as Trump appeared to merge these forces together in a manner that has merely appeared contradictory, then so has Brexit. The viability on the one hand of pursuing a free market Eldorado or, to quote Arron Banks, a 'Singapore on acid', with on the other hand, an acute reactionary nationalism, is too problematic to contain.

SIX | Consolidation and Mainstreaming

This book has investigated how a collection of right-wing ideologies have been transformed into movements and parties that
have made significant strides within the political culture of the US
and Europe. It has also suggested that whilst there are some very
definite commonalities between the different movements, contradictions exist that make the reality of the construction of a clear
alternative to neoliberalism more problematic. Despite such contradictions, the election of Trump and the experiences in Britain
with Brexit have produced a unique environment where the legitimacy of the post-cold war order is increasingly being contested
within the mainstream as opposed to the margins of politics. This
chapter will show how this contestation is also beginning to gain
a certain transatlantic character that has developed a convergence
around strategy and an attempt to de-legitimise what is regarded
as the political establishment. From here, it will show how the
counter-narratives that have been used in this form of contestation have increasingly become accepted as legitimate forms of
opposition within mainstream political discourse.

This can provide us with more indication of how far the
rhetoric of the far-right has gone in challenging the character
of the present order and what the implications of this might be.
As suggested in the Introduction, a war of position can be one
that takes a substantial amount of time or it can be one where a
hegemonic order is either re-solved or constructed over a short

period (Gramsci, 1971: 120–122). This can of course depend on the strength of an existing order. The social reproduction of the classical 19th-century liberal order which occupied the studies of Marx, Gramsci and Polanyi was one which took many twists and turns but at the same time maintained a hegemonic longevity. Its decline might have led to an embrace of nationalism and more towards a form of protectionism that emerged from the latter part of the 20th century through an era of imperialist expansion, but these were all geared towards maintaining the wider social relationships on which an expansive capitalism was based (Cox, 1987; Hobsbawm, 1987). The following century, however, saw similar periods where crises were more profound leading to periods of deep instability that would see a multitude of hegemonic combatants emerge in a confrontational manner.

Any mainstreaming of far-right ideas can also be used in a manner that can sustain the basic market principles of neoliberalism but also in a way that can aid its transformation. As we have seen in the last two chapters, both Reagan in the US and Thatcher in the UK used elements from the far-right in order to gain support. Here they looked to the extreme wings of their respective parties and the movements they influenced in order to bolster the support of their own wider projects. As a result the move to reach out to the religious and conservative right in the case of Reagan and the Monday Club in the case of Thatcher was designed to strengthen support for their own respective hegemonic projects (Diamond, 1995; Gamble, 1988). As we know, it was indeed these projects that laid the foundations for the contemporary neoliberal order.

The difference, however, between the Thatcher/Reagan case and the contemporary one is that whilst the former sought to co-opt right-wing elements and to normalise them into a project which contained a different point of focus, the current situation is one where the right-wing elements themselves are moving into the political centre in order to transform it (Hall, 1988; Mulloy, 2018). The establishment of the Tea Party and Trumpism in the US and the adoption of the nationalist rhetoric around Brexit in the UK have all looked to occupy space in the middle ground of politics. Thus instead of discourses that could previously be considered as 'fringe' or 'outsider' being included within a wider movement, it has been these discourses themselves that have looked to push their presence within the political mainstream. Both the Republican Party in the US and, to a lesser extent, the Conservative Party in the UK have seen a rhetorical form of popular nationalism emerge and attempt to gain ascendance (Herman and Muldoon, 2018). We have also seen that in certain countries in Europe this has emerged within the party system itself. Whilst before, parties which represented the right-wing fringe generally reflected that fringe position through the ballot box, they have now emerged as leading contenders.[1]

The Making of a Transnational Radical Right

I have questioned whether the growth of far-right movements could be seen as a truly global phenomena. Part of this was to assess the extent to which we could understand it as a basis for a hegemonic attack on the post-cold war order that appeared to emerge not just from Europe and North America but from elsewhere in the world. As suggested then, caution needs to be placed on equating populist developments in places such as Russia, India and South America with the right-wing movements that are occurring in Europe and the US. The co-ordination of ideas and outlooks between right-wing individuals and groups from the countries we might consider to be at the heart of the global economy has been more noticeable. It has been here where significant partnerships are beginning to be formed at a transatlantic level that has given the nationalist right far more legitimacy and coherence.

Discussions of partnerships have featured prominently within media circles within the last few years. *The Economist* depicted Trump, Putin, Farage and Le Pen as characters from the French Revolution banging the drum of a 'new nationalism' on the cover of their November 2016 edition, whilst news agencies across Europe have been quick to point out (often imagined) alliances between key populist leaders across the world (Ashkenas and Aisch, 2016). More substantial academic studies have looked at the tradition of partnerships between far-right groups from either side of the Atlantic. From neo-Nazi and white supremacist groups to conspiracy concepts such as cultural Marxism, significant partnerships have emerged which have developed both through traditional bonds between political organisations and through new media virtual networks (Jackson and Shekhovtsov, 2014). Yet, recent developments have seen relations grow between transatlantic partners that have moved beyond linkages between individuals and organisations and towards shared narratives.

In his understanding of contesting and the building of hegemony, Gramsci argued that ideas and assumptions are constructed by two types of intellectuals: the traditional intellectuals and the organic intellectuals (Gramsci, 1971: 6–23). Whilst the former appear as traditional politicians, teachers, clergyman etc. the latter disseminate knowledge through forms of popular culture. In terms of a war of position, the role of organic intellectuals is crucial as it can form the basis to contest the norms and assumptions inherent within a particular social order. If the basis for this form of contestation is drawn on similar lines across nations then it serves to strengthen the growth for an alternative set of assumptions. As we saw in the last chapter, the exchange of knowledge between the Brexit vote in the UK and the Trump campaign was strongly evident. Media columnists from popular right-wing outlets such as Fox News in the US and tabloids such as the *Daily Mail*, *The Sun* and the *Daily Express* in the UK have allowed certain synergies to be formed. Here, concepts such as 'globalism' have mutually entered the language with a 'globalist' denoting a common enemy.

The concept of a 'globalist' is one that appeared within world order conspiracies in the early 1990s and was originally synonymous with Pat Robertson's 1991 book (see Chapter 1). The BNP and the FN might have used the term to denounce the social process of globalisation, but the term 'globalist' as a noun had been used sparingly outside the US until recently. UKIP has centralised the term within its own language with its media outlets using the term throughout its comment pages (UKIP Daily News, 2019). Nigel Farage himself has been increasingly fond of its use and the phrase has also been used in depth by right-wing columnists in the UK. Prompted by Farage, Eurosceptic parties across Europe have also referred to the term to denote those within the EU that wish to promote multiculturalism. Marine Le Pen's *mondialisme* comes close to replicate the term, but *mondialisme* always developed a wider idea of a cultural process rather than one developed entirely in human agency (Eltchaninoff, 2017). Instead 'globalists' refers to a group of individuals which are conspiring to undermine national culture against the will of the public. As leading globalists are also categorised as being 'elites' then the two then naturally fit together well. Hence, what was initially used as a set of conspiracy theories that sought to impose a world government in order to contain American liberty, is one that has developed transnational proportions.

An intuition that a transatlantic movement was building was such that Steve Bannon took to a whirlwind tour across Europe in 2018 aiming to create a transnational force. His much publicised visit saw him urge parties such as AfD and the FN to forge a Europe-wide strategy in order to ensure that the 'nationalists' would put up a sustained front against the 'globalists' – this, he believed, would make up the key political battleground in the forthcoming years (Nougayrède, 2018). This would include establishing a group called The Movement which would be designed to promote 'globalist anti-globalism'. Bannon's tour saw him packing out halls in Prague and Budapest, singling out Viktor Orbán for particular praise and labelling him as the 'original Trump'. He also faced certain amounts of hostility from European parties over the idea of a European super party that would unite populist right-wing groups across the EU as a means to oppose it. For example, whilst the AfD had expressed interest in the idea of a collection of think tanks across Europe that develop nationalist strategies, its co-leader Alexander Gauland dismissed the idea that Bannon could make a significant contribution to any Europe-wide far-right project by claiming that 'Europe is not America'. Similarly, a more lukewarm response to any partnership was aired by the existing far-right grouping in the European Parliament, the Europe of Nations and Freedom that includes the FN and Geert Wilders' PVV. At the same time, Gerard Batten has been rather ambiguous when publically commenting on Bannon on social media – at times defending his position and at others declaring his reluctance to commit to a far-reaching project with him (James, 2018). In early 2019, a separate body within Europe was set up by Matteo Salvini of the Northern League called the European Alliance of People and Nations. Thus whilst Bannon did not succeed in setting up The Movement, it provided the impetus for a continental partnership.

It is with the British connections and through Breitbart that Bannon has looked towards seeking firmer forms of co-operation. The Leave.EU endeavour that saw Arron Banks, Leave.EU Director of Communications Andy Wigmore and Nigel Farage join the Trump campaign in the aftermath of Brexit has been the springboard for Anglo-American collaboration. A key figure here has been Gerry Gunster. Gunster, a US political strategist, was brought in to work on the Brexit campaign by Leave.EU and, in the words of Banks, had explained to them the idea that they should focus upon emotions and mythology, whilst rejecting facts during the campaign (Booth, Travis and Gentleman, 2016).[2] Gunster would later work with Bannon on Trump's campaign. Raheem Kassam also featured significantly on both sides of the Atlantic. Kassam was previously involved in Conservative Future before shifting to the right and becoming a key figure in Breitbart. Being from a Muslim background and having termed Islam a 'fascistic ideology', Kassam has become a popular figure particularly in the US where he has appeared regularly on Fox News and co-founded the London branch of Breitbart where he remained editor in chief until 2018. He was also a firm favourite of Bannon, who initially brought him into Breitbart and where his work with renowned right-wing columnist James Delingpole in starting up the London branch allowed Bannon to widen his connection and rhetoric.

As mentioned in the last chapter, the exchange of British right-wing figureheads with their American counterparts became highly prominent during the Brexit/Trump campaigns with a significant number originating in Britain but cutting their teeth with American audiences. Kassam joins a list that includes Watson and Yiannopoulos, who were influenced by the American traditions of conspiracy, the nature of the state and internationalism and have been shaped very much within that mind-set. In turn, their contributions to the shaping of far-right discourse in Britain have thus been heavily influenced by the American experience. Gerard Batten has been quick to involve both Watson and Yiannopoulos in UKIP as both look to build on this by spending more time concentrating on British politics, using their knowledge that has been very much shaped by American politics. Kassam has a longer association with UKIP, briefly putting together a leadership bid in 2016, before returning to the Breitbart offices both in London and the US.

The transatlantic development of far-right narratives is thus not geared on partnerships between parties and movements within specific countries but on distinct narratives which look to provide forms of universality to such narratives. Whilst the departure point for such narratives has been within the US and from American civil society, its development has taken a transnational form. The obsession of a global conspiracy has been a central feature of the American far-right and has provided the focal point for its transatlantic development. Yet, despite Bannon's best efforts, the growth of such a movement is stronger in certain places than others. Certain parties in Europe have thus been reluctant to commit to any formal partnership with those suggested by Steve Bannon, citing the vast difference between the cultural identities of Europe and the US. Indeed, some of the far-right groups are also distinctly anti-American in nature and would favour more of a connection with Russia than with the US (Polyakova, 2014).

It can be argued that transatlantic partnerships have been strongest in Anglo-America and increasingly through Anglo-American civil society, a position heightened by Trump and Brexit. In Kees van der Pijl's groundbreaking Marxist study of transatlantic class formation, he shows how the Lockean heartlands of Britain and the US provided a capitalist class that facilitated the development of modern capitalism (van der Pijl, 1998). A contemporary far-right is emerging along similar lines, with its objective to re-shape the social reproduction of such global capitalism. Yet, the networks and relationships created by right-wing narratives have gone further than can just be understood at a transatlantic level. Indeed the claims and counter-claims of the Trump–Putin connections that have dominated Trump's election and continue to dominate his period in office have been testament to that. Outside of the American–European sphere, new avenues for right-wing transnational collaboration have been further developed.

The post-Brexit imaginary on the right has produced a number of other ideas that build on transnational partnerships. These have looked to facilitate new – or, in reality, to rehash old – visions of the Anglosphere. Building on nostalgic narratives of the British empire, a new partnership between Britain and its prominent former colonies has long been the ambition of staunch conservative and far-right figures and politicians from both the UK and those in Australia, New Zealand and Canada as well as from the few overseas territories that remain under 'British rule'. Within the UK itself, these ideals were central to Euroscepticism from Britain's own entry to the European Economic Community (EEC) in the 1970s (Wellings, 2012). Indeed the seemingly para-doxical journey of the Monday Club saw it move from a body that opposed de-colonialisation yet would also opposed immigration from inhabitants of the said 'colonies' that it sought to continue to govern. As Euroscepticism became more prominent on the right, then partnerships with now Commonwealth countries became increasingly attractive. In reality this meant the developed and 'white' countries. Indeed, the Monday Club were to distin-guish between what it referred to as the 'new' Commonwealth – countries from Africa and South and East Asia – and the 'old' Commonwealth – effectively Australia, New Zealand, Canada and certain factions that supported the old apartheid-based regimes across southern Africa.

The re-establishment of the 'old Commonwealth' has become far more prominent in light of the Brexit vote. Under Gerard Batten, for example, UKIP was quick to publicise meetings with members of Pauline Hanson's One Nation and present them as kindred spirits on different geographical sides of the Commonwealth. Other Commonwealth-based Anglosphere partnerships are more developed. The idea of CANZUK was put forward by the New Zealand historian of the British Empire,

William McIntyre. Writing in the late 1960s he argued for a union between Australia, New Zealand, Canada and the UK which would continue the cultural and political aspirations of the empire (McIntyre, 1967). In light of the Brexit vote, CANZUK remerged initially through the observations of the American entrepreneur James Bennett, before subsequently being supported by a number of far-right, conservative and hyper-liberal think tanks as a means of re-kindling British exceptionalism at the global level and providing an alternative to the EU (Bell and Vucetic, 2018).

The victory of Bolsonaro has also opened up new avenues for right-wing networks to re-emerge between the US and South America in the manner they did during the cold war with American support for the military dictatorships and with the Milton Freedman-led economists – 'Chicago Boys' – that influenced Pinochet's regime in Chile in the 1970s. Not to miss such an opportunity, Bannon was quick to follow up his tour of Europe with a visit to Bolsonaro on his election trail, followed by an endorsement following his victory. *Infowars* appeared almost ecstatic over his victory, firmly portraying Bolsonaro as a central partner in the coalition against the 'globalist establishment' (Menahan, 2018). Official endorsements were to follow from Trump and Bolton. Yet, in terms of ideology, perhaps nowhere are the contradictory forces of market liberalism and national protectionism, which have marked the shape of the populist right, more evident. For on one level, Bolsonaro appears as the arch-typical embodiment of the neo-nationalism or authoritarian neoliberalism that we discussed in the Introduction. Indeed, *The Wall Street Journal*, who were ambiguous to Trump's own presidential aspirations, endorsed Bolsonaro's presidency on the grounds of his economic liberalisation being more significant to his populism (*The Wall Street Journal*, 2018). On the other hand, he appears to fit very well into the Trump mould, combining an almost chaotic form of reactionary nationalism alongside an economic rhetoric that appears more chaotic than anything one can firmly categorise (Spektor and Fasolin, 2018).

Mainstreaming the Far-Right

Not only have Trump and Brexit allowed for a convergence of far-right discourses, but rhetoric that was previously marginal has increasingly been seen as acting within the mainstream. For a war of position, this is a key movement in terms of the politics of contestation. For if a set of assumptions, ideas and forms of 'common-sense' are openly being challenged within the mainstream of political and civil society, as opposed to on its margins, then the possibility of transformation becomes far more possible. The idea that certain campaigns involved with the far-right – such as Islamophobia and immigration or, in the case of Europe, Euroscepticism – have entered mainstream debate has been discussed for some time (Ansari and Hafez, 2012; Brack and Startin, 2015). Indeed, concessions provided by mainstream parties on the issues of immigration, in fear of the march of the far-right, have seen some suggest that negativity around the process of immigration has already become a hegemonic idea, engrained within the political mainstream (Yilmaz, 2012).

Across Europe, the success of far-right parties has contributed electorally in a number of ways. For example, by entering government, parties such as the Austrian Freedom Party or the Danish People's Party that entered a governing coalition as a supporting player have seen their own objectives compromised. Yet, the same cannot be said of the increasing number of right-wing parties that have taken the main role in government. Fidesz and the Swiss People's Party have emerged as the main players in government, whilst Lega Nord in Italy has become the main political player under the wider right coalitional umbrella. Even, if other external constraints might exist on these parties, their presence as major players within the political process has naturally seen them at the forefront of political decision-making. At the same time, the political earthquakes that have occurred during this century, from Pim Fortuyn through to Marine Le Pen, have brought the question of the post-cold war consensus within Europe to the centre of debate. In this sense wider debate on the very nature of political society has seen far-right forms of opposition move to the mainstream (Akkerman, de Lange and Roodujin, 2016).

However, the Trump/Brexit factor has done more than merely bring things to the fore. Both have seen far-right discourses debated and dissected within the very corridors of power (Herman and Muldoon, 2018). For Trump, the establishment of support from the different facets of the nationalist right has seen such groups looking to establish a presence in support of the new administration. Many of the alt-right groups that came out in support for Trump during his presidential campaign were involved in the 'Unite the Right' rally that took place in Charlottesville, Virginia in August, 2017. Initially organised by the white supremacist online media group *The Daily Stormer*, a collection of groups, ranging from neo-Nazi organisations, to a variety of militias and a number of anti-Islamic groups marched carrying various neo-Nazi, Islamophobic and Confederate memorabilia. The clashes between the rally participators and the anti-fascist demonstrators that followed erupted into a violence that resulted in the death of Heather Heyer as a result of a car driven into the protestors by James Alex Fields Jr, a white supremacist on the rally who was later convicted of first-degree murder. Whilst the rally received widespread condemnation on Capitol Hill, Trump's response to the events, in which he refused to single out the alt-right participants, suggested the mainstream media's criticism of those attending was unfair.

Charlottesville occurred when Bannon was still at the White House. Bannon's influence on Trump's dealings with the mainstream media has been highly significant as has his own attack on the prevailing establishment (Green, 2017). His use of social media and of the term 'fake news' to describe traditional media outlets has been a central strategy of Trump. In doing so, he has served to de-legitimise established sources of information within civil society and directed them to alternative news sources instead. News outlets such as CNN, *The New York Times* and *The Washington Post* have been dismissed as being 'fake' by the president, with him refusing to entertain questions from those establishments. This has strengthened not just the appeal of agencies such as Breitbart but also alt-right and conspiracy-based media sources as Trump has increasingly used the politics of post-truth in order to maintain his support base (Ott, 2017).

The notion of a 'post-truth' society is one which places emotions ahead of concrete facts. As a result, any form of political fact – whether on the economy, on government statistics or on climate change – can be disputed (Sismondo, 2017). This follows the trend of scepticism towards 'experts' or at least 'experts' and traditional intellectuals that do not agree with a specific 'world view'. The post-truth environment has also been aided by social media and the internet, which have provided a space in which counter-narratives can be built and alternative forms of reasoning can develop. Trump has tapped into the potential of 'post-truth' by contributing to a myth that media firms are conspiring against him with the ultimate aim to remove him from office. Thus alternative 'truths' should be sought elsewhere (Ball, 2017). Whilst such alternative sources might be seen by their very nature as being marginal in their ability to provide a universal audience in order for a counter-narrative to develop, we have discussed how organisations and forums like *Infowars* can attract a readership comparable to that of mainstream media outlets. In addition, Trump has utilised Fox News – the Murdoch-backed populist news company that adopts a tabloid style of broadcasting and is the home to many of his supporters in the media – along with his personal tweets to mainstream his own form of a 'post-truth' world view further.

In the UK, post-referendum politics has seen many aspects of right-wing narratives enter the political mainstream and certain partnerships have emerged that would previously have been unimaginable (Stocker, 2017). The Tommy Robinson case did not just see UKIP move to lend their support to him but it also saw Batten address the Tommy Robinson march in London that was set up by the EDL as a means to free him. The march led to other regional counterparts across the UK which were marked by Islamophobic chanting and Nazi saluting. Many descended into violence. UKIP has also seen bloggers and right-wing social media activists join the party. Marcus Meechan, a YouTube performer who goes by the name Count Dunkula and who campaigns against political correctness and 'Islamification' on his site, joined the party in the aftermath of his conviction for racial hatred. The conviction followed a video in which a dog is trained to perform a Nazi salute after hearing commands such as 'gas the Jews' and 'Sieg Heil'. At the time, Meechan received support from right-wing conservative MPs such as Phillip Davies and several comedians who argued that his conviction was an attack on freedom of expression. Yet, many have suggested, Meechan's performance mirrored those in the alt-right in the US who use similar stunts for political effect (Bailey, 2018). Meechan was another who spoke alongside Batten at the Tommy Robinson march.

Meechan was joined both on the march and as a member of UKIP by fellow YouTuber, Carl Benjamin, alias Sargon of Akkad.

Benjamin made his name as an anti-feminist and a self-styled 'anti-progressive' who has espoused conspiracy theories to account for the emergence and popularity of equality campaigns around gender and race. He has been banned from Twitter, following a series of aggressive tweets aimed at endorsing violence against women in a series of arguments over the nature of political correctness. Many have seen this as finally ending the pretence that UKIP is not a far-right party (Mason, 2018). Indeed it was these endorsements from Batten that were used by Farage for justification in founding his new Brexit Party. Yet, the move towards engaging with more explicit forms of reactionary politics has become commonplace in Britain since the Brexit referendum. The hard-Brexit-endorsing members of the parliamentary Conservative Party have used social media to build upon the populist nationalism that emerged during the referendum. Included here are MPs such as the former novelist Nadine Dorries, whose tweets include claims that 'left-wing snowflakes' are conspiring against all forms of everyday British life, including 'killing comedy, tearing down historic statues, removing books from universities, removing Christ from Christmas and supressing free speech' (Dorries, 2017). Mimicking right-wing organic intellectuals such as tabloid media figures, politicians from mainstream parties are thus serving to bring such populism into mainstream debate.

Some of the more prominent figures within the Conservative Party since the referendum have been more active in seeking a hard Brexit. The rise in popularity of Jacob Rees-Mogg has been a case in point. Rees-Mogg has looked to install a vision of Britain that rekindles the memories of the Monday Club half a century earlier. Constantly referring back to the 19th century as a means of illustrating Britain's golden era of global supremacy, Rees-Mogg has been a symbolic figurehead for Leave Means Leave in campaigning for a hard Brexit (Rees-Mogg, 2018). Popularising himself as an 'English Gentleman', Rees-Mogg has added another dimension to the crude nationalism espoused by Banks and Farage, yet he also represents and embodies the form of aristocratic far-right exceptionalism that has long been a feature of the British far-right. This articulation has seen him presented as a traditional intellectual, of the sort that was a cornerstone of British civil society during the era of empire (Gramsci, 1985). Indeed, this has been reflected in his social media movement Moggmentum (a parody of Corbyn's Momentum), which has been quick to strengthen his image as a traditional intellect and an English gentlemen, and his association with far-right groups such as the Traditional Britain Group, which emerged out of the Monday Club.[3]

If Rees-Mogg has succeeded in making the image of the right-wing Eton-educated 'English gentleman' popular again in the Brexit era, then Boris Johnson has taken this a step further. Johnson has more than anyone been the key figure in the pro-hard-Brexit stance. Having failed to take over as prime minister from David Cameron, Johnson was appointed Foreign Secretary in Theresa May's cabinet in 2016 and promptly embarked upon a set of bizarre populist stances in the role that included using jingoistic names to refer to several of the countries that he was visiting and citing Kipling's colonial poem 'The Road to Mandalay' whilst visiting a sacred Buddhist temple in Myanmar. He remained in office despite these stunts and resigned his post in protest at May's Brexit proposals, thus giving himself the upper hand in appearing 'untouchable' by seeing out his term without being sacked in light of his behaviour. Since leaving the Foreign Office, his populist stunts have continued with an increase in Islamophobic and nationalist rhetoric, delivered in a number of pieces in the popular press (Johnson, 2018; Johnson and Hunt, 2018).

Perhaps more significant, however, has been the well-documented meetings that Johnson has had with Bannon. Whilst

Bannon has met with other key right-wing Conservative Party figures that include Rees-Mogg and also Michael Gove, his meetings with Johnson have forged a closer bond. In defending Johnson's outbursts against Islam, Bannon has confirmed that he and Johnson have chatted intensely on political strategy. He also suggested that Johnson would make an excellent leader and would be a perfect candidate in a wider right-nationalist project against globalism. In this sense, Johnson is courting a significant part of the Conservative Party towards adopting a strategy more in line with the rightward turn of the Trump-supporting segments of the Republican Party in the US. Studies on Conservative Party membership seem to back this trend, with the popularity of a harder Brexit increasingly significantly with the party since the referendum occurred (Alexandre-Collier, 2018).

At a wider level, Brexit has also seen an increasing mainstreaming of the campaigning for CANZUK. Writing in the arch-Conservative and Brexit-supporting newspaper, *The Daily Telegraph*, historian Andrew Roberts, popularised the idea, arguing that not only would it serve to rekindle and strengthen institutions of the leading Commonwealth countries (such as the monarchy) but would also serve to fill the void left by EU withdrawal, in the form of regional integration. Rather than relying on such regional integration, the four nations could facilitate the same economic and market integration, despite their location, as the EU, without resorting to its bureaucracy (Roberts, 2016). As discussed by Duncan Bell and Srdjan Vucetic, the plan has become discussed in Conservative circles across the four states, with interest, certainly on some form of renewed trade being expressed in Canada and Australia. Before Brexit, it had only really been discussed by individuals of the New Zealand right-wing party, the ACT, or by British Eurosceptics such Daniel Hannon – although UKIP did include a Commonwealth trading deal in its 2010 election. In light of Brexit a whole collection of prominent Brexiteers, from Banks and Farage to Rees-Mogg and Johnson, have all been quick to talk up an Anglosphere partnership (Bell and Vucetic, 2019).

The renewed interest in CANZUK saw Boris Johnson and International Trade Secretary Liam Fox[4] expand this vision, which became known as 'Empire 2.0'. In the light of the Brexit vote, both argued that an opportunity was there not just to create links with the advanced economies of the Commonwealth but to use it as a vehicle to offer a new form of international leadership across the Commonwealth as a whole. With the proposals gaining mainstream coverage, the discourse of British exceptionalism and imperial nostalgia, which had previously appeared at the margins of the Conservative Party and minority fringe organisations, was suddenly behind the vision for future policy (Eaton, 2018; Davis, 2019).

Wars of Position

The mainstreaming of these former far-right positions can be seen on one level as a demonstration that the current order is being contested and a war of position is occurring where the key principles and political virtues of the current order are being contested daily. The very fact that the Trump campaign and administration has promoted a 'post-truth' agenda demonstrates to a degree that all facets of the post-cold war neoliberal order are up for being questioned and challenged. Yet, despite the forms of opposition that Trump, Brexit and populist radical right parties have levied against global civil society, any sign of a coherent economic plan for the global political economy remains wanting. Thus we are left once more with the question we keep coming back to about the longevity of neoliberalism and its compatibility with the ideology of the far-right. Despite the mainstreaming of such right-wing opposition to many facets of cultural and social globalisation, the overriding economic challenge from the same opposition remains ambiguous. Indeed, one might say that the contradictions are even starker. As far-right narratives move closer to everyday life and forms of political common-sense become increasingly challenged through the normalisation of conspiracy-based theory and a rejuvenation of nationalist rhetoric, it would seem logical that a position on neoliberalism would be clearer. Instead, the economic illiteracy that marked the Trump campaign seems to have become more commonplace.

At the material level, these contradictions have been played out in a manner than reflects periods of crisis within a wider historical understanding of capitalism. Here the positioning of the reactionary right within the *longue-durée* of capitalism has been one which occurs both as a reflection of the nature of the international capitalist system itself and of a reaction of it. The competitive and uneven nature of capitalism at the geopolitical level is such that during times of crisis, state societies reproduce these within the national system, fuelling new avenues of class divisions based on ethnicity, race and national mythology (Saull, 2014; 2015). In turn, class dynamics are such that those that favour solutions to the crisis that will maintain their own capital interests rely upon such divisions as a means of maintaining the status quo. Yet, by doing so they also create solutions that cause wider friction within international capitalism, which can lead to a change in the way it is ordered.

For Steve Bannon and Marine Le Pen, such an economic solution remains simple. The promise of protectionism still appears the only solution that can accompany the rejection of globalism on other levels (Evans and Ivaldi, 2017). For others, such as Joseph Stiglitz, the drift towards protectionism seems likely to become more apparent as the rhetoric of Trump moves more and more towards tariff construction (Stiglitz, 2017). Certainly, Trump's administration has looked to contest the very fabric of multilateral free trade. This indeed does contest an economic norm that has become central to the confines of the post-cold war world order. Trade liberalisation has been one of the principle hallmarks of the contemporary order and the construction of permanent institutional bodies such as the World Trade Organisation (WTO), coupled with the vast increase in cross-regional trade agreements has led to its position as a central tenet of neoliberalism. Trump's rhetoric that free trade agreements have been levelled in a manner to undermine US productivity has been one that has sought to end the belief in its universal benefits (Sapir, 2017). However, as mentioned in Chapter 4, the attacks on free trade are done from a contradictory set of positions where Trump alternates his rhetoric so often to the point that is ceases to make much sense in attempting to analysing it.

The free market stance has become even more confusing. A successful position here would show how populism around immigration and – more consistently – the 'deep state' would be addressed through a radical re-endorsement of market forces. Ideologically at least, both the Tea Party and the economists for Brexit[5] imagined a form of free market Eldorado which would address the fallacies of a capitalism that has not been allowed to flourish because of regulatory bodies. Yet, what we have seen has been more confusion. The Tea Party moved increasingly towards nationalist concerns that compromised any market solution, whilst ideological free market Brexiteers moved to engage more and more with popular forms of nationalism in order to maintain the premise of a hard Brexit (Worth, 2017b). Arron Banks might have reflected the free market idealism of the economists for Brexit with his vision of 'Singapore on acid', but his media outlets' preoccupation with anti-immigration and anti-multiculturalism has tended to take precedence. The problems become even more significant when the Brexit vote itself was dominant in areas where manufacturing and industry was strong and any plan to produce a post-Brexit market radicalism would leave these areas even more vulnerable to market forces. Indeed, since the referendum, forms of free market radicalism have been played off with the pursuit of reactionary populism, centred on British nationalist renewal (Hopkin, 2017).

The mainstreaming of right-wing populism has thus led to a situation where many of the main social and cultural aspects that have resulted from the neoliberal world order are being contested in the manner that can be assumed during a war of position. However, the lack of the most crucial ingredient required for a war of position – that of a coherent alternative economic plan – has been lacking. This would form the main foundation for a new hegemonic project to develop and provide a comprehensive opportunity for wider transformation (Gramsci, 1971). We should also be aware of the observations made by Stuart Hall in this instance. Hall argued that the contours of hegemony are consistently shifting in a way that it has to be continuously worked upon in order for it to maintain legitimacy (Hall, 1988: 169). In this way, it can be suggested that the neoliberal order can adapt to the many turns that the far-right might deliver. In this way, the governing form of neoliberalism will not be under threat due to these reactionary forces but instead will be re-orientated. Indeed, many classical Marxist studies point to how far-right manoeuvres are utilised in different ways in order to maintain capital accumulation and to reduce the growth of socialist movements during times of crisis (Sweezy and Baran, 1966; Poulantzas, 1974; Holloway and Picciotto, 1979). A number of further studies have also shown us how the politics of race and racism have been used as a means of maintaining and legitimising forms of capitalism (Miles, 1986; Legassick, 1974).

Certainly it can be suggested that the post-crisis turn to the far-right has served to minimise debate on the longevity of neoliberalism. The debates over the future of the market system that were discussed in depth merely a decade ago in light of the credit crunch have very much been side-lined by the emergence of such right-wing rhetoric.

At the same time, the war of position levied by the right has been one that takes the terrains of hegemony seriously. From Bannon to Banks, the importance of the creation of grassroots movements has been stressed as a necessity so that the momentum seen with recent developments can be maintained. This realisation suggests that the protagonists behind these right-wing campaigns understand the logistics of how key forms of political common-sense can be contested and what is required for it to win the hearts and minds of the people. Indeed, an interesting paradox of such right-wing opposition is that whilst Gramsci himself has been demonised as a key inspirational figure in the globalist movement and within the 'cultural Marxism' which makes up a significant part of their critiques,[6] they seem to understand the tradition that he positioned himself in when understanding the dynamic of contestation (Brodkin and Strathmann, 2004). Therefore, whilst ambiguity continues to exist on the economic front, the forces of opposition have been such that the character and shape of the neoliberal order is certainly being shaped and re-evaluated by recent events.

Conclusion

In the aftermath of Brexit and Trump, the advances made by far-right ideas have been taken to a new level. Advances made by 'hard' Brexiteers in the UK have been accompanied by the development of the Trump administration coupled with its post-truth agenda. This has increasingly led to the inclusion of far-right arguments into mainstream debate. Whilst parts of Europe have seen populist radical right parties enter government, most have looked to keep or side-line far-right rhetoric from central debate. The developments in the US and the UK have not had this luxury as both have seen such debates occur at the very centre of government. As a result, such far-right arguments and outlooks, aided by social media and favourable media outlets, have become more prevalent within American and British political and civil society.

This mainstreaming of far-right rhetoric and what was previously considered 'far-right extremism' has been accompanied by significant moves towards a convergence around key ideas and outlooks on both sides of the Atlantic. Again, whilst Steve Bannon's attempts to forge a European alliance of nationalist movements were met with a great deal of scepticism from many in Europe, the differences between the American and European radical right are not anywhere near as wide as they appears. Alongside shared opposition to Islam and multiculturalism, narratives around globalism and conspiracies around globalists have become commonplace on both sides of the Atlantic. Thus, the imagined belief that liberals, socialists, feminists and 'cultural Marxists' have been engaged in creating a world geared towards undermining western values, which has long been a feature of right-wing opposition within American political society, has increasingly become the key characteristic of the radical right movements across Europe (Bergmann, 2018). In this sense, despite the geographical difference, a form of a right-wing response to the post-world order is gaining a certain amount of uniformity as a form of global opposition. The recent success of Jair Bolsonaro in Brazil, who has looked to engage supporters with similar narratives, creates the potential for such a movement to veer in a transamerican direction as well a transatlantic one.

Despite this, it remains difficult to assess the mobilisation of such rhetoric on the wider character of the post-crisis world order. As suggested in this chapter, there are many instances where we can show how a war of position is currently ongoing that will determine the future characteristic of any potential transformation of the neoliberal system. There are also many instances where we can see how even if such far-right forces continue to make advancements, the overriding neoliberal system might look to adjust and potentially strengthen its overall hegemonic character. At the same time, as we shall suggest in next chapter, the very fact that the far-right has failed to put forward any consistent economic outlook can play substantially into the hands of any response by the left. For, as the left has suffered electorally and ideologically since the economic crisis, its ability to recognise that the crisis was the result of the nature of the workings of neoliberalism does provide a significant advantage when looking for a response. It is also from this position that any left renewal must come from.

Conclusion: The Road to Renewal

There is no doubt that the rise of the far-right has been the most significant development within global political society since the end of the cold war. Whilst the events of 11 September 2001 have often been interpreted as a turning point against the optimism of the 1990s, particularly in terms of the reality of new security threats, it was the financial crisis that plunged the post-cold war neoliberal order into crisis. As with events in 1929, with the financial crisis that led to the final destruction of the last bastion of 19th-century liberalism, the political backlash has been provided by the right rather than the left. Yet, as we have seen throughout this book, the panic and doomsday scenarios that have been aired by several commentators prophesising on returning to the days of the 1930s are perhaps overblown and certainly guilty of historical determinism.[1] As we saw last chapter, new ways of articulating right-wing populism have certainly made their mark at the forefront of global politics but their form differs in nature from those in the 1930s. Whilst they have drawn from similar forms of conspiratorial logic and represent a significant danger to any form of progressive politics, they are geared towards different objectives. For whilst, some elements of the new populist right contain forms of neo-fascism that allude to pre-existing forms of white supremacy, the overriding radical right movement overwhelmingly distances itself from this.

The contemporary reactionary right is one that is historically specific to the contemporary world order. Its attack on globalisation – in the guises of globalism and of globalists – and on the cultural and social reproductions of globalisation can be seen as being its primary focus. In addition, as we have also seen, the content of wide-reaching far-right discourses has had a distinct American feel to it. Past eras of European nationalism, which were based upon blood and ethnicity and indeed were highly prominent in the fallout of the collapse of the Soviet Union and Yugoslavia in the early 1990s, have been superseded by a different form of nationalism (Hutchinson, 1994), which is one that has been geared towards a defence of what they believe is inherent within a nations' tradition against global forces.

The purpose of this book has been to assess the relevance of such social forces to the wider neoliberal world order that emerged from the ashes of the cold war (Worth, 2013). On one level here, these forces have been distinctly geared towards the destruction of such a world order. As Mark Rupert argued 20 or so years ago, the focal point of the attack from the right wing was on the very nature of the world order that they perceived had emerged since the end of the cold war and a commitment towards changing it (Rupert, 1997; 2000). This remains to this day and has flourished. Yet, its understanding of world order is not one that has been defined and driven through free market capitalism but by a set of elites and established mainstream political parties geared towards pursuing an undemocratic global society. The fallacy here is that by not tackling the faults of neoliberal economics head on, the material dynamics of the world order that it appears to be attacking remain more likely to survive.

This concluding chapter looks to do two things. It firstly seeks to provide an overview of the main findings of the book. Secondly, it aims to look at what is required for the left to respond to these developments. Here, an alternative hegemonic project that looks to construct an opposition to neoliberal capitalism geared around a democratic socialist political economy is desired (Worth, 2018b). Despite the general failings of social democracy in Europe and the decline of the so-called 'pink tide' in South America to envisage such a development, there have been some positive moves which allow us to tentatively envision the construction of such an alternative. Most recently, this has been seen with the campaigns of Bernie Sanders and more prominently Jeremy Corbyn, again within the domain of Anglo-American political society, which, whilst containing a number of problems, do offer some hope that the left might fashion a similar war of position.

Limitations of the Far-Right

There are a number of concluding observations that can be taken from the far-right. Firstly, in addressing the questions that were tentatively asked in the Introduction, the far-right can be seen within the Gramscian framework of a war of position but this does not necessarily mean that they appear opposed to the wider framework of neoliberalism. In terms of relating this to hegemony and to the framework of the construction of an alternative or 'counter'-hegemonic project that can challenge and replace neoliberalism, the claim that the far-right's brand of nationalism is in the process of establishing this is more difficult to substantiate. Part of the imagined future that such groups have might include a world where nations look to fulfil previous national cultural glories against the process of globalisation, but the idea that this will end up in a retreat back to the sort of competing forms of nationalism that were indicative of the inter-war years of the 20th century remains fanciful at the present. Therefore, in terms of wider questions of hegemonic transformation, it is difficult to claim that neoliberalism is on its last legs and that the nationalist right are necessarily geared towards its eradication. Yet, they are geared towards re-defining the way it operates.

This brings us to the second point. If far-right discourses serve to contest some of the main features of the contemporary order but do not necessarily represent a hegemonic challenge, how relevant are the equally tentative questions made in the Introduction and in the first two chapters regarding its economic contradictions? Here, the point was made that as one genre of right-wing opposition was looking towards protectionism and economic nationalism, the other favoured a more concentrated form of market governance. Therefore, due to such vast ideo-logical discrepancies, the radical right cannot be seen as repre-senting a coherent alternative to the status quo. This book has sought to demonstrate that this has been a significant feature of far-right forms of contestation. Indeed, Chapter 3 showed just how marked these positions were and how economic models were either placed in this oppositional manner or placed in such a form that could be described at best as opportunism and at worst as incoherent. Yet, whilst these might be a characteristic of right-wing movements and indeed one that does hinder any eco-nomic challenge to neoliberalism, there are other factors at play here as well. As we have seen, from not just the cases of Britain and the US but also from those across Europe, these economic positions are not necessarily ones that appear set in their differ-ences, but ones that drift and become both interchangeable and more contradictory as they develop.

As we have seen from the Tea Party and the libertarian tradi-tions in the US, the welfare chauvinism of certain European par-ties and from the market fundamentalism that has been implicit within some hard Brexiteers, the principles of economic liber-alism can become compromised and blurred when embarking upon populist campaigns that stimulate the forces of national-ism. This perhaps tells us more about the incompatibility of the forces of market economics and nationalism than it does about wider political strategy. For as we have seen through the discus-sions that neoliberalism can be seen as compatible with forms of nationalist renewal, it also serves to unleash a set of forces that appear incompatible (Betz, 1994; Harmes, 2012; Worth, 2014). At the same time, as we saw last chapter, when groups begin to gain greater prominence in other aspects of their campaigns, eco-nomic principles do become compromised and as a result often seem more contradictory than they did previously.

This brings us back to another observation that was posed at the beginning – one from Polanyi. To reiterate, rather than seeing nationalist social forces as a specific threat to the exist-ing market system, they instead represent its ultimate fallibility. Here they appear as forms of counter-movements that seek to protect society from some of the instabilities that occur from such market fallacy (Polanyi, 1944: 79–80). Ultimately, this has sown the seeds of destruction in the system and led to its ultimate demise amidst a rise in fascism and international catas-trophe (Hann and Hart, 2009: 4–5). Can the contemporary far-right be seen in a similar manner? In one way they certainly can. In their various guises – whether pro-market, anti-market or economically neutral – the far-right have looked to engage areas of popular concern that have resulted from neoliberal market governance. The popularity of anti-immigration campaigns, the attacks on the 'indigenous worker' and freedom of movement have all emerged from the failure of the market system that was seen with the fallout from the economic crisis.

Yet, far-right ideologies have also been geared – at least in their own eyes – towards transforming a world order, which they see to be dominated by liberal elites. In different ways their purpose is to challenge concessions made against national cultures that have arisen since the end of the cold war. Rather than operate to shield or protect such cultures from the excesses of global capitalism as such, they are geared towards ultimately transforming the very essence of the world order itself. Yet, it is this attack on an imagined mythical world that they have created themselves alongside the more general observations of contradictions and inconsistencies that shows their own limitations. The potential to see the far-right as a transformative force is thus limited by more than its inability to develop a coherent economic alternative to contemporary neoliberalism. Its own points of cohesion are based on certain connections that sustain the existence of such a mythical world. The erosion of what is understood as traditional life, culture and nationhood might have been constructed by globalists, elites and feminists within far-right narratives yet it has been the dangers of Islam and immigration that have largely bound them together. The post-Brexit/Trump environment might have looked to bring these right-wing narratives to a wider audience, but this has also added more legitimacy to this mythical world (Herman and Muldoon, 2018). The so-called 'post-truth' environment has developed from this situation to reinforce it.

These results have seen levels of inconsistency intensify alongside an increase in what can almost be termed as fantasy. Whilst this might have created a weakening of the overall legitimacy of neoliberal hegemony, it has lessened the potential for the far-right to challenge its actual overriding principle. Seen through wider class relations, this might serve existing social relations well. As the popularity of such narratives serve to deflect from the realities of economic crises, then social relations around the interests of free market capital can re-assert themselves (Albo and Panitch, 2019). This could play into the ideological interests of those free market radicals striving for a Hayekian utopia and who believe that a 'neoliberal populism' against the state provides an opportunity for this. However, the consequences which we have seen through Brexit and Trump's attack on free trade have suggested that the reverse is more likely and with the results being unable to serve such intentions (Morgan, 2017).

Such limitations, coupled with their contradictions and confusions, should serve to re-invigorate projects on the left that have the opportunity to take advantage of these shortcomings and also to bring an opposition back that confronts the economic realities of neoliberalism. As indicated in this book and elsewhere, the march of the right has to a degree come as a result of the failure of the left (Worth, 2013). The recent *gilets jaunes* in France have perhaps been the best testament to this, as they appear largely consistent with left-wing ideals, yet lack forms of political representation at large. In addition, due to those within the movement that appear to be more susceptible to far-right ideas, it could be utilised as further support for the FN (Damgé et al., 2018). Thus the poor performance and demise of many left-of-centre parties across Europe coupled with the more recent decline of the left in South America has positioned the left in retreat. Yet, the recent surges in popular support for left-wing figures have come from the UK and the US. Whilst containing several flaws in appearance, they provide potential avenues where a left-wing hegemonic alternative could be built. More importantly, they also provide a means of tackling far-right discourses head on.

Challenging the Far-Right

The seeds of resistance from the left within civil society since the global financial crisis have been well documented. Whilst a vast array of literature has been written that looks at the various strategies that have emerged in civil society to address the post-crisis world (for recent examples see, della Porta, 2015; Flescher Forminaya and Hayes, 2016; Bailey et al., 2017; Fishwick and Connolly, 2018), there has been significant comment recently on the inability of the left to convert this into electoral success (Jäger and Springler, 2015; Seymour, 2014; Worth, 2015). Examples of political parties from the left emerging to tackle austerity cuts and wider neoliberal policies have been well documented. From AKEL in Cyprus, through to Syriza and Podemos in Greece and Spain respectively and the Left Bloc in Portugal, all have sought to construct anti-austerity policies and an anti-neoliberal philosophy with varying degrees of success.[2] However, these have been overshadowed by parties on the right. Decline in support for traditional left parties such as the French Socialist Party and the German Social Democrat Party at recent legislative elections have limited any potential of such a response coming from traditional sources, aided in part by their own failure to construct a programme that reflects the civil discontent that has emerged post crisis.[3] Similar declines have been felt in Sweden, where the historically dominant Social Democrat Party slumped to its lowest share of the vote since 1908 at the 2018 election, whilst in Ireland, the Labour Party, which was traditionally a deal maker in government alongside the two 'civil war' parties (Fianna Fáil and Fine Gail) that emerged at the formation of the state, has slumped into obscurity (Adshead, 2018).

Yet, whilst these developments were occurring in Europe, the campaign of Bernie Sanders in the 2016 Democratic Primaries provided a left-wing response to the right-wing populism of Trump in his bid to gain the Republican nomination. Sanders presented a self-styled democratic socialist alternative to the centrist campaign of Hillary Clinton. Sanders looked to build on the wave of protest that occurred with Occupy Wall Street and the alternative globalisation movements that emerged from forums such as the American Social Forum. He would also gain from the anti-war movement that positioned itself in opposition to Clinton (Gautney, 2018). More significantly, Sanders attempted to develop an opposition that utilised a form of left-populism in order to secure support. His use of social media, engagement with grassroots movements and the framing of himself as an anti-elitist outsider drew further comparisons with Trump. The suggestion that left-populism can provide a useful strategy to counter the far-right and provide the basis for a left hegemonic alternative is not a new one (for a recent discussion see Charalambous and Ioannou, 2019). Indeed, Gramsci's own framework for mobilisation was understood through his concept of the 'national-popular' (McNally, 2009). Here, a combination of organic movements and political organisations combined to situate themselves along cultural, social and economic lines so that a war of position could be launched. Practices such as religion, popular culture and national folklore became important agencies of engagement and necessary for contesting an existing order (Gramsci, 1971: 419–425).

If the Sanders campaign represented a moment for the left, then the Jeremy Corbyn revolution in Britain has been more substantial. Corbyn became leader of the Labour Party in 2015. Running on an anti-austerity ticket, Corbyn – who only just received the minimum number of nominations from the Parliamentary Labour Party (PLP) to be allowed to stand, stormed to victory against three moderate candidates. Since taking over as leader, the party has seen its membership reach over half a million, a clear 100,000 higher than the peak of Blair and New Labour. Corbyn has also suffered an unprecedented series of attacks from within the PLP, where a significant number have refused to serve under him and this has led to some within the shadow cabinet doubling up on jobs. A vote of no confidence after the Brexit vote, within a year of coming to office saw another leadership election which Corbyn won comfortable. Despite these attacks from within parliament, Momentum, an organisation made up of activists and supporters of Corbyn committed towards developing his support within wider society, was set up, and saw his stature as a popular figure substantially increase. A snap election called by Theresa May when substantially ahead in the polls in 2017 saw the Labour Party overhaul this lead and wipe out the Conservative Party's majority that they had picked up in 2015.

Corbyn's performance at the 2017 election was made even more remarkable considering that the British tabloid media's attack on him was one of the most severe in living memory (Temple, 2017). Momentum's ability to counter these through social media strategies became one of the significant stories of the campaign and led newspaper tycoon Rupert Murdoch himself to question the 'fairness' of such a medium in election campaigns (Beckett, 2017). It also provides us with insight into how such an alternative anti-establishment movement can be mobilised. For unlike the Brexit campaigns where a large proportion of the popular press favoured a leave vote, Corbyn was left exposed to a torrent of smears, attacks and personal abuse by the so-called 'fourth estate' of British political society. As with Trump and his supporters, Momentum have produced a set of counter-narratives to provide protection against such attacks, which has in turn led to accusations from the press that they appear as a 'cult', as a set of 'bullies' and 'thugs' and 'power crazed' (Pope, 2017; McTernan, 2016).

In the aftermath of Brexit and in light of the nationalist discourses that have emerged within Britain, Corbyn has seemingly facilitated the beginnings of a hegemonic challenge that draws from the general principles of socialism and looks to oppose the idea that austerity is a necessary function of economic life during crisis. In response to the far-right, this emerging challenge has many advantages. Most crucially it identifies neoliberalism as the cause of the problem and that social and cultural problems have developed as a direct result of the neoliberal economic model. John McDonnell, the shadow chancellor in Corbyn's team, identifies the term and its processes to highlight the main problems with contemporary society (McDonnell, 2017; 2018). The fact that the term has moved from academia to debates within society at large can be seen to be one huge advantage. Yet this advantage comes with other problems that need to be identified in order for any such movement to develop.

Firstly, debates continue to develop on the wider issues over whether populism can be used as an adequate strategy for the left or whether it promotes similar forms of irrationalism that are indicative of the right as these can be equally seen with the case of Corbyn and Momentum (Fassin, 2018; Mouffe, 2018; Charalambous and Ioannou, 2019). For whilst the former might add that the very success of Corbyn's Labour is indicative of its potential as the spearhead for a wider hegemonic combatant, the latter might point to recent occurrences within the party. Accusations that Momentum heckle at meetings where opponents are in attendance and have violently attacked those who have criticised Corbyn[4] have often been dismissed by the group as being part of a wider smear campaign by Blairites and the media. Here, the tendency has been to create divisions between 'neoliberal Blairites' within the party and Corbyn sympathisers, with the former often being categorised in simplistic terms. The problem here is that by creating divisions and dismissing all forms of mainstream criticism as ideological attacks, the opportunity to battle for ideas within the central terrains of civil society become more limited. Indeed, this was one of the criticisms that Stuart Hall had with the left in the 1980s when they were in opposition to Thatcher. Hall's warning was that adopting confrontational strategies rooted in stringent ideological positions would serve to limit the possibility of hegemonic contestation (Hall, 1988). His 'hard road to renewal' was one that would have to be fought across the wider dimensions of society and required forms of flexibility in order to sustain itself.

Secondly, a siege mentality approach can also hamper any advance to confront right-wing positions. In the growing hostile environmental of post-Brexit Britain, claims of anti-semitism within the Labour Party have seen right-wing commentators and politicians, previously associated with attacks on multiculturalism and Islam, compare the party under Corbyn with the growth of Nazism (for example, Littlejohn, 2017). The anti-semitic dispute within the Labour Party centred on claims that a minority of Labour Party activists used anti-semitic language when condemning Israeli actions in Palestine. This was heightened due to its initial refusal to accept the International Holocaust Remembrance Alliance's (IHRA) definition of anti-semitism due to its belief that it did not allow for legitimate criticisms of the Israeli state.[5] As a result this has allowed many on the right to re-assert their own support of Israel, whilst legitimising their own reactionary positions. The response by many was to point to more smears, which did not heal the rifts within the Jewish community and led to further condemnations. Perhaps the most ironic has been seen in a recent article by Norman Tebbit reiterating the increasingly popular right-wing argument that Nazism was a socialist project of 'national socialism' and always associated with the left (Tebbit, 2018). Tebbit, a hard right former member of the Monday Club who openly welcomed the satirical depiction of him as a fascist boot boy during the 1980s,[6] follows a trend whereby the reactionary right can take advantage of Momentum's hostility to mainstream political smearing, to further demonise them as the 'real extremists' whilst depicting moves to the right as being 'moderate' (Tebbit, 2018).

The advances Corbyn might have had appeared to international onlookers to provide a rare glimpse of political optimism for a left that has suffered to find its feet and cope with the advances made by the popular right after the financial crisis. Certainly, a left-wing anti-neoliberal surge in an established political organisation contained within the core of the world system is obviously going to attract interest. Yet, its shortcomings in terms of strategy remain significant and illustrate the huge difficulty of the road ahead. The final problem remains its most difficult. For whilst condemnations of neoliberal economics have been forthcoming alongside a commitment towards democratic socialism, we are still left to imagine exactly what sort of model this would actually entail.

Solving the International/National Riddle

One of the central problems that have stifled the left since the beginning of the 1990s has been how it should react to the decline of the different forms of socialism as an economic model. The neoliberal order saw the fall of the central style of state socialism as practised by the Soviet bloc alongside the decline of national forms of social democracy in the west, but a response from the left which looks to develop a renewal of socialism is yet to develop. The 1990s saw the development of the 'third way' approach to the economy, which aimed to direct the market towards realising the goals of social democracy (Giddens, 1998). The peak of this position was probably with the 'new' Labour governments of Blair in the UK and Schröder's period in office as leader of the Social Democrats in Germany in the late 1990s and early 2000s, but the decline in its popularity was already marked before the financial crisis destroyed its remaining credibility.

The financial crisis has seen centrist ideologies that favoured some sort of continuity become more and more unpopular, leading, as we have seen, to a significant decline in support for parties that previously endorsed the 'Third Way' before the crisis and traditional social democracy before that in the post-war era. As we have seen, the one exception has been with Corbyn's Labour Party, which has ideologically transformed itself from within rather than continue to follow a pro-austerity line. The commitments laid down by Syriza, Podemos, the Left Bloc in Portugal, Sanders in the US and the Labour Party in Britain have pledged an anti-austerity socialism without a comprehensive plan of action. The left in Portugal alongside the brief left–left coalition in Iceland after the crisis made some ground in terms of their pursuit of anti-austerity measures, but these were largely confined towards alternating debt/spending ratios as a means to reduce loan repayments. These do not address the wider claims that serve to reinvent a form of socialism which appears to have been killed off by neoliberal economic globalisation (Lavelle, 2016).

The main puzzle for the left has been on where such a socialism should be levied. The traditional model of 'left nationalism' is one that formed the basis of post-war models of social democracy, but the forces of globalisation have made a return to such a model as both problematic and inward looking as a result (Radice, 2000). Yet regional and global entities have not in any way even been imagined, let alone been in existence in a way that allows for any wider plan. The EU might have been seen as a potential space for such a development to grow – or at least to imagine the building of and the realisation that 'another Europe is possible', yet its uncompromising response over the sovereign debt crisis coupled alongside the Brexit referendum has seen this become increasingly unlikely. Equally there remains no viable understanding of how a social Europe might aim to work with other bodies within the global economy towards building a post-neoliberal world order, especially as such bodies have themselves become embedded into the neoliberal market system.

It is not the place of this study to suggest in any way how a post-neoliberal world could or should be constructed. Indeed, the form of a potential post-neoliberal or post-capitalist world has been discussed in depth elsewhere, even if the way to get to such a world is not as well developed (Mason, 2015; Srnicek and Williams, 2015). Yet, in order to tackle the advances of the far-right a number of points can be made in final conclusion. For the left to tackle and ultimately challenge the alternative forms of common-sense that are offered by radical populist movements from the right, it needs to have a strategy in place that distinguishes it as a form of opposition. This requires more than just a nod towards the mechanisms of class struggle. Whilst the process of class struggle might remain part of the working process of transformation, in terms of the wider historical process of dialectical materialism, more work is required within practice scholarship on how this should be facilitated and developed. One of the more disconcerting views that came out of Lexit – which was the left-wing argument for the UK to leave the EU – was an absence of any direction from those that claimed to support an internationalist strategy for Britain's exit (Callinicos, 2015; Ali, 2016). Some indeed went further and dismissed any need for this with the abstract conviction that such a move would naturally 'develop' out of class struggle (Jones, 2016). The lack of any meaningful discussion beyond this merely added to the nationalist discourse that had been developed by the leave campaigns.

Likewise, any attempt to engage with the 'progressive nationalism' of the past also needs to be rejected on a number of fronts. This does not just refer to a recognition that the forces of globalisation and the reconstruction of the state into a market entity over the last few decades make it highly problematic to retreat back towards the state interventionism of the past. This, however, requires more than recognition. For example, objectives such as common ownership of the economy need to be re-thought so that they are not necessarily thought of in terms of nationalisation but as forms of ownership managed at different spatial levels. Whilst the idea of co-operatives has always occupied a central role in left-wing thought, it remains a concept understood through the lens of 20th-century states. Thus, if internationalism or globalism is to be taken seriously, then strategies to make very real moves towards beginning to realise this need to be developed. The fallacy of the left since the end of the cold war has been in its inability to reinvent socialism beyond the level of the Keynesian-inspired mixed economy of the post-war era (or indeed the flawed practicality of Marxist-Leninism). If a challenge to neoliberalism is to be realised, then this failure must be prioritised and addressed (Lavelle, 2016).

At present, it is perhaps more useful to look towards developing a global mind-set when aiming to establish a presence within the wider war of position. Right-wing populism has been highly successful in attracting those who might have formerly had social democratic beliefs through protective nationalism, irrespective of the fact that their economic positions might appear entirely at odds with this. As a means to oppose this, it becomes imperative that the socio-cultural dynamics needed in order to build hegemonic alternatives are global in context. For, whilst the left might be able to illustrate that the flaws in the world order appear primarily due to their economic conditions, without a global vision to tackle this, such an advantage becomes irrelevant.

In terms of the longevity of the neoliberal order, the seeds of destruction that Polanyi identified in the 1940s when reflecting upon the end of the Victorian era might very well have been placed in the contemporary system (Polanyi, 1944: 218–228). The presence and emergence of a collection of movements and groups around a wide populist nationalist far-right ideology has made a significant impact on the global political system in the aftermath of neoliberalism's first big crisis. However, despite the effects of this being noted strongly at the centre of the neoliberal system in the US and the UK, its economic dynamics are such that it is more likely to be re-shaped and perhaps even initially tentatively strengthened than suffer a quick death. Yet, as a hegemonic project it has been significantly weakened. Not only has the far-right in its many guises unleashed a whole collection of forces that have served to create great divisions within political and civil society, but in doing so it has led to a series of morbid symptoms in the wider neoliberal system itself. It now remains for the progressives to take note of the situation and to respond.

Notes

INTRODUCTION

1 Critical IPE can be understood as a body of work within the field of international political economy that seeks to move beyond the confines of states' interaction with economic affairs and look at the wider processes of world order, capitalism and transformation (Cox, 1987; Murphy and Tooze, 1991; Abbott and Worth, 2002; Shields, Bruff and McCartney, 2011).

2 Gramsci was sentenced to 20 years in 1926 to 'stop his brain from working' and despite being moved to a set of clinics whilst in captivity was not to be released before he was too ill to leave hospital. He died in 1937, shortly after his 'release'.

3 Passive revolution was a term and a concept that was used interchangeably throughout Gramsci's work. He used it to understand forms of historical transformation and as a concept it has become associated with how a state metamorphoses over time. Contemporary accounts employ passive revolution to show how states have looked towards a revolutionary break either to throw off the shackles of feudalism or to gain statehood/independence and then see social relations re-orientate themselves around the forces of modern capitalism (see Morton, 2010).

4 In the Buttigieg translation, this reads 'in this interregnum, morbid phenomena of the most varied kind come to pass' (Gramsci, 1996: 33).

5 The Whig government of 1830–1842 set the foundations of the liberal state through the instigation of the 1832 Reform Act, which saw electoral power shift from the landowners to the factory owners and the Poor Law Amendment Act, which drastically reformed welfare to allow for the freedom of labour. The ascension of the Tory Party in 1842 saw them split over the repeal of the protectionist Corn Law which saw them collapse and allowed the Whigs (or Liberals as they became in the 1850s) to dominate mid-19th-century British politics.

ONE

1 The Italian Social Movement or Movimento Sociale Italiano emerged
   as a neo-fascist party that appeared as the largest post-war fascist party
   in Europe, with many of its followers actively involved in the state under
   Mussolini. Whilst it died out as an electoral force relatively quickly, it
   established a number of key networks internationally by the late 1960s
   that were influential in the construction of right-wing social movements
   across Europe.

2 An attack by Federal officers on the range of the Branch Davidians –
   a religious sect which had settled as a group in Texas – issued by the
   Bureau of Alcohol, Tobacco and Firearms (ATF) led to a 51-day stand-
   out in which 76 people died.

3 Referred to as the *zapadnik* tradition or *zapadniki*, it took its roots from
   the Decembrist Uprising in 1825, against Alexander I, which looked to
   modernise the Russian state within the traditions of European liberalism.

4 This was a claim made by the US polling firm, Public Policy Polling
   in 2013. See Olga Oksman, 'Conspiracy Craze: Why 12 Million
   Americans Believe Alien Lizards Rule Us', www.theguardian.com/
   lifeandstyle/2016/apr/07/conspiracy-theory-paranoia-aliens-illuminati-
   beyonce-vaccines-cliven-bundy-jfk.

5 The Flemish nationalist Vlaams Bloc was one of the more significant
   far-right nationalist parties in Europe, Founded in 1978, it gained significantly in the 1990s before reaching a peak in 2003 and 2004 (see
   Chapter 3). In the aftermath of the Flemish parliamentary elections
   where it won a quarter of the vote, the party was dissolved for breach-
   ing the Belgian constitutional laws on race. It reformed under the name
   Vlaams Belang, but its subsequent support has dropped.

TWO

1 At the 2009 G20 summit in London, a commitment was given towards
   reforming the financial system and of looking to place wider forms of
   regulations over a global economy that had become too de-regulated.

2 The Leefbaar Nederland party was founded in 1999 as an attempt to
   forge together a collection of local politicians that challenged the hier-
   archies of central government by appearing 'local-first' and 'populist' in
   their campaigns at municipal elections. It formally disbanded in 2007.

3 For an overview of Le Pen in the Israeli media, see Manfred Gerstenfeld,
   'The Relationship between Israel and Marine Le Pen', *Jerusalem Post*

28 March 2017 and Ido Vock 'There's Nothing "Post-Fascist" or Jew-Friendly about Marine Le Pen – or Her Voters', *Haaretz* 17 April 2017.

4 Brazil, Russia, India, China and South Africa, who represent the sum of the 'emerging world powers'. Initially a term (BRIC) used by economist Jim O'Neil, the BRIC group met for their first summit in 2009, before adding South Africa the following year.

THREE

1 For example, the British National Party (BNP), who, under Nick Griffin made great strides at the time to make official linkages with the NF.

2 This is not to say that the FN has not suffered splits. Indeed, Bruno Mégret's faction split from the party to form the Mouvement National Républicain in the late 1990s, yet the party managed to survive this and rebuild.

3 The *Independent* in London for example termed them 'neo-Nazi' when commenting on their advances at the 2014 General Election, see www.independent.co.uk/news/world/europe/concerns-as-neo-nazi-jobbik-party-wins-20-of-hungary-vote-9244541.html.

4 In their case, the Poor Law Amendment Act overhauled the Elizabethan parish welfare relief by setting up the notorious workhouses.

5 This was first brought up in 2000 and went through a number of court rulings before the final one deeming it illegal in 2004. During this time Vlaams Blok gained greater support as they were seen to 'uphold free speech' against the political establishment and therefore increased their support due to the judicial process.

6 The term 'solidarity' is retained in the Declarations of Principles by referring to culture and civil society and government's role to nurture this. See Vlaams Belang, www.vlaamsbelang.org/beginselverklaring/.

FOUR

1 For wider reference, see the archive at the Hoover Institution Library & Archives, Radical Right Collection: John Birch Society, Liberty Lobby (Box 32); Radical Right Collection: Anti-Communism (Box 56); Radical Right Collection: America for Americas (Box 104); Radical Right Collection: Christian Victory; Common Sense (Box 105), all accessed in April 2018.

2 One of the statistics that is much quoted is that the federal debt tripled during the Reagan administration, seeing the US move from becoming the leading crediting nation to the leading debtor nation.

3 The Liberty Lobby's resurgence was brief as it folded in 2001.

4 Perhaps the most extreme here is Scott Lively and Kevin Abrams' *The Pink Swastika*, which argues that Nazism was in fact tied into a wider international conspiracy which placed homosexuality and the eradication of heterosexuality at its heart.

5 Jones himself has been known to overestimate this. In August 2018, Infowars was ranked 664 among most visited websites in the News and Media category and 4,217 worldwide.

6 See, for example, George W. Bush, Speech 'The Spirit of Liberty: At Home, in the World', New York City, 2017 and 'Is Being an American and a Globalist at Odds', George W. Bush Institute, www.bushcenter. org/catalyst/immigration/rooney-boot-american-globalist.html.

7 This reflects the majority of Tea Party nominees that campaigned for Republican nomination at the 2012 presidential elections – for example Newt Gingrich and Michelle Bachmann, who both stood with varying degree of backing from Tea Party members.

8 For example, Tea Party Patriot groups in Northern California and Southern Oregon have used meetings as a vehicle for the Jefferson state movement that seeks to break away and set up its own state based on a pledge that Thomas Jefferson had made to establish a Republic of the Pacific (Leeds, 2018).

9 In an interview with George Hawley for his book *Making Sense of the Alt-Right*, Gottfried distances himself from the term and describes white nationalism as 'living on another planet', yet he also adds that one of his resentments of white nationalism is due to the fact that multiculturalism was invented by 'white westerners' (Hawley, 2017: 52).

10 Given Hawley's definition of the term, he is quick to point out that this is not necessarily true. For example, unlike the *Daily Stormer* or Stormfront, Breitbart have not supported material that backs explicit forms of white supremacy. As an alternative, he refers to Breitbart as 'alt-lite' (Hawley, 2017: 129).

FIVE

1 Since the Labour Party replaced the Liberals as the main opposition to the Conservatives from the 1920s, the Liberals were largely side-lined from British politics until a split in the Labour Party in the early 1980s saw it gain greater traction and gradually increase its parliamentary representation until it went into coalition with the Conservative Party in 2010–2015, where it experienced record losses. The Irish Parliamentary Party prior to partition in 1921 and the Scottish Nationalist Party after 2010 have also made significant inroads into the two-party system, in terms of parliamentary representation.

2 Interview with Neil Hamilton, January 2018.

3 Nigel Farage emerged from a well-known privately educated boarding school to become a commodity broker; Banks profited from the family-run South African diamond trade industry that stretched back to colonial times; Johnson and Rees-Mogg were Oxford-educated Old Etonians, with the latter being the son of a life peer.

4 The Referendum Party was founded by the financial tycoon James Goldsmith as a reaction against John Mayor's pro-European stance during his time as leader of the Conservative Party. It was disbanded after the General Election 1997, where it made little impact.

5 The 2010–2015 government was a Conservative Party-led coalition with the pro-European Liberal Democrats.

6 Ironically, on the British version of Trump's *The Apprentice*, where she gained notoriety by walking out. Her media career has seen her as a columnist with the *Daily Mail* and previously the Murdoch owned *Sun* newspaper.

7 Article 50 is a clause that was put on the Lisbon Treaty that allows states to negotiate a withdrawal from the EU. The withdrawal process is set at two years.

8 The exact splits were: Scotland 62–38% remain, Northern Ireland 56–44% remain, Wales 52–48% leave, London 60–40% remain, South East England 52–48% leave, South West England 53–47% leave, West Midlands 59–41% leave, East Midlands 59–41% leave, East of England 56–44% leave, North East England 58–42% leave, North West England 54–46% leave and Yorkshire and Humber 58–42% leave.

9 The Social Democratic Party broke away from the Labour Party in 1981 and made a pact with the Liberals. The 25 per cent of the vote that they received allowed the Conservative Party to win a landslide.

10 Interview with Neil Hamilton, January 2018.

SIX

1 As we have seen from the first two chapters, certain far-right parties had made significant strides forward before others. Austria's Freedom Party and the Swiss People's Party were already gaining large shares of the vote and popularity in the 1990s, and through Pim Fortuyn we had already seen the short-lived effect of a populist party emerge in the aftermath of 9/11.

2 Gunster has been the subject of a number of enquiries into the behaviour of Leave.EU in the aftermath of the referendum. This has included questions on the nature of his role and payments to him from Leave. EU that were not declared. Banks subsequently dismissed these as an attempt by elites to silence their 'anti-establishment' presence.

3 The Traditional British Group believe in non-white repatriation, a reduction in the welfare state, an end to multiculturalism and a hard Brexit.

4 The position of Secretary of State for International Trade was a post created in light of the Brexit vote and was geared towards negotiating potential international trade deals after the UK exits the EU. Perhaps more than any other position in the post-Brexit atmosphere of chaos, Liam Fox's tenure has been met by blunders, miscalculations, confusion and, at times, an ignorance of the workings of international trade.

5 A body of free marketers that look to draw on classical models of economic liberalism to show how benefits would emerge from leaving the EU. The figurehead here is Patrick Minford, a significant advisor to Margaret Thatcher in the 1980s.

6 This use of Gramsci was illustrated in Chapter 6 with writers such as Melanie Phillips. The demonisation of Gramsci goes further back than this with many American-based conspiracy theorists using him as one of the major figures responsible for the attack on national culture (Heer, 2017).

CONCLUSION

1 See for example editorials in CNN, *The Washington Post*, *The Guardian* and *The Times*.

2 Podemos have not been in government to date. Portugal's Left Bloc have been much more successful in office than Syriza and AKEL, both of which submitted to stringent austerity programmes.

3 The German SDP dropped to just over 20 per cent of the vote in the 2017 elections, which was the worst since coming second to the Nazi landslide in 1933. The French Socialist Party slumped to 7.5 per cent in the French National Assembly elections of the same year, by far their lowest since the founding of the Fifth Republic.

4 This was mentioned when Angela Eagle, a challenger to Corbyn for the leadership in the aftermath of Brexit, claimed she was targeted and had her offices vandalised.

5 The Labour Party accepted the IHRA's definition in full in September 2018.

6 Norman Tebbit was dressed up as a fascist puppet during the popular long-running weekly political satirical television programme *Spitting Image* in the 1980s and 1990s. In an interview in a later documentary of the show, he commented on how he liked the depiction (Yorkshire TV, 2006).

Bibliography

Abbas, T. (2017) 'Ethnicity and Politics in Contextualising Far Right and Islamic Extremism' *Perspectives on Terrorism* 11 (3): 54–61.

Abbott, J. and Worth, O. (eds.) (2002) *Critical Perspectives on International Political Economy*. Basingstoke: Palgrave.

Achcar, G. (2018) 'Morbid Symptoms: What Did Gramsci Mean and How Does It Apply to Our Time?' *International Socialist Review* 108. https://isreview.org/issue/108/morbid-symptoms.

Adshead, M. (2018) 'Who's Left in the Wake of Irish Austerity' *Capital & Class* 42 (2): 205–227.

Agh, A. (2016) 'The Decline of Democracy in East-Central Europe: Hungary as Worst-Case Scenario' *Problems of Post-Communism* 63 (5/6): 277–287.

Akkerman, T., de Lange, S. and Roodujin, M. (2016) *Radical Right Wing Populist Parties in Western Europe: Into the Mainstream?* London: Routledge.

Alavi, H. (1972) 'The State in Post-Colonial Societies: Pakistan and Bangladesh' *New Left Review* 74: 58–81.

Albo, G. and Panitch, L. (2019) *A World Turned Upside Down: Socialist Register 2019*. London: Merlin Press.

Alexandre-Collier, A. (2018) 'From Soft to Hard Brexit: UKIP's Not So Invisible Influence on the Eurosceptic Radicalisation of the Conservative Party since 2015' in Herman, L.E. and Muldoon, J. (eds.) *Trumping the Mainstream: The Conquest of Democratic Politics by the Populist Radical Right*. London and New York: Routledge.

Ali, T. (2016) 'The Left Case against the EU', Speech given at Lexit: The Left Leave EU Campaign Rally, London 13 June.

Alternative für Deutschland (2017) 'Election Program'. www.afd.de/wahlprogramm/.

America for Americans (1969) 'What's Wrong with America: Our National Debt Plus the Money Changers Spell Ruin for the USA', Hoover Institution Library & Archive, 'Radical Right Collection: America for Americans', Box 104. Palo Alto, CA: Stanford University.

American Mercury Magazine (1953) 'Bankers and International Government', Hoover Institution Library & Archive, 'Radical Right Collection: John Birch Society; Liberty Lobby', Box 32. Palo Alto, CA: Stanford University.

Anderson, B. (1991) *Imagined Communities*. London: Verso.

Anderson, J. and Bjørklund, T. (1990) 'Structural Changes and New Cleavages: The Progress Parties in Denmark and Norway' *Acta Sociologica* 33 (3): 195–217.

Anievas, A. and Saull, R. (2019) 'Reassessing the Cold War and the Far-Right' *International Studies Review*. https://doi.org/10.1093/isr/viz006.

Ansari, H. and Hafez, F. (eds.) (2012) *From the Far Right to the Mainstream: Islamophobia in Party Politics and the Media*. Chicago, IL: University of Chicago Press.

Anti-Defamation League (ADL) (2003) 'Unravelling Anti-Semitic 9/11 Conspiracy Theories', ADL. www.adl.org/sites/default/files/documents/ assets/pdf/combating-hate/anti-semitic-9-11-conspiracsay-theories.pdf.

Antón Mellón, J. (2013) 'The *idées-force* of the European New Right: A New Paradigm' in Mammone, A., Godin, E. and Jenkins, B. (eds.) *Varieties of Right-Wing Extremism in Europe*. London: Routledge.

Art, D. (2011) *Inside the Radical Right*. Cambridge: Cambridge University Press.

Ashbee, E. (2017) *The Trump Revolt*. Manchester: Manchester University Press.

Ashkenas, J. and Aisch, G. (2016) 'European Populism in the Age of Donald Trump', *New York Times*. www.nytimes.com/interactive/2016/12/05/ world/europe/populism-in-age-of-trump.html.

Aydin-Duzgit, S. and Keyman, E. (2017) 'The Trump Presidency and the Rise of Populism in the Global Context', Istanbul Policy Center. Istanbul: Istanbul Policy Center.

Aytac, S. and Onis, Z. (2014) 'Varieties of Populism in a Changing Global Context: The Divergent Paths of Erdogan and Kirchnerismo' *Comparative Politics* 47 (1): 41–59.

Bacevich, A. (2002) *American Empire*. Cambridge, MA: Harvard University Press.

Backer, J. (1978) *The Decision to Divide Germany*. Durham, NC: Duke University Press.

Bailey, D., Clua-Losada, M., Huke, N. and Ribera-Almandoz, O. (2017) *Beyond Defeat and Austerity*. London: Routledge.

Bailey, L. (2018) 'The Far-Right Use Online Jokes to Launder Right-Wing Ideology, and Mainstream Comedians Are Helping Them Do It' *i-news*. https://inews.co.uk/news/long-reads/online-right-launder-ideology/.

Bakir, V. and McStay, A. (2018) 'Fake News and the Economy of Emotions' *Digital Journalism* 6 (2): 154–175.

Ball, J. (2017) *Post Truth: How Bullshit Conquered the World*. London: Biteback.

Ball, M. (2016) 'Did the Tea Party Create Donald Trump?' *The Atlantic* 10 May.

Banks, A. (2017a) *The Bad Books of Brexit*. London: Biteback.

Banks, A. (2017b) 'Leave.EU Will Support a Right-Wing Momentum'. https://twitter.com/Arron_banks.

Bar-On, T. (2018) 'The Radical Right and Nationalism' in Rydgren, J. (ed.) *The Oxford Handbook of the Radical Right*. Oxford: Oxford University Press.

Barber, B. (1996) *Jihad vs McWorld*. New York: Ballantine Books.

Barkun, M. (2003) *A Culture of Conspiracy: Apocalyptic Visions in Contemporary America*. Berkeley, CA: University of California Press.

Barkun, M. (2017) 'President Trump and the Fringe' *Terrorism and Political Violence* 29 (3): 437–443.

Bastow, S. (1997) 'Front National Economy Policy: From Neoliberalism to Protectionism' *Modern and Contemporary France* 5 (1): 61–72.

Batten, G. (2018) 'Twitter Page'. https://twitter.com/GerardBattenMEP?ref_src=twsrc%5Egoogle%7Ctwcamp%5Eserp%7Ctwgr%5Eauthor.

BBC (2014) 'Ex Tory Donor Arron Banks Gives £1 Million to UKIP'. www.bbc.com/news/uk-politics-29438653.

Beasley, C. (2008) 'Rethinking Hegemonic Masculinity in a Globalizing World' *Men and Masculinities* 11 (1): 86–103.

Beckett, C. (2017) 'Did Broadcast Stage-Management Create a Vacuum for Social Media' in Thorsen, E., Jackson, D. and Lillekar, D. (eds.) *UK Election Analysis: Voters, Media and the Campaign: Early Reflections from Leading Academics*. Bournemouth: Bournemouth University.

Bell, D. and Vucetic, S. (2019) 'Brexit, CANZUK and the Legacy of Empire' *British Journal of Politics and International Relations* Forthcoming.

Berglund, H. (2011) 'Hindu Nationalism and Gender: A Challenge to the Indian Women's Movement' *International Feminist Journal of Politics* 13 (1): 83–99.

Bergmann, E. (2017) *Nordic Nationalism and Right-Wing Populist Politics*. London: Palgrave.

Bergmann, E. (2018) *Conspiracy and Populism: The Politics of Misinformation*. London: Palgrave.

Berlet, C. (1995) 'The Violence of Right-Wing Populism' *Peace Review* 7 (3/4): 283–288.

Berlet, C. (2012) 'Reframing Populist Resentments in the Tea Party Movement' in Rosenthal, L. and Trost, C. (eds.) *Steep: The Precipitous Rise of the Tea Party*. Berkeley, CA: University of California Press.

Berlet, C. and Lyons, M. (2000) *Right-Wing Populism in America: Too Close for Comfort*. New York: Guilford Press.

Bessner, D. and Sparke, M. (2018) 'Don't Let His Trade Policy Fool You: Trump Is a Neoliberal' *Washington Post* 22 March.

Betz, H.-G. (1993) 'The Two Faces of Radical Right-Wing Populism in Western Europe' *Review of Politics* 55 (4): 663–685.

Betz, H.-G. (1994) *Radical Right Wing Populism in Western Europe*. New York: St. Martin's Press.

Betz, H.-G. (1999) 'Contemporary Right-Wing Radicalism in Europe' *Contemporary European History* 8 (2): 299–316.

Betz, H.-G. and Johnson, C. (2004) 'Against the Current – Stemming the Tide: The Nostalgic Ideology of the Contemporary Radical Populist Right' *Journal of Political Ideologies* 9 (3): 311–327.

von Beyme, K. (1988) *Right Wing Extremism in Western Europe*. London: Frank Cass.

Bieler, A. (2014) 'Transnational Labour Solidarity in (the) Crisis' *Global Labour Journal* 5 (2): 114–133.

Bieler, A. and Morton, A. (2018) *Global Capitalism, Global War, Global Crisis*. Cambridge: Cambridge University Press.

Birchfield, V. (2005) 'Jose Bove and the Globalisation Counter-Movement in France: A Polanyian Interpretation' *Review of International Studies* 31 (3): 581–598.

Blyth, M. (2013) *Austerity: The History of a Dangerous Idea*. Oxford: Oxford University Press.

Bokhari, A. and Yiannopoulos, M. (2016) 'Brexit: Why the Globalists Lost', Breitbart 24 June. www.breitbart.com/milo/2016/06/24/the-end-of-globalism/.

Bonefeld, W. (2013) 'Human Economy and Social Policy: On Ordoliberalism and Political Authority' *History of the Human Sciences* 26 (2): 106–125.

Booth, R., Travis, A. and Gentleman, A. (2016) 'Leave Donor Plans New Party to Replace UKIP – Possibly without Farage' *The Guardian* 19 June.

Brack, N. and Startin, N. (2015) 'Introduction: Euroscepticism from the Margins to the Mainstream' *International Political Science Review* 36 (3): 239–249.

Bratich, J. (2009) *Conspiracy Panics: Political Rationality and Popular Cultures*. Albany, NY: State University of New York Press.

British Election Results (2005) '2005 General Election Results', Electoral Commission. London: Electoral Commission.

British Election Results (2010) '2010 General Election Results', Electoral Commission. London: Electoral Commission.

British National Party (BNP) (2010) *Democracy, Freedom, Culture and Identity: British National Party Manifesto 2010*. Welshpool: British National Party.

Brodkin, K. and Strathmann, C. (2004) 'The Struggle for Hearts and Minds' *Labor Studies* 29 (3): 1–24.

Bruff, I. (2014) 'The Rise of Authoritarian Neoliberalism' *Rethinking Marxism* 26 (1): 113–129.

Bruff, I. (2017) 'Authoritarian Neoliberalism and the Myth of Free Market', Progress in Political Economy. http://ppesydney.net/authoritarian-neoliberalism-myth-free-markets/.

Buchanan, P. (1996) 'An American Economy for the Americans' 12 April. http://buchanan.org/blog/an-american-economy-for-americans-186.

Buchanan, P. (1998) 'Free Trade Is Not Free', Address to the Chicago Council on Foreign Relations, 18 November.

Buchanan, P. (2002) 'Bush and World Government' 3 July. http://buchanan.org/blog/pjb-bush-and-world-government-462.

Buchanan, P. (2007) 'George W. Bush: Globalist' 12 October. http://buchanan.org/blog/pjb-george-w-bush-globalist-867.

Burghart, D. (2012) 'View from the Top: Report on Six National Tea Party Organizations' in Rosenthal, L. and Trost, C. (eds.) *Steep: The Precipitous Rise of the Tea Party*. Berkeley, CA: University of California Press.

Bush, G. (1990) 'Address before a Joint Session of the Congress on the Persian Gulf Crisis and the Federal Budget Deficit'. www.presidency.ucsb.edu/ws/?pid=18820.

Buszynski, L. (1995) 'Russia and the West: Towards Renewed Geopolitical Rivalry' *Survival* 37 (3): 104–125.

Butko, T. (2004) 'Revelation and Revolution: A Gramscian Approach to the Rise of Political Islam' *British Journal of Middle Eastern Studies* 31 (1): 41–62.

Cahill, D. (2014) *The End of Laissez-Faire?* London: Edward Elgar.

Cahill, D. and Konings, M. (2017) *Neoliberalism*. London: John Wiley & Sons.

Cahill, D., Cooper, M., Konings, M. and Primrose, M. (eds.) (2018) *The Sage Handbook of Neoliberalism*. London: Sage.

Callinicos, A. (2015) 'The Internationalist Case against the European Union' *International Socialism* 148.

Cardoso, H. (2001) *Charting a New Course: The Politics of Globalisation and Social Transformation*. Lanham, MD: Rowman & Littlefield.

Carroll, W. (2014) 'Far Right Parties and Movements in Europe, Japan and the Tea Party in the US: A Comparative Analysis' *Journal of Power, Politics and Governance* 2 (2): 205–222.

Castaneda, J. (2006) 'Latin America's Left Turn' *Foreign Affairs* 85 (3): 28–43.

Castells, M. (1996) *The Network Society*. Oxford: Blackwell.

Castells, M. (1997) *The Power of Identity*. Oxford: Blackwell.

Chacko, P. and Jayasuriya, K. (2017) 'Trump, the Authoritarian Populist Revolt and the Future of the Rule Based Order in Asia' *Australian Journal of International Affairs* 72 (2): 121–127.

Chambers, D. (1965) *Hooded Americanism: The First Century of the Ku Klux Klan 1865–1965*. New York: Doubleday.

Charalambous, G. and Ioannou, G. (eds.) (2019) *Left Radicalism and Populism in Europe*. London: Routledge.

Chase-Dunn, C. (1990) 'Resistance to Imperialism: Semiperipheral Actors' *Review* 13 (1): 1–31.

Chase-Dunn, C., Kawano, Y. and Brewer, B. (2000) 'Trade Globalization since 1795' *American Sociological Review* 65 (1): 77–95.

Chin, C. and Mittelman, J. (2000) 'Conceptualising Resistance to Globalization' in Gills, B. (ed.) *Globalization and the Politics of Resistance*. Basingstoke: Palgrave.

Chodor, T. (2015) *Neoliberal Hegemony and the Pink Tide in Latin America: Breaking Up with TINA?* London: Palgrave.

Christian Coalition (1992) 'Address and Pleas for Funds'. Washington DC: Christian Coalition.

Clarke, H., Goodwin, M. and Whiteley, P. (2017) *Brexit: Why Britain Voted to Leave the European Union*. Oxford: Oxford University Press.

Coles, T. (2017) *President Trump Inc: How Big Business and Neo-liberalism Empower Populism and the Far Right*. West Hoathly: Clairview Books.

Connell, R. (2005) *Masculinities*. Sydney: Allen & Unwin.

Copsey, N. (2008) *Contemporary British Fascism: The British National Party and the Quest for Legitimacy*. London: Palgrave.

Copsey, N. and Macklin, G. (eds.) (2011) *British National Party: Contemporary Perspectives*. London: Routledge.

Coulter, A. (2017) 'How Feminism Killed the Family' *Fox News*. www.youtube.com/watch?v=DmwENiT4TNc.

Council on American Relations (1949) 'Proposals to Abolish the US', Hoover Institution Library & Archive, 'Radical Right Collection: United Nations and World Federalism', Box 43. Palo Alto, CA: Stanford University.

Cox, M. and Durham, M. (2000) 'The Politics of Anger: The Extreme Right in the US' in Hainsworth, P. (ed.) *The Politics of the Extreme Right: From the Margins to the Mainstream*. London: Pinter.

Cox, R. (1987) *Power, Production and World Order: Social Forces in the Making of History*. New York: Columbia University Press.

Cox, R. (1991) 'Real Socialism in Historical Perspective' in Milliband, R. and Panitch, L. (eds.) *Communist Regimes: The Aftermath*. London: Merlin Press.

Crehan, K. (2016) *Gramsci's Common Sense: Inequality and Its Narratives*. Durham, NC: Duke University Press.

Cronin, M. (ed.) (1996) *The Failure of British Fascism*. London: Palgrave.

Crouch, C. (2011) *The Strange Non-Death of Neoliberalism*. Cambridge: Polity Press.

Curato, N. (2017) 'Flirting with Authoritarian Fantasies? Rodrigo Duterte and the New Terms of Philippine Populism' *Journal of Contemporary Asia* 47 (1): 142–153.

Dahrendorf, R. (1990) *Reflections on the Revolution in Europe*. New York: Random House.

Daily Mail (2017) 'Margaret Thatcher Is My Role Model' 28 October.

Dale, G. (2010) *Karl Polanyi: The Limits of the Market*. Cambridge: Polity Press.

Damgé, R., Durand, A., Vaudano, M., Baruch, J. and Breteau, P. (2018) 'Sur un axe de Mélenchon à Le Pen, où se situent les revendications des gilets jaunes' *Le Monde* 10 December.

Daughters of the American Revolution (1965) 'NATO, the US Constitution and World Government', Hoover Institution Library & Archive, 'Radical Right Collection: John Birch Society; Liberty Lobby', Box 32. Palo Alto, CA: Stanford University.

Davidson, N. (2014) 'The Far Right and the "Needs of Capital"' in Saull, R., Anievas, A., Davidson, N. and Fabry, A. (eds.) *The Longue Durée of the Far-Right: An International Historical Sociology*. London: Routledge.

Davidson, N. and Saull, R. (2017) 'Neoliberalism: A Contradictory Embrace' *Critical Sociology* 43 (4–5): 707–724.

Davies, P. and Lynch, D. (2002) *The Routledge Companion to Fascism and the Far Right*. London: Routledge.

Davis, A. (2019) *India and the Anglosphere: Race, Identity and Hierarchy in International Relations*. London: Routledge.

De Sio, L. and Paparo, A. (eds.) (2018) *The Years of Challengers? Issues, Public Opinion and Elections in Western Europe in 2017*. Rome: CISE.

Deckman, M. (2016) *Tea Party Women*. New York: New York University Press.

Delingpole, J. (2011) 'How the BBC Fell for a Marxist Plot to Destroy Civilisation from Within' *Daily Mail* 27 September.

Dentith, M. (2014) *The Philosophy of Conspiracy Theory*. London: Palgrave.

Devlin, J. (1999) *Slavophiles and Commissars: Enemies of Democracy in Modern Russia*. London: Palgrave.

Dewinter, F. (2002) 'Het groene totalitarisme: Dem kolonisatie van Europa!' Speech given at the Colloquium 'Karel Martelstrichting', Antwerp 20 November.

Diamond Archive (1991) 'Committee to Avert a Mid-East Holocaust: Rothbard, Paul, Buchanan', Diamond Archive. Berkeley, CA: University of California.

Diamond Archive (1992–1997) 'Radical Right Files of the 1990s', Diamond Archive 98/70. Berkeley, CA: University of California.

Diamond, S. (1995) *Road to Dominion: Right Wing Movements and Political Power in the United States*. New York: Guilford Press.

Døving, C. (2010) 'Anti-Semitism and Islamophobia: A Comparison of Imposed Group Identities' *Tidsskrift for Islamforskning - Islam og minoriteter* 2: 52–76.

Dorey, P. (1996) *British Politics since 1945*. London: Wiley.

Dorries, N. (2017) 'Left Wing Snowflakes Are Killing Comedy …'. https://twitter.com/nadinedorries/status/945973216778031110?lang=en 27 December.

Downes, G. (2009) 'China and India: The New Powerhouses of the Semi-Periphery' in Worth, O. and Moore, P. (eds.) *Globalisation and the 'New' Semi-Peripheries*. London: Palgrave.

Dumenil, G. and Levy, D. (2011) *The Crisis of Neoliberalism*. Cambridge, MA: Harvard University Press.

Duncan, F. (2006) 'A Decade of Christian Democratic Decline: The Dilemmas of the CDU, OVP and CDA in the 1990s' *Government and Opposition* 41 (4): 469–490.

Dunn, B. (2017) 'Against Neoliberalism as a Concept' *Capital & Class* 41 (3): 435–454.

Eaton, G. (2018) 'The Commonwealth Delusion: Why Empire 2.0 Is No Substitute for the EU' *New Statesman*. www.newstatesman.com/politics/uk/2018/04/commonwealth-delusion-why-empire-20-no-substitute-eu.

Eatwell, R. (2000) 'The Extreme Right and British Exceptionalism: The Primacy of Politics' in Hainsworth, P. (ed.) *The Extreme Right in Western Europe*. London: Routledge.

The Economist (2016) 'The New Nationalism' *The Economist* November/December.

Ehrenberg-Shannon, B. and Wisniewska, A. (2017) 'How Education Level Is the Biggest Predictor of Support for Geert Wilder' *Financial Times* 2 March.

Eilinas, A. (2013) 'The Rise of Golden Dawn: The New Face of the Far Right in Greece' *South European Society and Politics* 18 (4): 543–565.

Eltchaninoff, M. (2017) *Inside the Mind of Le Pen*. London: Hurst.

Encarnacion, O. (2018) 'Bolsonaro Can't Destroy Brazilian Democracy' *Foreign Policy*. https://foreignpolicy.com/2018/11/01/bolsonaro-cant-destroy-brazilian-democracy/.

Enloe, C. (1973) *Ethnic Conflict and Political Development*. Columbus, GA: Little, Brown and Company.

Ennser-Jedenastik, L. (2016) 'A Welfare-State for Whom? A Group-Based Account of the Austrian Freedom Party's Social Policy Profile' *Swiss Political Science Review* 22 (3): 409–427.

Eriksen, T., Laidlaw, T., Mair, J., Martin, K. and Venkatesan, S. (2015) 'The Concept of Neoliberalism Has Become an Obstacle to the Anthropological Understanding of the Twenty First Century' *Journal of the Royal Anthropological Institute* 21 (4): 911–923.

Erk, J. (2005) 'From Vlaams Blok to Vlaams Belang: The Belgium Far-Right Renames Itself' *West European Politics* 28 (3): 493–502.

Esen, B. and Gumuscu, S. (2016) 'Rising Competitive Authoritarianism in Turkey' *Third World Quarterly* 37 (9): 1581–1606.

Evans, G. and Menon, A. (2017) *Brexit and British Politics*. Cambridge: Polity Press.

Evans, J. and Ivaldi, G. (2017) 'An Atypical "Honeymoon" Election? Contextual and Strategic Opportunities in the 2017 French Legislative Elections' *French Politics* 15 (3): 322–339.

Evans, J. and Ivaldi, G. (2018) *The 2017 French Presidential Election: A Political Reformation*. London: Palgrave.

Evans, T. (2011) 'The Limits of Tolerance: Islam as Counter-Hegemony' *Review in International Studies* 37 (4): 1751–1773.

Farah, J. (2010) *The Tea Party Manifesto: A Vision for an American Rebirth*. Washington, DC: WND Books.

Fassin, E. (2018) *Populism: Right and Left*. Chicago, IL: Prickly Paradigm Press.

Fielding, N. (1981) *The National Front*. London: Routledge & Kegan Paul.

Fieltz, M. and Laloire, L. (eds.) (2016) *Trouble on the Far Right: Contemporary Right Wing Strategies and Practices in Europe*. Bielefeld: Transcript.

Filip, B. (2012) 'Polanyi and Hayek on Freedom, the State and Economics' *International Journal of Political Economy* 41 (4): 69–87.

Financial Times (2016) 'Britain Has Had Enough of Experts, Says Gove' *Financial Times* 3 June.

Finchelstein, F. (2018) 'Trumpism in Spreading in Latin America' *Washington Post*. www.washingtonpost.com/outlook/2018/09/18/trumpism-is-spreading-latin-america/?noredirect=on&utm_term=.846043c3c336.

Fischer, A. and Tepe, D. (2011) 'What's Critical about Critical Theory? Feminist Materialism, Intersectionality and the Social Totality of the Frankfurt School' in Shields, S., McCartney, H. and Bruff, I. (eds.) *Critical International Political Economy: Dialogue, Debate and Dissensus*. London: Palgrave.

Fishwick, A. and Connolly, H. (eds.) (2018) *Austerity and Working Class Resistance*. London: Rowman & Littlefield.

Flåten, L.T. (2016) *Hindu Nationalism, History and Identity in India: Narrating a Hindu Past under the BJP*. London: Routledge.

Flescher Forminaya, C. and Hayes, G. (2016) 'Special Issue: Resisting Austerity: Collective Action in Europe in Wake of the Financial Crisis' *Social Movement Studies* 16 (1).

Foley, M. (2007) *American Credo: The Place of Ideas in US Politics*. Oxford: Oxford University Press.

Ford, R. and Goodwin, M. (2014) *Revolt on the Right: Explaining Support for the Radical Right in Britain*. London: Routledge.

Fortuyn, P. (1997) *Tegen de islamisering van onze cultuur: Nederlandse identiteit als fundament*. Amsterdam: W.W. Bruna.

Fortuyn, P. (2002) *De puinhopen van acht jaar Paars*. Uithoorn: Karakter.

Fowlie, C. (2018) 'Britain's Far Right since 1967: A Bibliographic Survey' in Copsey, N. and Worley, M. (eds.) *Tomorrow Belongs to Us: The British Far Right since 1967*. London: Routledge.

Fransen, J. (2017) 'Jayda Fransen@JaydaBF' Twitter. https://twitter.com/jaydabf?lang=en.

Fraser, N. (2017) 'The End of Progressive Neoliberalism' *Dissent* 2 January. www.dissentmagazine.org/online_articles/progressive-neoliberalism-reactionary-populism-nancy-fraser.

Fukuyama, F. (1992) *The End of History and the Last Man*. London: Penguin.

Gabriel, S. (2016) 'Interview' Funke Media Group, June.

Gamble, A. (1988) *The Free Economy and the Strong State: The Politics of Thatcherism*. London: Palgrave.

Gamble, A. (1996) *Hayek: The Iron Cage of Liberty*. Boulder, CO: Westview Press.

Gamble, A. (2009) *The Spectre at the Feast*. London: Palgrave.

Gauchet, M. (1997) 'Right and Left' in Nora, P. and Kritzman, L. (eds.) *Realms of Memory: Conflicts and Division*. New York: Columbia University Press.

Gautney, H. (2018) *Crashing the Party: From the Bernie Sanders Campaign to a Progressive Movement*. London: Verso.

Ghodsee, K. (2008) 'Left-Wing, Right-Wing, Everything: Xenophobia, Neo-totalitarianism and Populist Politics in Bulgaria' *Problems of Post-Communism* 55 (3): 26–39.

Giddens, A. (1998) *The Third Way*. Cambridge: Polity Press.

Golden Dawn (2015) 'National Plan for 2015'. www.xryshaygh.com/assets/files/xa_ethniko_sxedio.pdf.

Golden Dawn (2018) 'Information and Statement of Intent'. www.xryshaygh.com/en/information.

Gough, J. (2017) 'Brexit, Xenophobia and Left Strategy Now' *Capital & Class* 41 (2): 366–372.

Gramsci, A. (1971) *Selections from the Prison Notebooks*. London: Lawrence and Wishart.

Gramsci, A. (1985) *Selections from the Cultural Notebooks*. London: Lawrence.

Gramsci, A. (1996) *Antonio Gramsci: Prison Notebooks Volume 2*. New York: Columbia University Press.

Gramsci, A. (2007) *Antonio Gramsci: Prison Notebooks Volume 3*. New York: Columbia University Press.

Green, J. (2017) *Devil's Bargain*. Melbourne: Scribe.

Griffin, D. (2004) *The New Pearl Harbour*. Gloucestershire: Arris Books.

Griffin, N. (2002) 'Cults, Jets and Greed: The Frantic Rush to "One World"'. www.bnp.org.uk/articles/rush_globalism.htm.

Griffin, N. (2007) 'The Crisis of Globalism' *Identity* November. London: BNP.

Griffin, N. (2009) 'UK Needs Nationalist Answers to Globalism' *Russia Today* 19 August.

Griffin, R. (2000) 'Interregnum or Endgame? The Radical Right in the "Post-Fascist" Era' *Journal of Political Ideologies* 5 (2): 163–178.

Griffin, R. and Feldman, M. (eds.) (2003) *Fascism: Critical Concepts in Political Science*, Volume 5. London: Routledge.

Guess, A., Nyhan, B. and Reifler, J. (2018) 'Selective Exposure to Misinformation: Evidence from the Consumption of Fake News during the 2016 US Presidential Campaign' Dartmouth. www.dartmouth.edu/~nyhan/fake-news-2016.pdf.

Hafez, M. and Mullins, C. (2015) 'The Radicalization Puzzle: A Theoretical Synthesis of Empirical Approaches to Hometown Extremism' *Studies in Conflict and Terrorism* 38 (11): 958–975.

Hainsworth, P. (ed.) (2000) *The Extreme Right in Western Europe*. London: Routledge.

Hainsworth, P. (2004) 'The Extreme Right in France: The Rise and Rise of Jean-Marie Le Pen's Front National' *Representation* 40 (2): 101–111.

Hall, S. (1988) *The Hard Road to Renewal*. London: Verso.

Hall, S. (1998) 'The Great Moving Nowhere Show' *Marxism Today* Nov/Dec: 9–14.

Halliday, F. (1999) 'Islamophobia Reconsidered' *Ethnic and Racial Studies* 22 (5): 892–902.

Hallin, D. (2019) 'Mediatisation, Neoliberalism and Populisms: The Case of Trump' *Contemporary Social Science* 14 (1): 14–25.

Hamilton, A. (1791/2016) *Report on the Subject of Manufactures*. Scotts Valley, CA: Create Space.

Han, K.-J. (2015) 'The Impact of Radical Right-Wing Parties on the Positions of Mainstream Parties Regarding Multiculturalism' *West European Politics* 38 (3): 557–576.

Hann, C. and Hart, K. (eds.) (2009) *Market and Society: The Great Transformation Today*. Cambridge: Cambridge University Press.

Harmes, A. (2012) 'The Rise of Neoliberal Nationalism' *Review of International Political Economy* 19 (1): 59–86.

Harrop, M., England, J. and Husbands, C. (1980) 'The Bases of National Front Support' *Political Studies* 28 (2): 271–283.

Hawley, C. (2016) *Right-Wing Critics of American Conservatism*. Lawrence, KS: University Press of Kansas.

Hawley, C. (2017) *Making Sense of the Alt-Right*. New York: Columbia University Press.

Haynes, J. (2002) *Politics in the Developing World*. Oxford: Blackwell.

Haynes, J. (2007) *Religion and Development: Conflict or Cooperation?* London: Palgrave.

Heer, J. (2017) 'Trump's Racism and the Myth of Cultural Marxism' *New Republic*. https://newrepublic.com/article/144317/trumps-racism-myth-cultural-marxism.

Heffernan, R. (2000) *New Labour and Thatcherism: Political Change in Britain*. London: Palgrave.

Henderson, A., Jeffery, C., Wincott, D. and Wyn Jones, R. (2017) 'How Brexit Was Made in England' *British Journal of Politics and International Relations* 19 (4): 631–646.

Henissart, P. (1970) *Wolves in the City: The Death of French Algeria*. London: Simon & Schuster.

Herman, L. and Muldoon, J. (eds.) (2018) *Trumping the Mainstream*. London: Routledge.

Hitler, A. (1925/1992) *Mein Kampf*. London: Pimlico.

Hobsbawm, E. (1987) *The Age of Empire*. London: Weidenfeld & Nicolson.

Holloway, J. and Picciotto, S. (1979) *State and Capital: A Marxist Debate*. London: Edward Arnold.

Home Office (UK) (2017) 'Hate Crime England and Wales 2016–2017'. www.gov.uk/government/statistics/hate-crime-england-and-wales-2016-to-2017.

Hoover Institution Library & Archive (2018) 'Radical Right Collection: John Birch Society; Liberty Lobby', Box 32. Palo Alto, CA: Stanford University (accessed April 2018).

Hoover Institution Library & Archive (2018) 'Radical Right Collection: United Nations and World Federalism', Box 43. Palo Alto, CA: Stanford University (accessed April 2018).

Hoover Institution Library & Archive (2018) 'Radical Right Collection: United Nations and World Federalism', Box 44. Palo Alto, CA: Stanford University (accessed April 2018).

Hoover Institution Library & Archive (2018) 'Radical Right Collection: Anti-Communism', Box 56. Palo Alto, CA: Stanford University (accessed April 2018).

Hoover Institution Library & Archive (2018) 'Radical Right Collection: Patriotism', Box 57. Palo Alto, CA: Stanford University (accessed April 2018).

Hoover Institution Library & Archive (2018) 'Radical Right Collection: The Illuminati', Box 66. Palo Alto, CA: Stanford University (accessed April 2018).

Hoover Institution Library & Archive (2018) 'Radical Right Collection: America for Americans', Box 104. Palo Alto, CA: Stanford University (accessed April 2018).

Hoover Institution Library & Archive (2018) 'Radical Right Collection: Christian Victory; Common Sense', Box 105. Palo Alto, CA: Stanford University (accessed April 2018).

Hoover Institution Library & Archive (2018) 'Radical Right Collection: John Birch Society', Box 106. Palo Alto, CA: Stanford University (accessed April 2018).

Hope, C. (2019) 'New Brexit Party Has More Than £1 Million in Pledges and Slate of Over 200 Candidates Including Nigel Farage' *Daily Telegraph* 1 February.

Hopkin, J. (2017) 'When Polanyi Met Farage: Market Fundamentalism, Economic Nationalism and Britain's Exit from the European Union' *British Journal of Politics and International Relations* 19 (3): 465–478.

Hopkins, K. (2018) 'Femi-Nazi's'. https://twitter.com/KTHopkins/status/1049645849637281793.

Hroub, K. (2011) *Political Islam: Content versus Ideology*. London: Saqi.

Huntington, S. (1996) *The Clash of Civilisations and the Remaking of World Order*. New York: Simon & Schuster.

Hutchinson, J. (1994) *Modern Nationalism*. London: Fontana.

Hyman, R. (2015) 'Three Scenarios for Industrial Relations in Europe' *International Labour Review* 154 (1): 5–14.

Icke, D. (2001) *Children of the Matrix*. Daisy Hill, Queensland: Bridge of Love Publications.

Ignazi, P. (2003) *Extreme Right Parties in Western Europe*. Oxford: Oxford University Press.

Ikenberry, J. (2018) 'The End of the Liberal International Order?' *International Affairs* 94 (1): 7–23.

Inglehart, R. (1971) 'The Silent Revolution in Europe: Intergenerational Change in Post-Industrial Societies' *American Political Science Review* 65 (4): 991–1071.

Inglehart, R. and Norris, P. (2016) 'Pippa, Trump, Brexit, and the Rise of Populism: Economic Have-Nots and Cultural Backlash', HKS Working Paper No. RWP16-026. http://dx.doi.org/10.2139/ssrn.2818659.

Inglehart, R. and Norris, P. (2017) 'Trump and the Populist Authoritarian Parties: *The Silent Revolution* in Reverse' *Perspectives on Politics* 15 (2): 443–454.

Ivadi, G. and Mazzoleni, O. (2017) 'The Racial Right Politics of Economic Nationalism: A Comparison between the French Front National (FN) and the Swiss People's Party (SVP)', HAL. https://halshs.archives-ouvertes.fr/halshs-01635302/.

Jackson, P. (2014) 'Accumulative Extremism: The Post-War Tradition of Anglo American Neo-Nazi Activism' in Jackson, P. and Shekhovtsov, A.

(eds.) *The Post-War Anglo-American Far Right: A Special Relationship of Hate*. London: Palgrave.

Jackson, P. (2016) '"Thatcher the Betrayer!" May, Thatcher and the Downfall of the National Front' *Paul Jackson's Blog*. https:// paulnicholasjackson.wordpress.com/2016/10/10/thatcher-the-betrayer-may-thatcher-and-the-downfall-of-the-national-front/.

Jackson, P. and Shekhovtsov, A. (eds.) (2014) *The Post-War Anglo-American Far Right: A Special Relationship of Hate*. London: Palgrave.

Jacobs, S. (2011) 'Globalisation, Anti-globalisation and the Jewish "Question"' *European Review of History: Revue européenne d'histoire* 18 (1): 45–56.

Jacques, M. (1998) 'Wrong' *Marxism Today* Nov/Dec: 1–2.

Jaffrelot, C. (2016) 'The Hindu Nationalist Strategy of Stigmatisation and Emulation of "Threatening Others": An Indian Style Fascism?' in Koenig, L. and Chaudhuri, B. (eds.) *Politics of the 'Other' in India and China: Western Concepts in Non-Western Contexts*. London: Routledge.

Jäger, J. and Springler, E. (2015) 'Debating the Future of Europe: Critical Political Economy and Post-Keynesian Perspectives' in Jäger, J. and Springler, E. (eds.) *Asymmetric Crisis in Europe and Possible Futures: Critical Political Economy and Post-Keynesian Perspectives*. London: Routledge.

James, W. (2018) 'UKIP Will Not Join Steve Bannon's Anti-EU Movement, Says Leader'. www.reuters.com/article/us-britain-eu-ukip/ ukip-will-not-join-steve-bannons-anti-eu-movement-says-leader-idUSKCN1M10Q8.

Jervis, R., Gavin, F., Rovner, J. and Labrosse, D. (eds.) (2018) *Chaos in the Liberal Order: The Trump Presidency and International Politics in the Twenty First Century*. New York: Columbia University Press.

Jessop, B. and Overbeek, H. (2018) *Transnational Capital and Class Fractions: The Amsterdam School Perspective Reconsidered*. London: Routledge.

Jobbik (2010) 'Radical Change: A Guide to Jobbik's Parliamentary Electoral Manifesto for National Self-determination and Social Justice'. www. jobbik.com/sites/default/files/Jobbik-RADICALCHANGE2010.pdf.

Jobbik (2018) 'Policies: The Economy'. www.jobbik.com/policies.

John Birch Society (1996) *The New American Special Report: Conspiracy for Global Control*. Appleton, WI: JBS.

John Birch Society (2009) 'Get the US out of the UN: 50 Years On', John Birch Society. www.jbs.org/action-projects/get-us-out-of-the-united-nations.

Johnson, B. (2018) 'Denmark Got It Wrong. Yes, the Burka Is Oppressive and Ridiculous – But That's Still No Reason to Ban It' *The Daily Telegraph* 5 August.

Johnson, B. and Hunt, J. (2018) 'Chequers Debate' *Mail on Sunday* 9 September.

Jones, L. (2016) 'The EU Referendum: Brexit, the Politics of Scale and State Transformation' *The Disorder of Things*. https://thedisorderofthings. com/2016/05/24/the-eu-referendum-brexit-the-politics-of-scale-and-state-transformation/.

Kagarlitsky, B. (2008) *Empire of the Periphery: Russia and the World System*. London: Pluto Press.

Kaldor, M. (1999) *New and Old Wars: Organised Violence in a Global Era*. Palo Alto, CA: Stanford University Press.

Kaltwasser, C. and Mudde, C. (2017) *Populism: A Very Short Introduction*. Oxford: Oxford University Press.

Kaufman, E. (2016) 'It's NOT the Economy, Stupid: Brexit as a Story of Personal Values'. http://eprints.lse.ac.uk/71585/1/blogs.lse.ac.uk-Its%20NOT%20the%20economy%20stupid%20Brexit%20as%20a%20 story%20of%20personal%20values.pdf.

Keith, J. (1995) *Black Helicopters Over America: Strikeforce for the New World Order*. San Francisco, CA: Last Gasp.

Kellner, D. (2016) *American Nightmare: Donald Trump, Media Spectacle and Authoritarian Populism*. Rotterdam: Sense.

Kennedy, P. (1993) *Preparing for the Twenty First Century*. London: Fontana Press.

Kennedy, S. (2018) 'Trump's "Co-ordinated Chaos" May Be Part of a Grand Strategy, One That Doesn't Bode Well for China' *South China Morning Post* 18 April.

Keohane, R. (1984) *After Hegemony*. Princeton, NJ: Princeton University Press.

Kiely, R. (2017) 'From Authoritarian Liberalism to Economic Technology: Neoliberalism, Politics and De-Democratisation' *Critical Sociology* 4–5 (1): 725–745.

Kiely, R. (2018) *The Neoliberal Paradox*. London: Edward Elgar.

Kiely, R. and Saull, R. (2017) 'Neoliberalism and the Far Right: An Introduction' *Critical Sociology* 43 (6): 821–829.

King, M. (2014) 'UKIP: A New Monday Club?' https://anewnatureblog. wordpress.com/2014/11/03/ukip-the-new-monday-club/.

Kitschelt, H. (2004) *Diversification and Reconfiguration of Party Systems in Postindustrial Democracies*. Bonn: Friedrich Ebert Stiftung.

Knight, P. (2008) 'Outrageous Conspiracy Theories: Popular and Official Responses to 9/11 in Germany and the United States' *New German Critique* 103: 165–193.

Kofman, E. and Youngs, G. (1996) *Globalization: Theory and Practice*. London: Pinter.

Kotz, D. (2015) *The Rise and Fall of Neoliberal Capitalism*. Cambridge, MA: Harvard University Press.

Krouwel, A. (2012) 'The Polarised Nature of the Dutch System and the Volatility of the Electorate Ensure That Any "Victory for the Centre" Is

Likely to Be Short Lived'. http://blogs.lse.ac.uk/europpblog/2012/09/19/dutch-election-parties/.

Kutiyski, Y. (2016) 'The Achilles Heel of Bulgaria's Patriotic Front: Contemporary Right-Wing Strategies and Practices in Europe' in Fieltz, M. and Laloire, L. (eds.) *Trouble on the Far Right: Contemporary Right Wing Strategies and Practices in Europe*. Bielefeld: Transcript.

Kyriaz, A. (2016) 'Ultranationalist Discourses of Exclusion: A Comparison between the Hungarian Jobbik and the Greek Golden Dawn' *Journal of Ethnic and Migration Studies* 42 (15): 2528–2547.

Labour Research Department (1969) *Powell and His Allies*. London: Labour Party.

Landler, M. (2017) 'Trump the Insurgent, Breaks with 70 Years of American Foreign Policy', *New York Times*. www.nytimes.com/2017/12/28/us/politics/trump-world-diplomacy.html.

Lane, D. (1997) *The Rise and Fall of State Socialism*. Cambridge: Polity Press.

de Lange, S. (2011) 'Fortuyn versus Wilders: An Agency-Based Approach to Radical Right Party Building' *West European Politics* 34 (6): 1229–1249.

Lavelle, A. (2016) *The Death of Social Democracy*. London: Routledge.

Layton-Henry, Z. (1978) 'Race, Electoral Strategy and the Major Parties' *Parliamentary Affairs* 30 (1): 268–281.

Le Pen, M. (2017) 'Protectionnisme intelligent' Elysee: Le Grand Debat, C News.

Lechner, F. and Boli, J. (eds.) (2000) *The Globalization Reader*. Oxford: Blackwell.

Leeds, T. (2018) 'The Jefferson Movement: An Ethnography Study', Paper to the Center for Right-Wing Studies, University of California, Berkeley.

Legassick, M. (1974) 'South Africa: Capital Accumulation and Violence' *Economy and Society* 3: 253–291.

Libby, R. (2015) 'Has the Tea Party Eclipsed the Republican Establishment in the 2016 Presidential Elections?' *Journal of Political Science and Public Affairs* 3 (3): 183. doi:10.4172/2332-0761.1000183.

List, F. (2005) *The National System of Political Economy*. New York: Cosimo.

Littlejohn, R. (2014) *Littlejohn's Lost World*. London: Penguin.

Littlejohn, R. (2017) 'Once in the Shadows, Anti-Semitism Is Now Entrenched at the Poisoned Heart of the Labour Party' *Daily Mail* 27 September.

Lowndes, J. (2012) 'The Past and Future of Race in the Tea Party Movement' in Rosenthal, L. and Trost, C. (eds.) *Steep: The Precipitous Rise of the Tea Party*. Berkeley, CA: University of California Press.

Lyons, M. (2017) *Ctrl-Alt-Delete: An Anti-Fascist Report on the Alternative Right*. Montreal: Kersplebedeb.

Major, A. (2014) *Architects of Austerity: International Finance and the Politics of Growth*. Stanford, CA: Stanford University Press.

Mamdani, M. (2005) *Good Muslim, Bad Muslim: America, the Cold War and the Roots of Terror*. New York: Harmony.

Mandaville, P. (2007) *Global Political Islam*. London: Routledge.

Marcks, H. (2016) 'Don't Call Me Right! The Strategy of Normalization in German Right-Wing Extremism' in Fieltz, M. and Laloire, L. (eds.) *Trouble on the Far Right: Contemporary Right Wing Strategies and Practices in Europe*. Bielefeld: Transcript.

Margry, P. (2003) 'The Murder of Pim Fortuyn and Collective Emotions: Hype, Hysteria and Holiness in the Netherlands?' *Ethofoor* 16: 102–127.

Marx, K. (1967) *The Eighteenth Brumaire of Louis Bonaparte*. Moscow: Progress Publishers.

Marx, K. (1981) *Capital Volume 3*. London: Penguin.

Mason, P. (2015) *PostCapitalism: A Guide to our Future*. London: Allen Lane.

Mason, P. (2016) 'Are We Living through Another 1930s?' *The Guardian* 1 August.

Mason, P. (2018) 'UKIPs Turn to the Alt-Right Is a Warning Sign: We Need to Fight Back' *New Statesman* 27 June.

Mayer, N. (2005) 'Votes populaires, vote populistes' *Hermès* 42 (2): 161–166.

Mayer, W. (2016) *Islamic Jihad, Cultural Marxism and the Transformation of the West*. San Fransisco, CA: Pipeline Media.

Mayor, A. (2014) *Architects of Austerity*. Palo Alto, CA: Stanford University Press.

McAlister, M. (2003) 'Prophecy, Politics and the Popular: The *Left Behind* Series and Christian Fundamentalism "New World Order"' *The South Atlantic Quarterly* 102 (4): 773–798.

McBride, S. and Evans, B. (eds.) (2017) *The Austerity State*. Toronto: University of Toronto Press.

McDonnell, J. (2017) 'Labour Has Broken the Neoliberal Grip on Intellectual Thought' *The Guardian* 25 June.

McDonnell, J. (2018) 'Neoliberalism Has Failed: Labour's Ideas Are the New Mainstream' *Labour List*. https://labourlist.org/2018/05/john-mcdonnell-neoliberalism-has-failed-labours-ideas-are-the-new-mainstream/.

McHugh, M. (2018) 'In the Age of Trump: Populist Backlash and Progressive Resistance Create Divergent State Immigrant Integration Contexts', Transatlantic Council on Migration. Washington, DC: Migration Policy Institute.

McIntyre, W. (1967) *Colonies into Commonwealth*. London: Blandford Press.

McNally, M. (2009) 'Gramsci's Internationalism, the National-Popular and the Alternative Globalisation Movement' in M. McNally and

J. Schwarzmantel (eds.) *Gramsci and Global Politics: Hegemony and Resistance*. London: Routledge.

McTernan, J. (2016) 'The Idiots in Momentum Will Destroy Themselves before They Destroy Labour' *Daily Telegraph* 8 February.

Mead, W. (2011) 'The Tea Party and American Foreign Policy: What Populism Means to Globalism' *Foreign Affairs* 90 (2): 28–44.

Mead, W. (2018) 'How Trump Plans to Change the World' *The Wall Street Journal* 9 July.

Mellon, J., Evans, G., Fieldhouse, E., Green, J. and Prosser, C. (2018) 'Brexit or Corbyn? Campaign and Inter-Election Vote Switching in the 2017 UK General Election' *Parliamentary Affairs* 71 (4): 719–737.

Menahan, C. (2018) '"Brazil's Trump" Jair Bolsonaro Wins Stunning Victory after Surviving Left-Wing Assassination Attempt' *Inforwars*. www.infowars.com/brazils-trump-jair-bolsonaro-wins-stunning-victory-after-surviving-left-wing-assassination-attempt/.

Miles, R. (1986) 'Labour Migration, Racism, and Capital Accumulation in Western Europe since 1945: An Overview' *Capital & Class* 10 (1): 49–86.

Mirowski, P. (2013) *Never Let a Serious Crisis Go to Waste*. London: Pluto Press.

von Mises, L. (1934) *The Theory of Money and Credit*. London: Jonathan Cape.

Moffitt, B. (2016) *The Global Rise of Populism*. Palo Alto, CA: Stanford University Press.

Monbiot, G. (2016) 'Neoliberalism: The Ideology at the Root of All Our Problems' *The Guardian* 15 April.

Morgan, J. (2017) 'Brexit: Be Careful What You Wish For' *Globalizations* 14 (1): 118–126.

Morton, A. (2010) 'The Continuum of Passive Revolution' *Capital & Class* 34 (3): 315–342.

Mouffe, C. (2018) *For a Left Populism*. London: Verso.

Mudde, C. (2000) *The Ideology of the Extreme Right*. Manchester: Manchester University Press.

Mudde, C. (2007) *Populist Radical Right Parties in Europe*. Cambridge: Cambridge University Press.

Mudde, C. (2016) 'Europe's Populist Surge: A Long Time in the Making' *Foreign Affairs* Nov/Dec: 25–30.

Mudde, C. and Van Holsteyn, J. (2000) 'The Netherlands: Explaining the Limited Success of the Extreme Right' in Hainsworth, P. (ed.) *The Extreme Right in Western Europe*. London: Routledge.

Mufson, S. and Lynch, D. (2018) 'Breaking from GOC Orthodoxy, Trump Increasingly Deciding Winners and Losers in the Economy' *Washington Post* 1 June.

Muggah, R. and Winter, B. (2017) 'Is Populism Making a Comeback in Latin America' *Foreign Affairs* 23 October.

Mulloy, D. (2018) *Enemies of the State: The Radical Right from FDR to Trump*. London: Rowman & Littlefield.

Mun, T. (1628/2017) *England's Treasure by Foreign Trade*. London: Creative Media.

Munck, R. (2007) *Globalization and Contestation: The New Great Counter-Movement*. London: Routledge.

Murphy, C. and Tooze, R. (eds.) (1991) *The New International Political Economy*. Boulder, CO: Lynne Rienner.

Namusoke, E. (2016) 'A Divided Family: Race, the Commonwealth and Brexit' *The Roundtable: The Commonwealth Journal of International Affairs* 105 (5): 463–478.

Neiwert, D. (2017) *Alt America: The Rise of the Radical Right in the Age of Trump*. London: Verso.

Nelson, D. (2018) *Trump's First Year*. Charlottesville, VA: University of Virginia Press.

Neumann, I. (1996) *Russia and the Idea of Europe*. London: Routledge.

Norris, P. (2005) *Radical Right: Voters and Parties in the Electoral Market*. Cambridge: Cambridge University Press.

Nougayrède, N. (2018) 'Bannon Is on a Far-Right Mission to Radicalise Europe' *The Guardian* 6 June.

Olmsted, K. (2009) *Real Enemies: Conspiracy Theories and American Democracy: World War I to 9/11*. Oxford: Oxford University Press.

Olteanu, T. (2017) 'Gender Relations and the Freedom Party of Austria (FPÖ)' *Perspective Politice* 10 (1): 75–82

Ott, B. (2017) 'The Age of Twitter: Donald J. Trump and the Politics of Debasement' *Critical Studies in Media Communication* 34 (1): 59–68.

Overbeek, H. and van Apeldoorn, B. (eds.) (2012) *Neoliberalism in Crisis*. London: Palgrave.

Panagiotopoulos, V. (2017) 'Meet Denmark's New Anti-Islam, Anti-Immigration and Anti-Tax Party'. www.politico.eu/article/meet-denmarks-new-anti-islam-anti-immigration-anti-tax-party-nye-borgerlige-new-right-pernille-vermund/.

Panitch, L. and Albo, G. (2015) *Socialist Register 2016: The Politics of the Right*. London: Merlin Press.

Panitch, L. and Gindin, S. (2018) *The Socialist Challenge Today: Syriza, Sanders, Corbyn*. London: Merlin Press.

Panizza, F. and Miorelli, R. (2009) 'Populism and Democracy in Latin America' *Ethics and International Affairs* 23 (1): 39–46.

Paul, R. (2008) *The Revolution: A Manifesto*. New York: Grand Central Publishing.

Paul, R. (2009) *End the Fed*. New York: Grand Central Publishing.

Paul, R. (2016) 'What Could America Learn from the Swiss', Voices of Liberty. https://voicesofliberty.com/2016/05/10/what-america-could-learn-from-the-swiss-ron-paul-interviews-claudio-grass/.

Peck, J. (2010) *Constructions of Neoliberal Reason*. Oxford: Oxford University Press.

Perlmutter, T. (2015) 'A Narrowing Gyre? The Lega Nord and the Shifting Balance of Italian Immigration Policy' *Ethnic and Racial Studies* 38 (8): 1339–1345.

Peter, M. (2017) 'The End of Neoliberal Globalisation and the Rise of Authoritarian Populism' *Educational Philosophy and Theory* 50 (4): 323–325.

Peto, A. (2016) 'How Are the Anti-Gender Movements Changing Gender Studies as a Profession?' *Religion & Gender* 6 (2): 297–299.

Phillips, M. (2009) 'We Were Fools to Think That the Fall of the Berlin Wall Has Killed Off the Far Left: They Are Back – and Attacking Us from Within' *Daily Mail* 11 November.

Picciotto, S. (1991) 'The Internationalisation of the State' *Capital & Class* 15 (1): 43–63.

van der Pijl, K. (1998) *Transnational Classes and International Relations*. London: Routledge.

Pitchford, M. (2011) *The Conservative Party and the Extreme Right 1945–75*. Manchester: Manchester University Press.

Plummer, B. (ed.) (2003) *Window on Freedom: Race, Civil Rights and Foreign Affairs 1945–1988*. Chapel Hill, NC: University of North Carolina Press.

Polanyi, K. (1944/2001) *The Great Transformation: The Political and Economic Origins of Our Time*. Boston, MA: Beacon Press.

Polyakova, A. (2014) 'Strange Bedfellows: Putin and Europe's Far Right' *World Affairs* 177 (3): 36–40.

Pope, C. (2017) 'How Populism Took Hold' *Progress*. www.progressonline.org.uk/2017/06/27/how-left-populism-took-hold/.

della Porta, D. (2015) *Social Movements in Times of Austerity*. Cambridge: Polity Press.

Posner, S. (2016) 'How Donald Trump's New Campaign Chief Created an Online Haven for White Nationalists', MotherJones. www.motherjones.com/politics/2016/08/stephen-bannon-donald-trump-alt-right-breitbart-news/.

Poulantzas, N. (1974) *Fascism and Dictatorship: The Third International and the Problem of Fascism*. London: New Left Books.

Premdas, R. (1992) *Ethnic Conflict and Development: The Case of Guyana*. New York: United Nations Institute for Social Development.

Prowe, D. (1994) 'Classic Fascism and the New Radical Right in Western Europe: Comparisons and Contrasts' *Contemporary European History* 3 (3): 289–313.

Pugh, M. (2006) *Hurray for the Blackshirts! Fascists and Fascism in Britain between the Wars*. London: Pimlico.

PVV (2010) 'Manifesto General Election 2010'. www.pvv.nl/.

Question Time (2009) *Question Time*, 22 October, BBC.

Quigley, A. (2017) 'Trump Expresses Support for French Candidate Le Pen'. www.politico.com/story/2017/04/21/trump-supports-marine-le-pen-237464.

Radice, H. (2000) 'Responses to Globalisation: A Critique of Progressive Nationalism' *New Political Economy* 5 (1): 5–19.

Rees-Mogg, J. (2018) 'My Vision for a Global-Facing, Outward Looking Post-Brexit Britain' Brexit Central. https://brexitcentral.com/vision-global-facing-outward-looking-post-brexit-britain/.

Remmer, K. (2012) 'The Rise of Leftist-Populist Governance in Latin America' *Comparative Political Studies* 45 (8): 947–972.

Riedlsperger, M. (1998) 'The Freedom Party of Austria: From Protest to Radical Right Populism' in Betz, H.-G. and Immerfall, S. (eds.) *The New Politics of the Right: Neo Populist Parties and Movements in Established Democracies*. New York: St. Martin's Press.

Roberts, A. (2016) 'CANZUK: After Brexit, Canada, Australia, New Zealand and Britain Can Unite as a Pillar of Western Civilisation' *Daily Telegraph* 13 September.

Robertson, P. (1991) *The New World Order*. Dallas, TX: Word.

Robertson, P. (1992) 'Address and Plea for Funds'. Washington DC: Christian Coalition.

Robinson, N. (2012) 'The Edges of Europe: The "Eastern Marches" and the Problematic Nature a "Wider Europe"' in Strange, G. and Worth, O. (eds.) *European Regionalism and the Left*. Manchester: Manchester University Press.

Robinson, T. (2018) 'Tommy Meets: UKIP Leader Gerard Batten', YouTube. www.youtube.com/watch?v=IKAdiM2pYsQ.

Rojecki, A. (2017) 'Trumpism and the American Politics of Insecurity' *The Washington Quarterly* 39 (4): 65–81.

Rosenthal, L. and Trost, C. (2012) 'Introduction: The Rise of the Tea Party' in Rosenthal, L. and Trost, C. (eds.) *Steep: The Precipitous Rise of the Tea Party*. Berkeley, CA: University of California Press.

Roth, S. (2018) 'Introduction: Contemporary Counter-Movements in the Age of Brexit and Trump' *Sociology Research Online* 23 (2): 496–506.

Rothbard, M. (1987) 'The Myths of Reaganomics', Memo to Mises Institute Members, Mises Institute. https://mises.org/library/myths-reaganomics.

Roy, J.-P. (1998) 'Le programme économique et social du Front National en France' in Delwit, P., De Waele, J.-M. and Rea, A. (eds.) *L'extreme driote en France et en Belgique*. Brussels: Editions Complex.

Runnymede Trust (1997) *Islamophobia: A Challenge to Us All*. London: Runnymede Trust.

Rupert, M. (1997) 'Globalisation and Contested Common Sense in the United States' in Chin, C. and Mittelman, J. (eds.) *Innovation and Transformation in International Studies*. Cambridge: Cambridge University Press.

Rupert, M. (2000) *Ideologies of Globalization*. London: Routledge.

Rydgren, J. (ed.) (2017) *The Oxford Handbook of the Radical Right*. Oxford: Oxford University Press.

Said, E. (1978) *Orientalism*. New York: Pantheon Books.

Sapir, J. (2017) 'President Trump and Free Trade' *Real World Economic Review* 79. www.paecon.net/PAEReview/issue79/Sapir79.pdf.

Saull, R. (2014) 'The Origins and Persistence of the Far-Right: Capital, Class and the Pathologies of Liberal Politics' in Saull, R., Anievas, A., Davidson, N. and Fabry, A. (eds.) *The Longue Durée of the Far-Right: An International Historical Sociology*. London: Routledge.

Saull, R. (2015) 'Capitalist Development and the Rise and "Fall" of the Far Right' *Critical Sociology* 41 (4/5): 619–639.

Saull, R. (2018) 'Racism and Far Right Imaginaries within Neoliberal Political Economy' *New Political Economy* 23 (5): 588–608. https://doi.org/10.1080/13563467.2017.1417370.

Saull, R. and Anievas, A. (2019) 'Rethinking the Far Right and the Cold War: Fascist Legacies in the Making of the Liberal Order' *International Studies Review* Forthcoming.

Saull, R., Anievas, A., Davidson, N. and Fabry, A. (eds.) (2014) *The Longue Durée of the Far-Right: An International Historical Sociology*. London: Routledge.

Schiavone, M. (2016) *Austerity and the Labour Movement*. Albany, NY: State University of New York Press.

Schipani, A. (2017) 'Rightwing Populist Firebrand Eyes Presidency in Brazil' *Financial Times* 11 November.

Schoen, D. (1977) *Enoch Powell and the Powellites*. London: Palgrave.

Schram, S. and Pavlovskaya, M. (eds.) (2017) *Rethinking Neoliberalism: Rethinking the Disciplinary Regime*. London: Routledge.

Schroeder, R. (2018) *Social Theory after the Internet: Media, Technology and Globalization*. London: UCL.

Seton-Watson, H. (1985) 'What Is Europe, Where Is Europe: From Mystique to Politique' *Encounter* July/Aug: 9–16.

Seyd, P. (1972) 'Factionalism in the Conservative Party: The Monday Club' *Government and Opposition* 7 (4): 464–487.

Seymour, R. (2014) *Against Austerity: How Can We Fix the Crisis They Made*. London: Pluto Press.

Sheridan, L. (2006) 'Islamophobia Pre-and-Post-September 11th, 2001' *Journal of Interpersonal Violence* 21 (3): 317–336.

Shields, S. (2007) 'From Socialist Solidarity to Neo-Populist Neo-liberalisation? The Paradoxes of Poland's Post-Communist Transition' *Capital & Class* 31 (3): 159–178.

Shields, S. (2012) 'Opposing Neoliberalism? Poland's renewed populism and Post-Communist Transition' *Third World Quarterly* 33 (2): 359–381.

Shields, S. (2014) 'Poland's Recombinant Far-Right Populism and the Reconfiguration of Post-Communist Neoliberalism' in Saull, R., Anievas, A., Davidson, N. and Fabry, A. (eds.) *The Longue Durée of the Far-Right: An International Historical Sociology.* London: Routledge.

Shields, S. (2015) 'Neoliberalism Redux: Poland's Recombinant Populism and Its Alternatives' *Critical Sociology* 41 (4–5): 659–678.

Shields, S., Bruff, I. and McCartney, H. (eds.) (2011) *Critical International Political Economy.* London: Palgrave.

Short, N. (2014) '*Passato e presente?* Gramsci's Analysis of Fascism and the Far-Right' in Saull, R., Anievas, A., Davidson, N. and Fabry, A. (eds.) *The Longue Durée of the Far-Right: An International Historical Sociology.* London: Routledge.

Silver, B. and Arrighi, G. (2003) 'Polanyi's "Double Movement": The Belle Epoques of British and US Hegemony Compared' *Politics & Society* 31 (2): 325–355.

Simon, R. (2009) 'Upper Volta with Gas? Russia as a Semi-Peripheral State' in Worth, O. and Moore, P. *Globalisation and the 'New' Semi-Peripheries.* London: Palgrave.

Simon, R. (2010) 'Passive Revolution, Perestroika and the Emergence of the New Russia' *Capital & Class* 34 (3): 429–448.

Sismondo, S. (2017) 'Post-Truth?' *Social Studies of Science* 47 (1): 3–6.

Skenderovic, R. (2007) 'Immigration and the Radical Right in Switzerland: Ideology, Discourse, Opportunity' *Patterns of Prejudice* 41 (2): 155–176.

Skenderovic, R. (2009) *The Radical Right in Switzerland: Continuity and Change.* Oxford: Berghahn Books.

Sklair, L. (2001) *The Transnational Capitalist Class.* London: Wiley.

Skocpol, T. and Williamson, V. (2012) *The Tea Party and the Remaking of Republican Conservatism.* Oxford: Oxford University Press.

Somer, M. (2016) 'Understanding Turkey's Democratic Breakdown: Old vs New and Indigenous vs Global Authoritarianism' *South East European and Black Sea Studies* 16 (4): 481–503.

Southern Poverty Law Center (2018) 'Alt Right'. www.splcenter.org/fighting-hate/extremist-files/ideology/alt-right.

Spark, A. (2000) 'Conjuring Order: The New World Order and Conspiracy Theories of Globalisation' *The Sociological Review* 48 (2): 46–62.

The Spectator (2006) 'How to Beat the BNP' *The Spectator* 22 April.

Spektor, M. and Fasolin, G. (2018) 'Brazil and the United States: Will President Bolsonaro Bandwagon' *E-International Relations*. www.e-ir.info/author/matias-spektor-and-guilherme-fasol/.

Springer, S., Birch, K. and MacLeavy, J. (2016) *The Handbook of Neoliberalism*. London: Routledge.

Srnicek, N. and Williams, A. (2015) *Inventing the Future: PostCapitalism and a World without Work*. London: Verso.

Stahl, J. (2011) 'Where Did 9/11 Conspiracies Come From?' *Slate*. www.slate.com/articles/news_and_politics/trutherism/2011/09/where_did_911_conspiracies_come_from.html.

Steger, M. (2005) *Globalism: Market Ideology Meet Terrorism*. Lanham: Rowman & Littlefield.

Stempel, C., Hargrove, T. and Stempel, G. (2007) 'Media Use: Social Structures and Belief in 9/11 Conspiracy' *Journal of Mass Communication Quarterly* 84 (2): 353–372.

Stephens, B. (2016) 'The Return of the 1930s' *The Wall Street Journal* 7 March.

Stiglitz, J. (2017) *Globalisation and Its Discontents Revisited: Anti-Globalisation in the Era of Trump*. New York: W.W. Norton.

Stocker, P. (2017) *English Uprising: Brexit and the Mainstreaming of the Far-Right*. New York: Melville House Publishing.

Stone, R. (2017) 'White Guilt, Cultural Marxism and Public Monuments' *UKIP Daily* 17 September.

SVP (2015) 'Manifestos 2015–2019'. www.svp-international.ch/index.php/en/about-us/svp-s-party-manifesto.

Swank, D. and Betz, H.-G. (2003) 'Globalization, the Welfare State and Right-Wing Populism in Western Europe' *Socio-Economic Review* 1 (2): 215–245.

Sweezy, P. and Baran, P. (1966) *Monopoly Capitalism*. New York: Monthly Review Press.

Swyngedouw, M. (2000) 'Belgium: Explaining the Relationship between *Vlaams Blok* and the City of Antwerp' in Hainsworth, P. (ed.) *The Extreme Right in Western Europe*. London: Routledge.

Sygkelos, Y. (2015) 'Nationalism versus European Integration: The Case of Ataka' *East European Quarterly* 43 (2/3): 163–188.

Talev, M. (2017) 'Bannon Calls for 44% Tax for Incomes above $5 Million'. www.bloomberg.com/news/articles/2017-07-26/bannon-is-said-to-call-for-44-tax-on-incomes-above-5-million.

Tansel, C.-B. (2017) *States of Discipline: Authoritarian Neoliberalism and the Contested Reproduction of Capitalist Order*. London: Rowman & Littlefield.

Tarr, D. and Benenson, B. (2013) *Elections A to Z*. Moline, IL: QC Press.

Taylor, F. (2011) *Exercising Hitler: The Occupation and Denazification of Germany*. London: Bloomsbury.

Tea Party (2015) 'Tea Party Manifesto'. www.teaparty.org/about-us/.

Tea Party Patriots (2018) 'Our Vision and Manifesto'. www.teapartypatriots. org/ourvision/.

Tebbit, N. (2018) 'A History Lesson for Those Who Would Smear the Moderate Right: The Nazis Were Socialist' *Daily Telegraph* 24 September.

Teehankee, J. (2016) 'Duterte's Resurgent Nationalism in the Philippines: A Discursive Institutionalist Analysis' *Journal of Current South East Asian Affairs* 35 (3): 69–89.

Tempest, M. (2004) 'Howard Attacks BNP "Thugs" in Burnley' *The Guardian* 19 February.

Temple, M. (2017) 'It's the Sun Wot Lost It' in Thorsen, E., Jackson, D. and Lillekar, D. (eds.) *UK Election Analysis: Voters, Media and the Campaign: Early Reflections from Leading Academics*. Bournemouth: Bournemouth University.

Thomas, S. (2005) *The Global Resurgence of Religion and the Transformation of International Relations*. Basingstoke: London.

Thurlow, R. (1998) *Fascism in Britain: A History 1918–1945*. London: I.B. Tauris.

Time (2017) 'Donald Trump's New World Order Puts Nation Over Globe' *Time Magazine* 12 January.

Träbert, A. (2017) 'At the Mercy of *Femocracy*? Networks and Ideological Links between Far-Right Movements and the Anti-Feminist Men's Rights Movements' in Köttig, M., Bitzan, R. and Petö, A. (eds.) *Gender and Far-Right Politics in Europe*. London: Palgrave.

Tribe, K. (2010) 'Max Weber and the "New Economics"' in Hagemann, H., Nishizama, T. and Ikeda, Y. (eds.) *Austrian Economics in Transition*. London: Palgrave.

Trump Campaign Poster (2016) 'Globalism vs Nationalism'. New York: Trump Presidential Campaign.

Turner, J. (2014) *Religious Ideology and the Roots of the Global Jihad: Salafi Jihadism and International Order*. London: Palgrave.

UK Polling Report (2015) 'Election Guide 15'. http://ukpollingreport. co.uk/2015guide.

UK Polling Report (2018) 'Voting Intention 2010–2018'. http:// ukpollingreport.co.uk/voting-intention-2.

UKIP (2010) *UKIP Manifesto April 2010: Empowering the People*. Newton Abbot: United Kingdom Independence Party.

UKIP (2015) *Belief in Britain: 2015 General Election Manifesto*. Newton Abbot: United Kingdom Independence Party.

UKIP Daily News (2019) www.ukipdaily.com.

United Patriots of Bulgaria (2017) 'Declarations'. http://obedinenipatrioti.com.

Uscinski, J. and Parent, J. (2014) *American Conspiracy Theories*. Oxford: Oxford University Press.

Vanaik, A. (2017) *The Rise of Hindu Authoritarianism*. London: Verso.

Vieten, U. and Poynting, S. (2016) 'Contemporary Far-Right Racist Populism in Europe' *Journal of Intercultural Studies* 37 (6): 533–540.

Vlaams Belang (2018) 'First, Our People'. www.vlaamsbelang.org/eerst-onze-mensen-3/.

Vlcek, W. (2009) 'A Semi-Periphery to Global Capital: Global Governance and Lines of Flight for Caribbean Offshore Financial Centres' in Worth, O. and Moore, P. *Globalisation and the 'New' Semi-Peripheries*. London: Palgrave.

Vossen, K. (2016) *The Power of Populism: Geert Wilders and the Party of Freedom in the Netherlands*. London: Routledge.

The Wall Street Journal (2018) 'Brazilian Swamp Drainer' 8 October. www.e-ir.info/author/matias-spektor-and-guilherme-fasol/.

Ward, C. and Voas, D. (2011) 'The Emergence of Conspirituality' *Journal of Contemporary Religion* 26 (1): 103–121.

The Washington Post (2018) 'In Trump Some Fear the End of the World Order' 8 June.

Watson, M. (2017) 'Brexit, the Left Behind and the Let Down: The Political Abstraction of "the Economy" and the UK's EU Referendum' *British Politics* 13 (1): 17–30.

Webber, J. (2017) *The Last Days of Oppression and the First Days of the Same: The Politics and Economics of the New Latin American Left*. London: Haymarket.

Webster, N. (1921) *World Revolution: The Plot against Civilisation*. London: Small, Maynard & Company.

Wellings, B. (2012) *English Nationalism and Euroscepticism: Losing the Peace*. Berne: Peter Lang.

Whiteley, P. (1979) 'The National Front Vote in the 1977 GLC Elections: An Aggregate Data Analysis' *British Journal of Political Science* 9 (3): 370–380.

Wilkey, D. (2006) 'A Christian Looks at the Religious Right: New World Order Review'. https://web.archive.org/web/20100124032720/http://www.livingston.net/wilkyjr/link26.htm.

Williams, Z. (2015) 'Feminazi: The Go-To Term for Trolls to Silence Women' *The Guardian* 15 September.

Wilson, G. (2017) 'Brexit, Trump and the Special Relationship' *British Journal of Politics and International Relations* 19 (3): 543–557.

Wilson, J. (2015) '"Cultural Marxism": A Uniting Theory for Rightwingers Who Like to Play the Victim' *The Guardian* 15 January.

Winlow, S., Hall, S. and Treadwell, J. (2017) *The Rise of the Right: English Nationalism and the Transformation of Working-Class Politics*. Bristol: Policy Press.

Wodak, R. and Pelinka, A. (eds.) (2002) *The Haider Phenomenon*. London: Transaction.

Women Against Feminism (2017) http://womenagainstfeminism.com/.

World Bank Group (2016) *International Migration Stock*, Report 2016.

Worth, O. (2002) 'The Janus-Like Character of Counter-hegemony: Progressive and Nationalist Responses to Neoliberalism' *Global Society* 16 (3): 297–315.

Worth, O. (2009) 'Unravelling the Putin Myth: Strong or Weak Caesar?' *Politics* 29 (1): 53–61.

Worth, O. (2013) *Resistance in the Era of Austerity*. London: Zed Books.

Worth, O. (2014) 'The Far Right and Neoliberalism: Willing Partner or Hegemonic Opponent?' in Saull, R., Anievas, A., Davidson, N. and Fabry, A. (eds.) *The Longue Durée of the Far-Right: An International Historical Sociology*. London: Routledge.

Worth, O. (2015) *Rethinking Hegemony*. London: Palgrave.

Worth, O. (2017a) 'Globalisation and the 'Far-Right' Turn in International Affairs' *Irish Studies in International Affairs* 28: 19–28.

Worth, O. (2017b) 'Reviving Hayek's Dream' *Globalizations* 14 (1): 104–109.

Worth, O. (2018a) 'The Role of Women's Leadership in the Masculinist Construction of Global Far Right', Paper presented to the *International Feminist Journal of Politics* Conference, San Francisco.

Worth, O. (2018b) 'The Battle of Hegemony: Resistance and Neo-liberal Restructuring in Post-Crisis Europe' *Comparative European Politics* 16 (1): 126–142.

Worth, O. and Abbott, J. (2006) 'Land of False Hope? The Contradictions of British Opposition to Globalisation' *Globalizations* 3 (1): 49–63.

Yilmaz, F. (2012) 'Right Wing Hegemony and Immigration: How the Populist Far Right Achieved Hegemony through the Immigration Debate in Europe' *Current Sociology* 60 (3): 368–381.

Yorkshire TV (2006) 'The Best of Spitting Image' Yorkshire TV, ITV.

YouGov (2016) 'How Britain Voted'. https://yougov.co.uk/news/2016/06/27/how-britain-voted/.

Zaslove, A. (2011) *The Re-invention of the European Radical Right: Populism, Regionalism, and the Italian Lega Nord*. Montreal: McGill-Queen's University Press.

Zeskind, L. (2012) 'A Nation Dispossessed: The Tea Party Movement and Race' *Critical Sociology* 38 (4): 495–509.

Index

ZED

Zed is a platform for marginalised voices across the globe.

It is the world's largest publishing collective and a world leading example of alternative, non-hierarchical business practice.

It has no CEO, no MD and no bosses and is owned and managed by its workers who are all on equal pay.

It makes its content available in as many languages as possible.

It publishes content critical of oppressive power structures and regimes.

It publishes content that changes its readers' thinking.

It publishes content that other publishers won't and that the establishment finds threatening.

It has been subject to repeated acts of censorship by states and corporations.

It fights all forms of censorship.

It is financially and ideologically independent of any party, corporation, state or individual.

Its books are shared all over the world.

www.zedbooks.net
@ZedBooks